Death in Mount Rainier
National Park

DEATH IN MOUNT RAINIER NATIONAL PARK

Stories of Accidents and Foolhardiness on the Northwest's Most Iconic Peak

TRACY SALCEDO

Guilford, Connecticut

An imprint of The Rowman & Littlefield Publishing Group, Inc.
4501 Forbes Blvd., Ste. 200
Lanham, MD 20706
www.rowman.com

Distributed by NATIONAL BOOK NETWORK

British Library Cataloguing in Publication Information available

Library of Congress Cataloging-in-Publication Data available

ISBN 978-1-4930-2694-4 (paperback)
ISBN 978-1-4930-2695-1 (e-book)

♾™ The paper used in this publication meets the minimum requirements of American National Standard for Information Sciences—Permanence of Paper for Printed Library Materials, ANSI/ NISO Z39.48-1992.

Printed in the United States of America

CONTENTS

Introduction

Mount Rainier National Park maintains a list of more than four hundred visitors who have died or disappeared in the park since the late 1800s. Their names and dates of death are recorded, along with location and a brief description of the circumstances if known. This "fatality list," which you can find online, is a stark reminder that, even though the park resonates with beauty, it has a deadly edge.

Three columns of the list are labeled Activity, Factor, and Cause. Sometimes these follow a logical course. For instance, if the deceased were in an aircraft when they perished, the activity is flying, the factor is a plane crash, and the cause of death is "traumatic injury." Same with victims of car or motorcycle crashes: activity = driving; factor = vehicle accident; cause of death = traumatic injury.

But in other cases, the lines blur and neat categories fail. When a ranger loses his or her life in a fall while attempting to evacuate a stricken mountaineer from a glacier, is the activity climbing or rescue? When a hiker plunges off a trail to her death and her companion's role in the "accident" is suspicious, is the cause a fall? Or is it murder?

Perhaps the toughest to put in a box is the heart attack victim. On the fatality list, heart attacks strike campers, hikers, skiers, snowshoers—participants of nearly every conceivable activity in the park. Is the factor overexertion? Hypothermia? Age?

Then again, ultimately, cardiac arrest defines death for all of us. In this book it's considered a natural cause. Considering some of the unnatural causes that have led to deaths in the park—and I don't mean to be flippant—the unexpected heart attack seems like a pretty good way to go.

We define our lives in many ways: father, brother, son, climber, salesman; mother, sister, daughter, skier, doctor. When I've been able to find the resources, I've set out to illuminate not only the circumstances surrounding a death but also who the person was, and what they left behind. In a perfect world, I'd have been able to give each of Rainier's dead equal time and space, but that hasn't been possible. Not every record is detailed; some of the stories are lost in time and obscurity. My research took me in many different directions—into newspaper accounts, journals, books, and National Park Service records. But I did not seek out or interview families: The logistics were too daunting, and I didn't want to reopen emotional wounds. Thus, my sources are primarily secondary. That said, if families or friends would like to touch base about a loved one who perished on Rainier, or if you discover an error of fact or an omission that can be remedied in a subsequent printing, I invite the contact and the opportunity to hear more, remedy, and share.

It should come as no surprise that park service officials aren't enthused about a book that focuses on death in Mount Rainier National Park. For good reason. The numbers help put things in perspective. Between 1904 and 2016, nearly 95 million people visited the park; as of the end of 2017, fewer than 450 people have landed on the fatality list. Clearly a person's chance of surviving a visit to Rainier far exceeds his chance of dying there.

There's also the danger that readers might be tempted to visit sites where accidents have occurred—a concern that takes on urgency when it comes to deaths that took place high on the mountain. Unless you are in excellent physical condition, properly outfitted, and well versed in mountaineering techniques and glacier travel, Rainier's alpine zone should be contemplated only from trails, camps, and vista points low on the volcano's slopes. Even if you are fit and experienced, the high ground demands respect, confidence, wariness, an arsenal of gear, and, in most cases, a good guide. As you read about how mountaineers—some neophytes, some experts—have lost their lives on the mountain, be open to learning how to avoid the circumstances that resulted in their deaths. If you are lucky enough to travel in the airy places where they lay down a final time, remember them and heed their lessons. In addition to being climbers—or rafters, or motorists, or hikers—they are teachers.

A couple of notes on the details: On occasion, names, dates, and circumstances surrounding a death varied from source to source. I deferred, in most of these instances, to the park record. But I have noted where inconsistencies occur. Also, as I've slotted stories into particular chapters, I've taken into account nuances and complications gleaned from newspaper accounts, accident reports, and archival records. It's not always a neat fit, but every story, no matter how brief, has a place in this book.

And a personal note: While this book was in draft, wildfire destroyed much of my hometown. Both during the blaze and in its immediate aftermath, I witnessed firsthand, both with eyes and heart, the work that first responders—rescuers—do. I hope I've adequately captured the heroism and dedication of Rainier's rangers and search-and-rescue teams in these stories. I am forever awed and indebted.

Finally, I invite you to meditate on Mount Rainier's iconic power as you read. If you were to toss pictures of the world's greatest mountains on a table in front of the average person, the ones that stand alone are the ones that stand out. America has some ringers in that category, many of them part of the Cascade Range. The big volcanoes rise above the ranges that surround them like diamonds in the sky. In that way, Rainier is typical. But it's bigger, brighter, bolder. In terms of destructive power alone, the peak has spectacular potential. It looks at Saint Helens, which erupted in 1980, and says, "I can do that better." It looks at Lassen, which erupted in 1915, and says, "What was that? A hiccup?"

Rainier's ability to attract the eye and the imagination like a great white magnet is what led to its preservation as a national park. These are tales of the macabre, of the unimaginable, of surprisingly few incidents of foolhardiness and more of just bad luck. The stories in this book offer glimpses into the lives of dynamic and tragic characters, and the mountain itself is one of them. Whatever you might take away from this book, I hope you also come away with a sense of Rainier's majesty, its potential, and its standalone power.

A Brief History of Peak and Park

FOR THOUSANDS OF YEARS BEFORE MOUNT RAINIER NATIONAL PARK started keeping records of those who perished within its boundaries, people lived and died in proximity to the peak. There's no written record of who, how, or where first peoples lost their lives in what would become America's fifth national park in 1899. But the Nisqually, Puyallup, Yakama, Cowlitz, Squaxin Island, Muckleshoot, and their ancestors were passionate about the rugged terrain, wild weather, and magnetic draw of the peak called *Tacoma*. Their long history on the mountain is evidence of Tacoma's power, both spiritual and volcanic.

Tacoma's influence on the landscape and culture of the Pacific Northwest following the arrival of the white man, from the days of privateers and settlers to the days of rangers and tourists, is undeniable. To appreciate why people want to be in the park and on the mountain—and thus why some of them die there—it helps to understand how peak and park came into existence.

Fire and Ice

There may come a time when a book about the 400-plus deaths recorded on the slopes of Mount Rainier over 129 years pales beside lives lost in a disaster born of a single volcanic event. That's because Mount Rainier, the tallest volcano in the Cascade Range, is only sleeping.

But even at rest, the forces that have reshaped the volcano's silhouette and reconfigured the surrounding landscape simmer just beneath the surface. One telling sign are the steam vents on the summit; these vents blast hot air, creating caves in the ice cap on the crater. The caves have been a hot-cold refuge, on occasion, for climbers caught in the storms that frequently boil up at the summit. Mountaineers tell tales of overheating on one side of their bodies while the other side is frostnipped.

Rainier—along with the other iconic peaks of the Cascade Range, including Mount Hood, Mount Saint Helens, Mount Baker, Glacier Peak, Mount Adams, Crater Lake, Mount Shasta, and Lassen Peak—is a product of the collision of tectonic plates along the Pacific Ring of Fire. These fractured pieces of the earth's crust shift on a molten substrate, grinding and subsiding, generating heat and instability that results in volcanic activity and earthquakes. This activity occurs along the plate boundaries from South America to the West Coast of the United States to Japan and Indonesia.

Mount Rainier's eruptive history dates back about a half million years; it is considered a young composite volcano (or stratovolcano). Repeated eruptions over the eons have sculpted the iconic cone that now rises thousands of feet above the surrounding foothills. The composition of Rainier's lava flows is different from those that created the older, lower mountains surrounding the peak, and that difference is what caused it to rise higher than the rest. Both in time and in structure, the rocks of the rest of the Cascades are separate from those of Rainier. Thus, according to geologists, the "huge mass of the cone stands out in bold relief; towering 10,000 feet above the range beneath."

Though its underpinnings are molten, Mount Rainier is cloaked in ice. Its heights support more than twenty-five major glaciers. The Carbon Glacier contains the greatest volume of ice in the Lower 48; the Emmons Glacier covers the most area. While an eruption is certainly a concern, what's even more concerning is what volcanism can do to the mountain's frozen mantle. When rivers of molten rock and gas meet rivers of ice, the resulting lahars, or mudflows, are capable of completely remodeling surrounding landforms and, especially in heavily populated regions like Seattle and its suburbs, also capable of causing death and destruction on a massive scale.

What gives pause to researchers, park staff, government officials, and residents when contemplating the possibility, or inevitability, of a mudflow charging down the mountain's slopes is the evidence left by previous lahars. They've spooled down the mountain on numerous occasions, but the event that jumps to the forefront is the Osceola Mudflow, one of the largest to have taken place worldwide.

The Osceola flow occurred roughly 5,600 years ago, and the statistics associated with it are staggering. According to geologists, the flow essentially obliterated the summit of the volcano. Hot volcanic "gases and solutions" transformed the existing rock into clay, and the "spectacular" mudflow that followed "streamed down the Emmons Glacier and down valley for 70 miles . . . submerged the White River valley at the site of White River campground beneath more than 500 feet of mud and rock debris, including boulders as large as 15 feet in diameter [and] buried Enumclaw and Buckley under as much as 70 feet of mud."

The flow ultimately ranged from the mountaintop to Puget Sound. Any indigenous peoples living in its path would have been wiped out, their stories buried in mud and time.

More recently, glacial outburst floods have proven periodic reminders that even while Rainier sleeps, it is capable of wreaking havoc. Also called "jokulhlaups," these outbursts can follow rain-on-snow events, which loosen debris and water that has pooled under a glacier. "The jokulhlaup flood wave is a noisy, tumbling, churning mass of mud and rocks that is sometimes accompanied by local winds, thick dust clouds, and the smell of freshly crushed vegetation," the authors of a US Geological Survey report titled "Geology in Action—Jokulhlaups on Mount Rainier" wrote. "It sounds like a freight train as it travels down-valley at speeds of 10 miles per hour or more."

In 1947 a glacial outburst flood from the Kautz Glacier delivered fifty million cubic meters of debris into the Nisqually River. As described in one scientific reckoning, "a sea of moving boulders (up to 4 m in diameter) and thick, cement-like volcanic sand poured down on a front 1 km wide, buried the paved highway under 5 to 6.5 m of debris, and snapped off fir trees up to 1.6 m in diameter." The Kautz followed up with similar outbursts in 1960 and 1961.

Jokulhlaups have also been recorded on Tahoma Creek, downstream of the South Tahoma Glacier, in 1967, 1971, 1973, and three times in the late 1980s. Outburst floods have barreled down the Nisqually River at least eight times in the twentieth century. The most recent flooding along the river—and along streams throughout the park—occurred in 2006, when torrential rains resulted in massive damage to the park's infrastructure. Thankfully, however, no deaths have been recorded with these flows.

The upshot for visitors: Mount Rainier is in motion. From the prosaic, like wind, rain, and snow, to the exotic, like lahars and jokulhlaups, the volcano's beauty comes with barbs.

From Homeland to Parkland

Thoroughly exploring the 119-year history of Mount Rainier National Park is the stuff of another book. But aspects of the park's long evolution inform the stories that follow.

Archaeological evidence indicates that first peoples, including ancestors of the tribes that thrived in the region at the time of its "discovery," were present in what would become Mount Rainier National Park as early as nine thousand years ago. Colonization of the region by Europeans began with the arrival of Captain George Vancouver in 1792; the British mariner named the beacon he saw on the horizon *Rainier* for a colleague, Rear Admiral Peter Rainier, though the locals called the peak *Tacoma* (or some variation on the word).

Complex cultural myths grew up around the peak over the millennia, some of which persisted as explorers began probing the mountain wilderness in the eighteenth century. For the tribal people the mountain was a sacred site, and while they hunted and gathered on its flanks, they generally didn't venture onto its glaciated heights. Danger lurked there.

That didn't stop newcomers, some of whom set their sights on the summit of the great white cone no matter the perils. Earlier attempts were made, but the first recognized ascent was accomplished in 1870 by Hazard Stevens and Philemon Van Trump, accompanied for at least part of the distance by Sluiskin, a Klickitat Indian. Sluiskin refused to go to the summit and cautioned Stevens and Van Trump to stay away as well, warning that the crater contained a lake of fire and was guarded by a hostile spirit. Stevens and Van Trump ventured forth regardless, and came away with a mountaineering prize.

Explorers were followed by settlers, as was the case all along the west coast of what would become the United States. Manifest destiny had propelled Americans westward into the fertile woodlands of the Cascades, where timber, minerals, and fisheries all presented opportunities. Mount Rainier sat right in the middle of it all, now a beacon both for navigation and for prosperity.

The newcomers soon began to understand what the natives had long known: that Rainier was a special place, worthy of protection from commercial exploitation. The movement to preserve mountain and surroundings as a national park was homegrown. The locals saw what the protection of Yellowstone and Yosemite meant—a chance to set aside the pleasure ground in their backyard for posterity—and lobbied in the halls of Congress for the mountain's safekeeping. What had been forest reserve became the country's fifth national park on March 2, 1899.

That's when the formal record-keeping began. Suddenly it was important to know who was coming into the park and who was going out, who was climbing the peak and who was going for a more casual hike, who was camping and who was on a sightseeing tour by motorcar. These details were critical to making sure facilities and services were in place to accommodate the needs of visitors.

It also became important to know who perished in the park, and how. Keeping track of these details, no matter how grim or macabre, remains key to safeguarding lives. As you'll read in some of the stories that follow, park administration as it relates to the park's natural and man-made attractions—think climbing and climbing regulations, sightseeing and speed limits—plays a significant role in life and death on Mount Rainier.

Part 1: To the Summit

The summit of Mount Rainier is a magnet for American climbers. For some it's a home peak: They've spent their lifetimes exploring the mountain, experiencing it anew on each ascent. Some come to train: The volcano's crevassed glaciers, rugged rock cleavers, and oxygen-deprived heights serve as proving grounds for mountaineers intent on summiting more imposing icons like Denali in Alaska and the eight-thousand-meter giants of the Himalaya and Karakoram, including Mount Everest. Some come for a one-off experience: They've dreamt of standing atop Columbia Crest, and the time is finally right.

Most aspiring summiters are well prepared for their attempts. They've trained, assembled a team, secured an experienced guide, and understand the challenges that Rainier's steep terrain, broken glaciers, and great height present.

Others are neophytes—park visitors who arrive at Paradise and decide the sloping white cone doesn't look all that imposing. They set off in sneakers, their day packs (if they carry one) loaded with a sweatshirt, a cell phone, a ham sandwich, and a can of soda. Usually, Rainier turns these greenhorns around before any harm befalls them, as the altitude steals their breath and the cold cuts through their cotton T-shirts.

But even for the experienced, reaching the top of Mount Rainier is not a sure thing. Weather is the biggest unknown. Peaks like Rainier, piercing rarified levels of atmosphere, are notorious for creating their own storms. It may be calm and clear in the lowlands, and the sky surrounding the peak may be blue, but the formation of a lenticular cloud—the infamous cloud cap—on the summit portends an imminent pummeling by howling winds and driving snow. That said, fair weather and the absence of a telltale cloud is no guarantee of safety either. Warm temperatures and sunshine pose their own special hazards, melting the ice that locks rocks—and sometimes entire snow slopes—in place, unleashing dangerous rockfalls and avalanches.

Despite the dangers, in each year over the past decade more than ten thousand climbers have made an attempt on the summit. More than 75 percent of modern climbers aim for the summit via the Disappointment Cleaver/Ingraham Glacier route, and about half are successful. In earlier years the most popular way to the top was via another "cleaver," a term that refers to the rock buttresses separating one glacier from another on the volcano. The Gibraltar Ledges route, referenced in a number of the deaths associated with summit attempts when the park was younger, can still be climbed but has fallen out of favor; part of the ledge used in the ascent has collapsed, and the line has always been peppered with rockfall. Ascending to the summit via the Liberty Ridge—a rocky spine on the north face that separates two of Rainier's most daunting faces, the Willis Wall and the Liberty Wall—has also claimed a number of lives.

While these routes and a handful of others see the most traffic, a glimpse at a climber's map of the mountain reveals a web of possibilities and variations, thus the endless challenge. Between the physical variety and the added variable imposed by season and weather, successful and passionate mountaineers are never bored on Rainier.

What kills climbers, however, can be slotted fairly neatly into three categories: a fall (commonly into a crevasse); an avalanche; or exposure. What sets each incident apart are the circumstances, which are as unique as each climber who seeks the summit.

The stories of those who've perished while climbing the mountain provide windows into a world most people find hard to imagine—a world where men and women choose to expose themselves to conditions that will test their physical and mental strength in extraordinary ways. Their success or failure is determined not only by their fitness, but also by a mountain. It may seem harsh—and certainly assigning a human emotion to a mass of rock and ice is fraught—but Rainier doesn't care. And Rainier can't be controlled.

When climbers throw on their packs and strap on their crampons to ascend Rainier, they don't just carry their loved ones' photographs in their wallets. If they should freeze, fall in a crevasse, get crushed by an avalanche or tumble fatally down the ice, their wives, children, parents and siblings go with them. We survivors may not die on Rainier, but we are severely wounded, and while our wounds may get better with time, they never fully heal.

—Ashley Ryan, sister of climbing ranger Sean Ryan, who died on a rescue mission in 1995

CHAPTER 1

The Ranger and the Guide

The skilled professionals who work as guides on Mount Rainier have dedicated their lives to leading aspiring summiters up the mountain, not only braving the hazards inherent to alpine ascents, but also negotiating the tricky terrain of cranky clients, unprepared clients, and potentially litigious clients.

Rainier Mountaineering Inc. (RMI) has held a guide service concession in the park for decades. Two generations of Whittakers, a family with an impressive mountaineering résumé, have dedicated themselves to the park and peak. Twins Jim and Lou Whittaker began their impressive alpine careers on Rainier, where they honed the skills that would serve them well on bigger mountains in faraway places. Jim became the first American to summit Mount Everest in 1963, and Lou led the first American team to summit Everest via the North Col in 1984.

But Rainier was home turf. Between them, the twins have logged more than 330 Rainier ascents. Jim went on to found REI, a premier purveyor of all things outdoors, and Lou's RMI, based outside the park's Nisqually entrance in Ashford, has long been a go-to guide service on the mountain. In 1990 Lou Whittaker turned over leadership of RMI to his son Peter. Another son, Win, runs the Whittaker Bunkhouse, base camp for many an aspiring summiter. Both of the younger Whittakers are also accomplished mountaineers.

Two other guide services held concessions on Mount Rainier as of 2017: International Mountain Guides and Alpine Ascents International. The guides employed by each company have notched expeditions to impressive peaks around the globe, from the Himalaya to the Alaska

Range, from Patagonia to the Karakoram. Leaders from any of these out-fits are eminently qualified to guide an aspiring summiter to the top of Rainier, or to determine that such a goal is better gained another day.

Rainier serves a test piece with reasonable overhead for climbers. Climbing K2, or even Denali, requires an expedition and a hefty outlay of money and time; those factors alone limit how many people can launch an attempt on their summits. By comparison Rainier, charismatic and challenging for even the most seasoned alpinist, is a scenic two-hour drive from a major metropolitan area and, depending on route, conditions, and experience, can be climbed in a day, though most climbers take two or three days to complete the round-trip.

It's important to understand the basic challenges of a Rainier climb, and the necessary skills that guides (and rangers, and experienced moun-taineers) have mastered. The fact is that the ill-equipped and inexperi-enced don't stand a chance on Rainier's glaciers. Climbers must have a working understanding of safe travel on a glaciated peak, including how to use crampons (traction devices that attach to a boot and are equipped with spikes on the toes and underfoot), snow anchors (pretty much what they sound like), and an ice ax (a shaft with pointy ends that can be plunged into snow or ice to stop, or arrest, a fall).

When clients purchase summit packages from a service, as the bulk of Rainier's climbers do, they are schooled not only in what to expect in terms of weather, conditions, and physical effort on the mountain, but also in how to protect themselves and their teammates from potential dangers, including falls. They must be proficient in the use of specialized gear and in ropework, because they will be hitched together for safety as they ascend the peak. In the event someone along the rope slips, every person on that line must be prepared to arrest. As nearly every story that follows illustrates, a failure to gear up, or to properly use gear—or failure of the gear itself—plays a starring role in fatal accidents on Rainier.

Even though each guide service operates independently, in the event of trouble on Rainier, they become an efficient rescue team. Guides on the mountain at the time of an incident pool skills and resources and work closely with National Park Service climbing rangers to save lives.

Depending on the situation, other resources can be called in as well, including air support from nearby army bases.

The stories of heroic rescue efforts by guides to save stranded climbers, whether members of their own teams or from other groups, are foundational to the story of mountaineering on Rainier. Though this book focuses on lives lost despite the efforts of guides and climbing rangers, those who survive far outnumber those who have died. The events that unfolded in July 1929, which highlight the talents and sacrifices of guide Leon Brigham Sr. and ranger Charlie Browne, offer a vivid illustration of how success and failure can mesh in unexpected ways for climbers, guides, and rangers in an accident on the peak.

The Greathouse-Wetzel Tragedy

Six men succeeded in climbing Mount Rainier via the Ingraham Glacier and Gibraltar Ledges routes in early July 1929. But only four made it off the mountain alive.

The summit team set off from Paradise on July 1. The lead guide was Leon Brigham Sr.; his assistant guides were Forrest Greathouse and Robert Strobel. Their clients were Edwin Wetzel of Milwaukee, Wisconsin; Yandy Bradshaw of Cambridge, Massachusetts; and H. P. Weatherly, also from Cambridge. The ascent started out with the team climbing to Camp Muir, where they spent the night. The next day they made an early start in calm conditions, but as they climbed higher, Rainier slapped them with one of its hallmark challenges—sudden and freakishly bad weather.

"A blizzard was raging from the time that we crossed the crevasses above Comfort," Yandy Bradshaw wrote in his account of the climb. "Much of the time the wind was so strong that we had to lean over or get down on all fours in order to keep from being blown over."

By all accounts, Edwin Wetzel struggled throughout the ascent. Bradshaw refers to lead guide Brigham as "a superman" for helping to get the climber to the rim, writing, "He practically carried Wetzel the last half of the climb between Comfort and the Summit."

The team, flattened by the maelstrom, crawled the final five hundred feet to the crater rim, which they reached at about 8:30 a.m. After signing the registers, the climbers sought shelter in the summit steam caves, but the wind was "all around" and there was no respite, Brigham wrote in his account of the tragedy. With no alternative, the men started the descent.

As the storm continued to pummel the mountaineers, climber Wetzel became, in Bradshaw's words, "spent." He sat down repeatedly and wanted to slide down the icy summit crown; his teammates had to keep him "buttressed" upright. No report describes the exact nature of Wetzel's affliction, but altitude sickness, which can present with symptoms of mental confusion, might have been at play.

All hell broke loose at about 12,500 feet, as the team approached Camp Comfort. There, park superintendent O. A. Tomlinson wrote, "assistant guide Strobel slipped on the icy slope and slid into a crevasse about 100 feet deep, dragging his rope mates with him. Each of the men was knocked unconscious in the fall."

Bradshaw is more descriptive. "I thought we were nearing Camp Comfort, due to the extreme angle of snow and ice," he remembered, "when someone back of the line lost footing and swept down the forty-five-degree incline like a shot. We were unable to hold." All of the climbers attempted to set their ice axes but were unable to arrest, as the snow was "frozen hard and polished with ice particles."

"As we raced down the Mountain at breakneck speed, all went dark," Bradshaw wrote. "How we ever got out I don't know. I thought we were lost forever."

According to Tomlinson's report, Strobel was the first to recover his senses; he revived Brigham, the lead guide, who sent him on down the mountain alone to seek help. Brigham then turned his attention to the others still in the crevasse.

Greathouse was wedged in the narrowest part of the cleft, and was clearly seriously injured. "Brigham propped up his head, but he thought that the man was beyond help," Tomlinson wrote.

In Brigham's report, he details the crushing pain he felt upon his revival, and his focus on locating the gravely injured Greathouse. Upon gaining his feet, he identified Weatherly on a ledge above and Bradshaw, who had also found his way to standing. Using his ice ax, Brigham freed Weatherly's legs from blocks of ice that had pinned him to the ledge. Then the lead guide looked up and his face fell: "We were imprisoned between two narrow ice walls that ran straight and sheer up a hundred feet or more to a mass of overhanging ice and snow above." The climbers had landed on a ledge that Brigham believed was formed by collapsing snow. There was no obvious way out.

There's no indication that any of the men gave up, and giving up was not in the lead guide's nature. But Brigham writes of the difficult choices he had to make, and of the fog in his brain brought on by concussion, loss of blood, and cold. Strobel, who appeared to be in "good condition," had been dispatched to find a way out of the crevasse and then down to Camp Muir for help, but Brigham worried about the apprentice guide's lack of experience and the blizzard that might obscure his way. He considered sending the others on as well and remaining alone with Greathouse, his "poor chum," who appeared to be breathing lightly. But Brigham knew his friend was beyond help.

Brigham also knew he and the other men in the crevasse were in danger of freezing. They'd been in the storm for hours prior to the accident, and the cold of the crevasse was penetrating. Brigham made the decision to leave Greathouse behind while he and the other three survivors attempted self-rescue.

But Wetzel was also incapacitated. "He seemed utterly exhausted and incapable of making the effort required," Brigham remembered. Because time was precious, the guide advised the fatigued man to keep moving to keep warm while the others went ahead for help. He made sure Wetzel had food, in packs the climbers left behind, and moved on.

Brigham, Bradshaw, and Weatherly inched up ledges in the wall of the crevasse and punched through a hole, likely created by Strobel, onto the glacier's surface. "How Brigham was able to chop a man out and cut steps to a hole above is beyond me. . . . It all seems like a terrible dream. I am most lucky to be alive," Bradshaw wrote.

Given their injuries, the team's progress was slow as they continued their descent. A break in the storm clouds revealed Camp Comfort and the route down to Camp Muir, and Brigham, focused on getting help, moved forward with Bradshaw, while Weatherly lagged. Unbeknownst to the three ahead, Wetzel had climbed out of the crevasse after them.

Though no one knows exactly what transpired, apparently Wetzel became disoriented at Camp Comfort and "instead of following the others to the right, toward the Chutes, he went to the left, and slipped and fell down to the Ingraham Glacier," superintendent Tomlinson recorded. The men ahead, including lead guide Brigham, were unaware that their teammate had strayed dangerously off-route. Climber Weatherly, who also fell behind, notes the mental exhaustion brought on by the ordeal, and how that may have affected all decision-making in the aftermath of the fall. "Brig wasn't in his full senses," Weatherly wrote. "It was my impression that he did all he possibly could for the men particularly owing to his weakened and exhausted condition at the time."

When Strobel, the first man Brigham sent down the mountain, reached Camp Muir, he alerted the park to the disaster above and the formal rescue began. Ranger Charlie Browne made a heroic climb to Wetzel, who had fallen from Camp Comfort onto the ice of the Ingraham. He reached the man in the afternoon, as Wetzel was nearing the end. According to Browne, "This man had apparently slipped, slid, rolled and crawled for over a half mile on the glacier and possibly a thousand feet in elevation. . . . When I found him he was unconscious and, though still breathing, the spark of life was very low."

In his report, superintendent Tomlinson related that "Ranger Browne was unable to carry or drag unaided, the dying man from the place where he found him . . . so he hollowed out a place in the ice and snow to keep Wetzel from sliding further down the steep icy slope and returned to Camp Muir for help."

Meanwhile, a rescue party met Brigham and Bradshaw at the Beehive. Though they were injured and exhausted, the two climbers requested the rescuers continue up to help those higher on the mountain. The rescuers encountered Weatherly at Camp Misery, and Ranger Browne, though weary from his efforts on the Ingraham aiding Wetzel, helped the climber down the Chutes. Brigham, Bradshaw, and Weatherly would all be tended to at Camp Muir.

The persistent storm prevented further rescue or recovery efforts until the following day. Greathouse's remains were retrieved from the crevasse on July 7. Ranger Browne was lowered seventy-five feet into the abyss, where he chopped away the snow that had filled in around the dead guide and secured a rope so that the body could be raised and returned to Camp Muir and, finally, to his family.

In the wake of the accident and rescues, the park and its rangers received both praise and criticism. Robert Strobel was honored with the DeMolay medal from Tacoma's Masonic Temple in May 1930. Edwin Wetzel's family proposed installing a stone fireplace and plaque in the Paradise Community House to commemorate his life and in gratitude for the ranger's rescue efforts. This was politely rejected by National Park Service director Horace Albright himself, whose letter stated the park service had "a fundamental policy against the granting of authority for installation of various markers or monuments or things of that kind for the reason that if we make an exception in one case, it is very difficult to deny others." This policy remains in place today, though the national park does permit families to scatter the ashes of their loved ones, with restrictions.

As for recognition, a letter from superintendent Tomlinson notes that the rangers, including Charlie Browne, "feel that what they did was done as a matter of duty in serving park visitors and that your expression of [appreciation] is ample reward for their efforts."

Criticism of the guides focused on their decision to take tourists to the summit in spite of inclement weather conditions. Criticism leveled at the park focused on protection of climbers along the Gibraltar route. Tomlinson, with justification, responded to one critic shortly after the accident, lamenting the inclination of commentators "to rush into print and write articles criticising [sic] guides and others concerning whom they have no knowledge whatsoever. This of course must be expected." The park temporarily closed the Gibraltar route in the accident's aftermath, however, and when it reopened additional ropes had been placed in the chutes, a ladder was provided for crossing crevasses, and "footing along the ledge of Gibraltar" was "improved."

Brigham's Sons

Leon Brigham Sr. survived his intimate encounter with a crevasse. His first-born son would not.

Twenty-one-year-old Leon Brigham Jr. intended to follow in his father's footsteps. In an in-depth article in *Pacific NW Magazine*, published by the *Seattle Times*, the young man, called Juney, is described as a talented athlete and ball player, a member of his high school's football, basketball, and track teams, all coached by his father. He was raised on Rainier, climbing, hiking, and skiing. In pictures he appears a handsome young man—swinging from a boulder or watching his dad sign his ski school registration card. The *Times* article also shows young Juney at his father's bedside after the Greathouse-Wetzel tragedy.

It was natural that Brigham Jr. would want to climb Mount Rainier. On August 10, 1941, Juney was contemplating a summit expedition. The *Times* account describes a team of young men on a mountain hike (the park record notes, ambiguously, that they were on the Russell or Carbon glacier at the time of the incident). On the descent, they reached a crevasse. Seeing a snow bridge, Juney handed one end of his ice ax to a companion, Harrison Holland, and gripped the other end: on belay. When he stepped onto the bridge, it collapsed. The ice ax handle was wrenched from Holland's grasp and young Brigham fell into the void.

"Harrison looked into the crevasse, unable to see the bottom, unable to understand what had just happened. He didn't hear anything. Juney had just vanished," the article relates. Holland and the others attempted an unsuccessful rescue, then bolted for help. Rangers notified the Brigham family, and the senior Brigham rushed to the mountain to assist in the rescue. His son was found the next morning, buried under eight feet of snow. The article notes the young man's shirt was off; apparently he survived the fall, then succumbed to hypothermia. A friend carried his ashes to the summit fourteen days after the accident.

In 1973 Charles Brigham, Juney's younger brother, also tumbled into one of Rainier's crevasses, according to the *Times* piece. Charles Brigham and his daughter had summited, but on the descent Charles slipped and disappeared into a crack in the glacier. He landed on an "unstable chunk of ice," assured his daughter that he was fine, and climbed to safety.

CHAPTER 2

No Safety in Numbers

THERE'S COMFORT IN THE TRIBE. WHEN YOU ARE WITH PEOPLE WHO think like you do, who are tuned in to the environment like you are, and who are as capable as you are, confidence and a sense of security come easily. If one person gets in trouble, another is on hand to help. Your chance of success, no matter the task, is enhanced by companionship.

This holds true on any mountain. Climbing solo is generally discouraged; even two climbers are better than one. But sometimes the numbers just don't matter. The misstep of one can lead to the downfall of many. And sometimes, on peaks like Rainier, there is no misstep. A bad thing happens, and the whole tribe pays the price.

The Worst Accident in Mountaineering History

Eleven climbers lost their lives when a giant serac—a wall of ice—collapsed and swept them away in June 1981. It remains the worst accident in the history of American mountaineering as of summer 2017.

According to *American Alpine Journal*'s (*AAJ*) accident report, the weather was clear when the party, guided by Rainier Mountaineering Inc. (RMI), set out for the summit from Camp Muir. They were on the Disappointment Cleaver route; the six RMI guides were in charge of twenty-three clients. Three of the novice climbers opted out of the climb at Ingraham Flats, retreating to Camp Muir with one of the guides. The others forged ahead to the cleaver, where the "senior guide," John Day, called a halt. He wanted to scout the route ahead based on reports of increased avalanche danger above.

The clients waited near the edge of a crevasse and two guides, Gary Wilson and Tom O'Brien, stayed with them. Day and fellow guides Peter Whittaker and Michael Targett roped up and went ahead to reconnoiter, digging snow pits to test for avalanche danger. Determining it wasn't safe to proceed given the conditions, the three men turned back, intending to call the climb off.

That's when it happened. One of the survivors told the Associated Press (AP) that "all of a sudden, there was a crack and a snap. The thing I remember vividly was everybody going, 'Ooooh,' kind of like they were watching a Fourth of July display."

A wall of ice three hundred feet wide, by one estimate, had separated from the Ingraham Glacier. The ice fractured as it crashed eight hundred feet onto the slope below, breaking "into several massive ice blocks which crashed rapidly down the slope and creat[ed] an unusually large snow and ice avalanche," according to the *AAJ*. Another survivor recalled watching the collapse and ensuing massive slide, telling the AP that "for an instant no one moved as the ice roared down the glacier. Then the guides yelled to run."

Not everyone was able to sprint out of the avalanche path, however. When all was said and done, the eleven victims had either been swept into the nearby crevasse or were buried under "boulder-sized chunks of ice" that piled up to seventy feet deep on the mountainside.

The search for survivors began immediately. Two guides and one client remained at the scene while the other guides and the rest of the climbers descended to Camp Muir. Those that remained found "only a pack, an ice ax, and a headlamp." A small army—rangers, guides, independent climbers—ascended to the site to search for survivors, but the risks proved too great. Deteriorating weather and the possibility of another icefall forced the effort to be called off. Conditions allowed a brief resumption of the search the following day, but that too was fruitless and had to be abandoned when blizzard conditions buried the rubble in fresh snow. No further rescue was attempted. Given the scale of the disaster and the uncooperative weather, park officials determined that it would be both "futile" and hazardous to continue.

The bodies of the climbers were never recovered. "They are part of the mountain now," one of the rescuers told a wire service.

Guide Peter Whittaker, son of RMI founder and mountaineer Lou Whittaker, was twenty-two years old when the accident occurred. The deaths had a profound impact on the young guide, as well as others with the company, he told *Outside* magazine in December 1999. Some of the guides quit. Whittaker took a long break from Rainier in an effort "to get my head together."

"But I'd grown up on Mount Rainier. I loved the mountains. I thought, 'There must be a reason I was spared.' So I continued guiding and used everything I learned to prevent other accidents," Whittaker told the magazine.

The eleven who died that day included 19-year-old guide Tom O'Brien of Seattle and clients David Boulton, 29, and Gordon Heneage, 42, also both from Seattle; Mark Ernlund, 29, of Renton, Washington; Ronald Farrell (his age is 41 in the park record, but newspaper accounts say he was 21) and Craig Tippie, 28, of Bellevue, Washington; David Kidd, 30, of Arlington, Washington; Jonathan Laitone, 27, of Ann Arbor, Michigan; Ira Liedman, 30, of Hatfield, Pennsylvania; Michael Watts, 36, of Mercer Island, Washington; and Henry Matthews, 38, of Auburn, Washington.

Six Men Gone

In late May 2014, six men—two guides from Alpine Ascents International and four clients—headed to the summit via the Liberty Ridge route, one of the most difficult and desirable lines on the peak. The plan, according to the itinerary submitted to the National Park Service, was for the party to bivouac the first night, May 26, on Curtis Ridge; the next night at Thumb Rock; and the third night at Camp Schurman, which would serve as base camp for a summit attempt. The planned descent was via the Emmons Glacier, and the party was slated to be off the mountain by May 30.

But things didn't go as planned. There's no way of knowing exactly what happened, but what is known is that the six climbers fell more than 3,000 feet from a steep ridge at about 12,800 feet. They came to rest on the Carbon Glacier below the imposing Willis Wall, where a helicopter crew spotted their gear in an area of jumbled ice and snow, according to a *Seattle Times* report. There's a possibility that an icefall or avalanche swept them down the mountain as they climbed; it's also possible that the men were bivouacked on the ridge when the avalanche occurred.

Conditions at the recovery site were so dangerous that attempts to rescue or recover the victims could not proceed. The geography framing the glacier—the sheer Willis Wall and Liberty Cap above—shed rock and ice with increasing frequency as the weather grows warmer in the summer season, posing unacceptable avalanche and rockfall hazards for anyone climbing or searching below. The park maintained that recovery of any of the bodies would be done quickly and by air, if it at all. "There's no certainty that recovery is possible given the location," a park spokesperson told the Associated Press.

The men who died in the Liberty Ridge accident included guide Matt Hegeman, 38, of Truckee, California. Hegeman had climbed Rainier more than fifty times; was a veteran climber of fourteen-thousand-foot peaks in California, including one of Rainier's sister volcanoes, Mount Shasta; and had also climbed Aconcagua, one of the Seven Summits. Guide Eitan Green, 29, was a Colby College graduate and experienced mountaineer. Mark Mahaney, 26, of St. Paul, Minnesota, was remembered by family as an avid outdoorsman and had already summited the volcano once, as well as climbed Denali in Alaska. The other clients included Erik Kolb, 34, who worked in finance and lived in Brooklyn, New York, and Seattleites John Mullally, 40, employed by Microsoft, and Uday Marty, 40, an Intel vice president.

It Could Have Been Worse

A wet-snow avalanche triggered by warm, late-day weather conditions and, perhaps, by a climbing guide who slipped on a treacherous slope, slammed into two groups of roped climbers on the Disappointment Cleaver route in June 1998. Nine of the climbers survived the harrowing event; Patrick Nestler, 29, of Norwalk, Connecticut, did not.

Nestler was part of an RMI-guided climb on descent from the summit when the avalanche cut loose. A *Seattle Times* article records this observation from one of the survivors: "It felt like we were going down a waterfall."

Following the slide, a climber who came to rest above Nestler told the *Los Angeles Times* that the doomed young man "was in the worst predicament, dangling in mid-air nearly 100 feet below the ledge, out of sight of the others, suffering from various injuries and getting drenched by snowmelt." Rescuers weren't able to reach Nestler for hours after the slide; by then he had succumbed to exposure.

An *American Alpine Journal* account of the event and its aftermath notes that snow anchors placed by the two teams had been wrenched free by the slide. One anchor finally held, with climbers on the lines "entangled at the top of the cliff-bands." The victims were scattered at the scene: "One guide and one client were caught on the fixed line above the cliff. Three clients and one guide clung to the top of the cliff, tangled in the rocks and ropes. Three clients dangled below them on a cliff of ice and snow, while the solo client (Nestler) hung below a second cliff band in a waterfall of snowmelt."

The reports also describe a heroic rescue effort, employing RMI founder Lou Whittaker and noted Rainier climbing ranger Mike Gauthier, who'd climbed the mountain on his day off and, upon hearing of the accident, snowboarded down to the scene.

The victims, including Nestler, were saved from a longer fall when their ropes hitched up on rocks—otherwise they all might have tumbled another several hundred feet down the mountain, Gauthier told the *Seattle Times*. The article also noted that one of those ropes, with "five climbers attached, was so frayed that rescuers worried it would snap."

The tenuousness of the situation was further highlighted in the *AAJ* account: "The location was extremely hazardous with 40-degree icy slopes, 20-foot vertical rock bands, exposure to avalanche hang-fire and a 300-foot drop to the glacier below. . . . One of the distressed climbing teams was pendulumed over a refrigerator-sized rotten rock; the other clung to the cliff or dangled on a rope which was frayed to the inner strands and pulled tight over a sharp rock held by one picket!"

Rescuers worked diligently to secure and evacuate both the surviving climbers (eight suffered injuries in the event) and Nestler's remains. Litters were employed to get the most severely injured to the helicopters that flew them to medical facilities; others were able to hike down to safety.

CHAPTER 3

Experience Is No Guarantee

There are old climbers, and there are bold climbers, but there are no old bold climbers.

—A CLIMBER'S ADAGE

AS MOUNTAINEERS GET SMARTER, TECHNIQUES ARE REFINED, AND GEAR gets better, the long-lived truism paraphrased above has lost some of its relevance. While climbers like Alex Honnold, who scaled Yosemite's three-thousand-foot El Capitan without a rope, and Kilian Jornet, who reached the summit of Mount Everest twice in one week, continue to test the limits, even the neophyte, if properly outfitted, guided, and willing, has a good shot at reaching the summit of a mountain like Rainier and living to tell the tale.

A generation of mountaineers who cut their teeth on Mount Rainier—and then went on to climb other coveted, deadly peaks—have lived to tell their stories into their golden years. Jim and Lou Whittaker, as well as mountaineer Dee Molenaar, another sage of the volcano, are among the most well-known and respected of these elder summit statesmen.

But even the best and most experienced sometimes tragically fail.

Many Rainier summiters have logged impressive ascents elsewhere on the planet. The stories that follow chronicle the deaths of several climbers with international résumés whose careers ended on the volcano. Their passages also highlight another backcountry truism: You don't have to be on the steepest, or the highest, or the coldest, to meet your maker in the wild.

The Teacher and the Student

Willi Unsoeld was an alpinist of the finest pedigree. Over his long career, he climbed peaks in the Cascades, the Tetons, and the Sierra Nevada. He summited Everest in 1963 via the difficult and then-unclimbed West Ridge, and claimed the first ascent of Masherburn, another Himalayan peak.

He was also a father, husband, smokejumper, philosopher, theologian, teacher . . . "Willi was a very complex, wonderful human being," recalled Tom Hornbeim, one of his Everest teammates, in an *Outside* magazine interview about the 1963 expedition. As an experiential educator— Unsoeld was a faculty member at Evergreen State College, with a focus on outdoor education—Hornbeim noted that his friend had "inspired many young lives."

His daughter Nanda Devi was one of those inspired by her father's passion and experience. She was named for a Himalayan peak that had enchanted Willi (and, later, would enchant her). In 1976 the twenty-two-year-old Devi succumbed to illness on an attempted ascent of her namesake mountain with her father by her side. "We are not in charge in the face of reality and nature," Unsoeld said in the wake of Devi's death, "and in the final analysis, I wouldn't have it any other way."

Reality and nature, in the form of Mount Rainier, were in charge in 1979, when it unleashed an avalanche on the thoughtful mountaineer and his students near Cadaver Gap.

Unsoeld and his party, composed of twenty-one outdoor education students from Evergreen State, had been on the mountain for several days attempting to make the summit. Bad weather and hostile conditions kept them low on the peak at first, but one weather window allowed them to ascend to Camp Muir, and a second allowed them to climb to 11,800 feet, where they established a high camp.

But that was as close to the crest as they would get. Unsoeld and some of the party made an aborted summit attempt before a storm forced them to hunker down in tents near Gibraltar Rock on the Ingraham Glacier. In the face of worsening weather, Unsoeld made the decision to return to Camp Muir. The group was on the retreat when, according to the *American Alpine Journal* accident report, the first rope team triggered a slab avalanche with a "fracture line [that] measured the entire width of Cadaver Gap and had a depth of three feet in the center."

The slide swept the four climbers on the lead rope, including Unsoeld, five hundred feet down the mountain. The leader was buried under three feet of compacted snow and ice, and one of his students, twenty-one-year-old Janie Diepenbrock, of Sacramento, California, was also completely buried. Another member of the rope team, Frank Kaplan, was only partially buried, and upon extricating himself was able to free the fourth climber, Peter Miller, who had managed to punch an arm to the surface.

The rest of the team, which was above the fracture line and not caught in the slide, acted quickly to resuscitate Miller.

But it took longer to locate, and then to uncover, Unsoeld and Diepenbrock, with one of the rescuers following the rope that had hitched them together from climber to climber. Miller survived, but despite earnest efforts at CPR, Unsoeld and Diepenbrock did not.

The *AAJ* analysis of the incident reflects not only on the decisions that played into the outcome of the climb, but also on the skills that Unsoeld's outdoor program sought to instill in students. "The foundation upon which The Evergreen State College Outdoor Education Program is built is the belief that individuals need to engage in demanding physical and mental activities in order to acquire the strength and energy it takes to accomplish something worthwhile in life," the report states. "Climbers in general believe that the risks involved in climbing lead to the benefits. It is only a question, then, of whether the risks are entered into responsibly." In the end, the report concludes, "Unsoeld made reasonable judgments under the circumstances."

The annals of the *AAJ* also include a rebuttal to this view, authored by Jeremy Bernstein in a review of *Fatal Mountaineer: The High-Altitude Life and Death of Willi Unsoeld, American Himalayan Legend.* This is included not to disrespect Unsoeld, but to highlight how individuals may view and react to the same set of inputs in different ways, for better or worse. "The conditions were so bad that [noted climber] Yvon Chouinard was leaving the mountain because of his perception of the avalanche dangers," Bernstein wrote in 2003. "This did not stop Unsoeld. Nor did the potentially bad weather. The whole thing seems to me like sheer irresponsibility—almost suicidal. In France, where guides are sanctioned by the government, this sort of performance would have led to a trial and a probable jail sentence. As it was, it led to Unsoeld's death in avalanche along with that of a young woman whom he was guiding. That anyone survived was something of a miracle."

Regardless of whether blame can be laid, the passing of Unsoeld and Diepenbrock left a profound hole. "The empty space which has been left in our lives, as in so many others, often feels as deep as the crevasses Willi used to leap and as vast as the mountainous regions of the world that used to echo his joyous yodels," Unsoeld's widow, Jolene, wrote in the wake of his death. "Yet through our tears breaks an understanding smile, a shared recognition that here went two remarkable people doing what they chose to do, knowing that in the mountains they would find wondrous beauty along with risk and the lesson of each other."

Almost Old and Bold
An accomplished Norwegian climber, Arvid Lahti had not only reached the top of the world—twice in a single year—but had also logged a number of attempts and successful climbs of Himalayan peaks, as well as topped Aconcagua in Argentina and Mount Kilimanjaro in Tanzania.

But on March 26, 2016, Lahti succumbed to hypothermia on the Gibraltar Ledges route near the Beehive.

Lahti, 58, had reached the summit with partner and fellow alpinist Monique Richard, 41. Then a winter storm swept in, with high winds and temperatures dropping into the single digits. That night, according to the park record, a Mountaineers group at Camp Muir became concerned when the two climbers, who had left gear at the camp, didn't return. They contacted rangers to report the missing summiters. The park was also aware of a snowshoer in trouble on the Muir Snowfield; he had activated his SPOT device, a satellite GPS locator that can be homed in on by rescuers in backcountry emergencies. But rescue teams would not be able to begin their ascent to Camp Muir until daylight.

On the mountain, according to Richard, she and Lahti sought shelter from the wind and cold among the rocks on the route. But they had planned to be up and off within the day; they weren't prepared to spend the night on the peak. Richard wrote that though she was sure she would be the one to die of hypothermia in that long night, it was Lahti who was unable to survive the cold, and who perished in her arms.

In the morning, according to the park service, "the climbers at Camp Muir reported that a female climber had been heard screaming from above the Camp Muir area. They were able to assist her in getting to the shelter at Camp Muir." The snowshoer also made it back to Camp Muir, and both were airlifted off the mountain and to an area hospital.

A Chinook helicopter was dispatched and Lahti's body was spotted at about 10,600 feet, "about 400 vertical feet away from Camp Muir," the park reported. A couple of days later, on March 30, "the high winds abated" and four rangers were able to bring Lahti down off the mountain.

The park service notes, rightly, that climbers like Lahti and Richard, as well as snowshoers, skiers, and others who venture high onto Rainier, should be diligent about following weather forecasts, and be prepared for an emergency bivouac. Exactly what Lahti and Richard—or the unnamed snowshoer, for the matter—carried is not described. Though the storm was, in Richard's words, "unexpected by all," the lesson is clear: Carry the gear whether you think you'll need it or not.

A picture posted by Richard on Facebook following the tragedy shows her companion on descent from Rainier's summit, drenched in sunshine. Richard's tribute to her climbing partner, a montage of images from expeditions and adventures shared with Lahti over the years following their meeting on Mount Everest in 2012, is punctuated with smiles and mountain vistas. "I will carry your human legend," she pledged, and it's easy to imagine her keeping that promise on every mountain she's climbed since Lahti's passing.

A Calculated Risk

Fifty-one-year-old Donald McIntyre of Reno, Nevada, an experienced mountaineer and climbing guide, died on descent after reaching Rainier's summit via its challenging north face in July 1997. He and teammate Joel Koury, 37, another experienced climber from California, were on their way down to Camp Schurman when the accident occurred. A storm had enveloped the mountain, creating challenging conditions and depositing wet, new, slick snow. Koury was attempting to clean snow off his crampons when he lost purchase, and when he slipped, he took his partner with him. The two men fell 25 to 30 feet into a crevasse on the Emmons Glacier at about 13,500 feet. McIntyre's aortic artery was ruptured in the fall; he perished several hours later. Koury was injured, but with the help of rangers who arrived to assist in search and rescue he was able to descend to Camp Schurman. McIntyre's body was eventually airlifted off the glacier.

In a memorial in the *American Alpine Journal*, McIntyre's business partner in Sierra Mountain Guides, John Cleary, noted that McIntyre's twenty-year career as a mountaineer included expeditions around the world, and that he had "reached the summits of Changtse, the north peak of Mt. Everest, Denali in Alaska, the Matterhorn and the Eiger in Switzerland, and Peak Communism in the Soviet Union, among many others." McIntyre was also a veteran of the US Air Force, having served a tour of duty in Vietnam, and made a career as an investigator with the US Department of Energy.

"It's like a lot of things. There's calculated risk," Cleary told the *Seattle Times* after the accident. "High-altitude mountaineering is the most dangerous, followed by mountaineering in glacial terrain as in Mount Rainier. More people are seriously injured per capita mowing their lawns."

Power and Loss in Experience and Partnership
In May 2004 Peter Cooley, an experienced mountaineer with summits including Rainier and Denali notched on his ice ax, suffered a fall near the Black Pyramid on the Liberty Ridge route. According to friend and partner Scott Richards, who recounted the story to *News Tribune* reporter Craig Hill in 2009, the tragedy began to unfold when Cooley caught his crampon in a gaiter, then slid and fell over a twelve-foot cliff, sustaining a serious blow to the head. Richards knew they needed to get off the mountain to seek medical help, but a storm was building. He hacked a platform into the snow and set up a tent in the shelter of a "rock outcropping he hoped would protect them from the Volkswagen-size chunks of ice that regularly tumble down the mountain."

Richards then used his cell phone to call for help, initiating what Hill calls "one of the most intensive rescue attempts the park has ever seen." The gears were engaged, but bad weather pinned down the rescuers and the stranded climbers for an excruciating two days. During that time, Richards did everything in his power to keep Cooley comfortable and alive. One report describes how he kept the head wound clean and his friend warm. Richards even dripped water into Cooley's mouth when the stricken man could no longer drink. Meanwhile, the park service was able to airlift supplies to the stranded climbers, but the storm precluded a formal rescue.

A pair of rangers were finally able to climb to the aid of the two mountaineers, but with aircraft still grounded by storms, the only option for Cooley's evacuation appeared to be a long, roped descent over dangerous terrain. The rescuers got a break before the overland descent started, however: A weather window allowed a Chinook helicopter to pluck Cooley off the mountain and carry him to a local hospital. Unfortunately, Cooley died on the flight.

Hill's *News Tribune* story vividly exposes the rawness of such a loss, for the surviving climber, for the dead man's family, and for the rescuers. Climbing ranger Mike Gauthier describes the letdown the rescuers felt on learning of Cooley's death as "devastating." Cooley left behind a wife and three children. His parents, who had traveled to the mountain during the rescue attempts, were en route to the hospital when they got the news. For Richards, even years after the event, the accident and loss are "still vivid. I'm still sad."

CHAPTER 4

The Crevasse

OF ALL THE POTENTIAL WAYS A CLIMBER CAN DIE ON RAINIER, THE crevasse looms large. These gashes in glacial ice can be narrow enough to step across or so deep and wide that it's best to go around. They are as integral and unavoidable on glaciers as needles are on conifers. As rivers of ice, glaciers are always in motion, flowing over the contours of the bedrock below even as they grind away at that underpinning. The ice bends and dips, advances and retreats, sometimes traveling at different speeds in one location versus another. These stresses result in fractures that can be hundreds of feet deep, reaching into seemingly bottomless blue depths.

Time and time again, on Rainier as on other glaciated peaks, mountaineers have pitched into the glacial void. Yet crevasses are also part of mountaineering's appeal. Climbers aspiring to the world's highest peaks must develop and polish the skills needed to travel in crevassed terrain. They lower each other into the frigid rents to practice hauling each other out. How best to rig an anchor? How best to set up a pulley system that can safely hoist a companion back to the surface? How best to avoid ending up in a crevasse in the first place?

Despite best efforts, both in avoidance and in rescue, the maw of the crevasse opens at the end of a long slide, under a collapsing snow bridge, at the terminus of the avalanche. And taking the plunge can be deadly.

Frozen for One Hundred Years
If they haven't been ground to bits, they should emerge from the glacier any time now.

In August 1909 Joseph W. Stevens, of Trenton, New Jersey, and T. V. Callaghan, of Portland, Oregon, both about fifty years of age, vanished in a storm, presumably near Rainier's summit crater. Accounts in the park's fatality files, which include stories taken from the *Seattle Post-Intelligencer*, record that Stevens and Callaghan, "men of some means and experienced mountaineers with alpine records," set off to climb Rainier with another man, J. P. Stirley, despite cautions to "desist" in the face of weather that was "unfavorable."

As they climbed the cleaver between the Muir Snowfield and Gibraltar Rock, the storm grew more intense, and Stirley quit the team, retreating to Paradise. There, Stirley reported that his partners were likely in danger. But it was too late in the day to begin a search-and-rescue mission. Stevens and Callaghan were left to fend for themselves overnight on the mountain.

The next morning, rescuers recovered the climbers' alpenstocks and packs stashed behind a ledge of rocks near the crater. But drifting snow had "obliterated all tracks," and there was no sign of them. Still, the searchers held out: Callaghan was "very hardy and experienced, a naturalist and woodsman, well able to take care of [him]self under such conditions."

Driven back by persistent bad weather, two more days passed before mountain guide Jules Stampfler discovered "tracks leading toward a 500 ft. ice cliff" at the head of the White River Glacier, and circumstances led the rescuers to conclude that the storm had blown the men off the mountain. Likely lost in a crevasse and "encased in ice, the bodies will freeze and remain frozen until delivered by glacier at it's [*sic*] foot," a report in the file states. The following calculation was also made: Given estimates that the glacier moved ten inches per day, or a mile every seventeen years, and was six miles long, Callaghan and Stevens would likely emerge from the toe in "102 years." There's also a notation that a $10,000 trust fund might be established to cover a later search.

Then again, as a letter from superintendent O. A. Tomlinson observes, the two climbers "may be ground to pieces in the glacier and never reach the terminal moraines."

Seven Steps

These guys did just about everything right. They were experienced mountaineers. They trained. They chose to climb Liberty Ridge, one of the most difficult routes on Rainier, but they knew what they were up against, and they knew they were capable.

Still, as Jim Davidson recounts in a powerful memoir of the climb that claimed the life of his partner, Michael Price, in June 1992, the mountain demanded unexpected sacrifice and determination.

The men took three days and worked through both physical and mental exhaustion to successfully reach the summit on June 20. They spent the night on top, and woke the next morning to a beautiful day and the prospect of a straightforward descent via the Emmons and Winthrop Glaciers. But they were exhausted. To mitigate the physical strain they deviated from the beaten path, opting to glissade from point to point instead. Glissading is a controlled slide, but a slide nonetheless. To avoid straying dangerously off-route, Davidson and Price stayed within sight of the snow-packed trail, leapfrogging other climbers who were methodically walking downhill.

Thoughtfulness, unfortunately, does not guarantee safety. Calling a halt to reconnoiter, Davidson discovered he and his partner had glissaded dangerously close to a cliff. The two decided to return to the safety of the main trail, but as they worked across the splintered glacier to the path, the bottom dropped out. Davidson broke through a sun-weakened snow bridge, plunging eighty feet into a crevasse, and he brought Price down with him.

Crevasses are shape-shifters, opening and closing, splintering and shattering, compressing and flattening as the glaciers flow. The length of a fall and what the climber hits as he tumbles in—whether he wedges like a corkscrew, or tilts upside down, or is stripped of his gear—is a crapshoot. He can land on a ledge within reach of the lip, or he can drop for hundreds of feet into darkness. He can disappear forever. For better and worse, both Davidson and Price came to rest on a narrow ledge deep in the crevasse. Davidson was buried in an avalanche of snow from the snow bridge he'd broken through. Price landed on top. As Davidson frantically dug out, he witnessed his partner, battered in the fall, expire. Still, once he was free, Davidson tried to revive Price, tried to breathe for him, begged him to wake up. It took long, precious moments for the survivor to realize his companion was lost, to work through the anguish, to come to grips with both his fear of climbing solo out of the crevasse and the recognition that this was his only option. He needed to leave his partner behind.

He was alone, and he had to do this on his own.

The spirit of his climbing buddy sustained Davidson on the harrowing ascent. The young mountaineer rigged a system that allowed him some security as he climbed, using a handful of ice screws and an ice ax, which had been stripped from the climber's hand in the fall and had to be retrieved from even deeper in the crevasse. Whether as memory or specter, the dead man prodded and encouraged the living man, guiding him up a glacial wall that was overhanging in places and that, in ordinary circumstances, Davidson considered beyond his skill level.

When Davidson reached the surface, he realized he was only seven steps from safe passage over the crevasse, and a half-hour's walk from the security of Camp Schurman. He was able to yell for help, and rangers at the hut climbed to his aid. They provided compassionate care to Davidson, who was battered but not seriously injured, and they also acknowledged his remarkable achievement. Mike Gauthier, the climbing ranger who rappelled into the crevasse to retrieve Price's body, witnessed firsthand the rope work and gear placement Davidson employed to save his own life, and complimented the climber for engaging common sense and ingenuity even as he grappled with shell-shock, insecurity, and grief.

Precursor to the Ledge

James Tuttle, 44, and his partner, Lester Spross, 37, reconsidered their skill sets when they sought the summit of Mount Rainier in May 1991. Their original plan was to ascend via the Fuhrer Finger, but the Colorado climbers opted instead for the less technical Ingraham Glacier route, telling rangers their experience level wasn't adequate for the more challenging climb.

In the end, even the more standard route proved too much.

According to the *American Alpine Journal* account of their fatal accident, the two climbers were belaying each other across a crevasse at about twelve thousand feet when the snow bridge Spross was crossing gave way. Both climbers were sucked into the void. Spross landed on soft snow at the bottom of the crevasse, a fall of more than one hundred feet. His partner was wedged in a narrower part of the cleft above.

Spross worked for hours to free Tuttle, to no avail. Before he died—the park record notes compression was responsible for Tuttle's demise—the trapped climber urged Spross to save himself. "Don't die here with me," Tuttle told the younger man, according to the *AAJ*.

Spross survived the night and the next day in the crevasse, using his ice ax to access food and water in Tuttle's pack. A heavy snowfall enabled him to build a "cone" toward the surface, and with Tuttle's crampons strapped to his hands, Spross clawed his way to the surface of the glacier. The climber then wound down the mountain, reentering civilization and finding help upon reaching Box Canyon, miles from Paradise and the start of his odyssey.

Father and Daughter

A Tacoma firefighter and climbing instructor with the Mountaineers, Kurt Fengler, 34, organized a summit attempt on Rainier via the Emmons-Winthrop route in June 1987 to fulfill a promise to his fourteen-year-old daughter, Kirstan. The two made their attempt as part of a fifteen-person party that included other Mountaineers instructors, a party well equipped and well educated for the adventure.

According to the *American Alpine Journal*'s accident report, the team took every precaution before heading up the peak, including practicing self-arrest techniques and how to rig a pulley system for crevasse rescue. The weather was cooperative as well.

The trouble started when one of the teammates began to feel ill. Both Fenglers climbed to the rope team ahead to assess the situation and discuss options, and Kurt decided to help the sick man retreat while his daughter continued the climb. As the father and daughter were talking to another member of the party, the snow bridge they were standing on "opened right up," and Kurt, along with another man, dropped into the crevasse below. Kirstan, who was not far away and still roped to her father, didn't take the plunge.

The park record attributes Fengler's death to asphyxiation; according to the *AAJ* report, the climber was buried under about five feet of snow. When a rescuer reached the victim not long after the accident, Fengler was still alive. He squeezed the rescuer's hand and asked to have the rope that secured him loosened. But, tragically, by the time he was finally extracted nearly an hour later, he had passed on.

It Comes with a Cost

Sometimes, when climbers find themselves in life-threatening situations on Mount Rainier, rescue isn't possible. Sometimes a climber simply disappears into a crevasse, into a whiteout. Sometimes the terrain is too severe to navigate. Sometimes weather conditions are so ravaging they preclude rescue attempts by crews both on the ground and in the air. The same holds true for recovery of a climber's remains. Returning loved ones to their families is always the goal, but sometimes it simply isn't possible.

And then there's the cost. The National Park Service doesn't specifically charge to rescue climbers—the permit fees climbers pay are used to cover those expenses. But if rescue or recovery requires evacuation via a helicopter or private services are called into play, someone must pay. It'd be nice to think that such practicalities wouldn't matter in a tragedy, but money is a factor, leaving the families of victims with bills they didn't anticipate and the park service, which operates on a perpetually tight shoestring, digging deep for resources.

In Mount Rainier National Park, the issues surrounding what it costs to rescue a climber date back to the earliest days. Consider the case of J. A. Fritsch. When the climber fell into a crevasse on a summit attempt via the Gibraltar Rock route on September 15, 1916, he was rescued by his teammates and evacuated to Paradise. Though park records state he suffered "no apparent injuries," he died three days later.

The details of the accident, and Fritsch's subsequent demise, are laid out in letters from the park supervisor, DeWitt Raeburn, to W. H. Penner, Fritsch's brother-in-law. Fritsch fell about fifty feet into the crevasse and was successfully retrieved by his partners, but was shaken up enough that he and two teammates spent the night on the mountain together before attempting the descent to Paradise. In the immediate aftermath of the accident there were no indications that Fritsch had suffered grave injury. Still, the supervisor noted that "Otto Kurz, cook at the hotel, who was a member of the mountain party, said that Mr. Fritsch was out of his head and somewhat dazed when they got him out of the crevasse. He did not seem to know where he was and complained of pain in his back."

A rescue party climbed to his assistance, and Fritsch made it back to Paradise after a strenuous trip. He was able to walk some of the distance, but was "very much exhausted and chilled from the cold and appeared to be somewhat delirious at times." Still, upon examination, three physicians were in agreement that he was "not seriously injured." Having spoken with two nurses in the stricken man's attendance, the supervisor noted that even Fritsch "did not seem to think he was dangerously ill, he talked a great deal about his trip up the mountain, how it happened by his stepping across the first crevasse and he slipped into the second one; that it was simply an accident and he blamed no one but himself; that he expected to be out in a few days, and was going to Portland to climb Mount Hood." His death was, therefore, a "surprise."

Fritsch's fatality file contains accounts not only of his rescue, but also of the practicalities that followed his passing. W. H. Penner took care to ensure that bills for rescue and for services rendered before Fritsch's death were paid in full, including $10 for guide services; $131.45 for "services rendered" by employees of the Rainier National Park Company who helped with the rescue; $150 to T. H. Long for medical services; $5 for the Rainier National Park hotel bill; and $3.25 for the telegram notice of his death.

The notes also include this poignant detail: A ring worn by the climber went missing, and likely fell off during his rescue. But the memento meant enough to family members that they offered a reward for its recovery.

CHAPTER 5

Going It Alone

*The days are slipping back into their regular sequence again, named
and numbered; but our thoughts linger far away on the mountain.
Thus must, I feel, it ever be so, —how otherwise?*
—FROM A LETTER OF THANKS SENT TO THE PARK BY MR. AND
MRS. HARRY DELMAR FADDEN, SEAHURST PARK, MARCH 12,
1936, FOLLOWING THE DEATH OF THEIR SON

Delmar Fadden's story, no matter where you encounter it, is laced with
regret—regret that a young man's life was lost, regret that a young man
made poor choices. It's also a road map to how solo climbers on Mount
Rainier can avoid suffering the same fate.

In January 1936 the twenty-three-year-old mountaineer was alone,
high on the Emmons Glacier. He'd summited and was on the descent
when he slipped, tumbled down the icy face, and was knocked unconscious. He likely never woke up again. When he was found days after
he was reported missing, he lay face down on the slope, head downhill,
crampons up, and frozen solid.

The tragic story began to unfold when Delmar's twin, Donald,
informed the park that his brother had not returned from a ski trip into
Glacier Basin. Donald spoke up on January 24, more than a week after
Delmar had entered the park. The first report that the man was missing
had been made a few days before that. And by the time the park launched
a search on January 25, Fadden had been adventuring alone in Rainier, in
the harshest season, for more than ten days.

Fadden was no stranger to hardship in the mountains. This attempt on Rainier was his fourth in winter; the other three had ended in failure. Notes in Fadden's fatality file also mention a monthlong trek he'd made across the Olympic mountain range, during which he'd survived on foraged roots and fried ants.

According to accounts recorded by the park, though Fadden professed a ski trip when he set off on this January trek, he ultimately sought the summit. Knowing rangers would forbid the attempt, the climber circumvented protocol and snuck past the park's White River entrance station to gain access to his route. His self-confidence—some might call it arrogance—is clear in this comment from the file: "Donald also told of his brother's determination to do as he pleased relative to his trips."

Given his reputation, it's no wonder the park wasn't alerted to Fadden's attempt until the climber missed arrangements to meet up with his brother on time. Still, given Fadden's demonstrated ingenuity and experience, all involved held out hope.

As rescuers tracked Fadden's travels in the park, they discovered that the young man had camped in the "old hotel building erected by the Mount Rainier Mining Company"; the evidence included his skis, a few cooking utensils, and some food. "From the amount of food consumed . . . it was estimated he stayed at Glacier Basin at least two or three days," the rescuers wrote.

Fadden was tracked carefully though the woods and up the slopes to Steamboat Prow. By then his brother, Donald, had clued rangers in to his true goal. The rangers were skeptical: "Fadden might have been foolish enough to attempt the summit, however there was still a question in our minds if he really had attempted such a dangerous trip alone."

The search revealed no sign of camps on Emmons Glacier or at the base of the prow. Finding a snowshoe beside a crevasse, the rescuers discovered "that Fadden had not followed the logical or usual summit route, but rather had taken a short cut." With snow obscuring his tracks, there was no way to know for sure where the aspiring summiter was or what his condition might be.

The uncertainty of their son's fate plagued his parents. His father traveled to the mountain to wait while the search played out, on the ground and in the air. Even after the climber's body was finally spotted, by plane on January 29, Harry Fadden continued his vigil. He wanted to take his son home.

A recovery party was dispatched on January 30. Retrieving Fadden's remains entailed a long journey across unforgiving terrain, with the potential that those involved could be injured or worse. The team skied about twenty-four miles through the park and up onto the slopes, proceeding "at great personal risk," before they reached the fallen man.

Getting there proved only half the battle: The effort to bring Fadden down was complicated by freezing temperatures and difficult terrain. In mountaineer and climbing historian Dee Molenaar's account of the tragedy, the men were forced to anchor the body overnight at Steamboat Prow so they could retreat to Glacier Basin to nurse frostbitten extremities. "They worked in temperatures reported by Wendell Trosper as 'pushing the mercury to the bottom' of a thermometer that recorded to minus 25°F (57 degrees below freezing)," Molenaar wrote.

All the while, Mr. Fadden was waiting at the park's White River entrance with a hearse.

In his report on the incident, Rainier's chief ranger, John Davis, wrote this: "It is my belief that Fadden had not met his fate until well after the search had been started." He came to this conclusion based on the fact that, given the storms that had enveloped the peak in those January days, the climber hadn't been buried, but was found atop the snowpack.

"It is believed that he was camped high on the mountain in a crevasse or snow cave, where he was sheltered from winds and storms watching search parties and waiting for an opportunity to come down without detection," Davis wrote. The chief ranger noted that Fadden was wearing mukluks, moccasin-like footwear that provides great insulation from the cold but no grip on hard snow or ice, and that the climber had employed crampons. But the crampon on his left foot was missing, and Davis surmised the loss of the traction device may have caused his fall. Whatever the chain of events, Davis concluded, "it is evident that he had lost his footing and slid down the mountain, knocking himself unconscious and freezing to death before he could regain his senses."

"Delmar Fadden's life was cut short at its prime," Molenaar reflected, exploring the young man's motivations and passions in *The Challenge of Rainier*, his definitive history of climbing on Mount Rainier. "But his soul doubtless would have had it no other way."

Remembering the Soloists

Despite the park service's requirement that climbers have at least one partner, Ken Seifert, like Fadden, was determined to go it alone. And, as with Fadden, his climb didn't go well. The forty-one-year-old mountaineer died on his "unauthorized" summit bid in September 1991, after taking a fall on the Disappointment Cleaver route and pitching into a crevasse at 12,600 feet.

An American Alpine Club accident report describes a climber who seemed cavalier not only about the park's climbing regulations, which require special permission from the superintendent for solo climbers, but also about conditions on the mountain. "He was traveling without a pack, had an ice ax but no crampons, and was dressed in light clothing, even though the weather was changing, temperature dropping and snow beginning to freeze," the accident report states.

When Seifert met Rainier Mountaineering Inc. guides on the route, who advised him that a rescue/recovery was under way due to the adverse conditions, he reportedly offered to help. When he was turned down, he also chose to turn around and begin a descent. Witnesses say the accident happened when he caught his gaiter with his foot and began to slide, eventually coming to rest in the crevasse about eight hundred feet below.

In early June 2010 another solo climber, Mark Wedeven, disappeared in an avalanche on the Ingraham Glacier; the resident of Olympia is still missing and presumed dead, according to the park record. He was last seen at 11,700 feet on the route, bound for the summit, along with ten other climbers traveling alone or in separate small groups.

Wedeven was a father, an experienced mountaineer who'd logged a number of ascents of Rainier, and a survivor. While researching his heritage in Colombia in 2003, he was kidnapped and held hostage. His mother told *Mother Nature Network* that the kidnappers took her son to a graveyard, where he expected to be executed but instead was set free.

The twenty-nine-year-old Wedeven chose to make his ascent on a day when rangers had warned others to back away. Avalanche conditions on the mountain were severe when the incident occurred, park officials told reporters. Two of the mountain's guide services had pulled their teams off the route prior to the slide, having determined it was too hazardous to proceed. Wedeven and another solo climber had not checked in with rangers as required by the park before their climbs, and so had not been warned about the extreme danger.

The ten other climbers caught in the slide were successfully rescued, pulled from the debris by fellow climbers and guides.

CHAPTER 6

Tales from the Routes

By one count, there are more than sixty named routes to the summit of Mount Rainier. Pick a glacier, pick a cleaver, pick a chute or a wall, and if the ambition and skill level of your climbing team is a match, you can make an attempt.

Ascents via the Disappointment Cleaver and Ingraham Glacier are far and away the most common these days, but other routes also have gained prominence over the years, including challenging climbs on the mountain's north face, such as Liberty Ridge. Whether the accidents involved avalanche, crevasse, exposure, or something else, the stories that follow have been assigned to these most prominent routes and approaches, in the hope they might pass along some wisdom to the climbers who choose the same paths.

Losses on most of the routes covered in this chapter are listed in chronological order. Both short and long, the stories illustrate the difficulties and the consequences of encounters with foul weather, adverse conditions, and bad luck. The brevity of some of the chronicles reflects, in most cases, my inability to locate media coverage of the accidents, which occasionally is a function of the fact that the accidents occurred long ago. Here, as throughout this book, please remember that a single-sentence memory isn't intended to reflect a lack of respect or diminish the impact of a loss on family and friends. Perhaps, in time, the resources needed to flesh out abbreviated stories will come to light, ready to share.

The Muir Snowfield

If it's a whiteout, you should just sit down.
        —Advice about route-finding on the Muir Snowfield

Named for celebrated naturalist John Muir, father of the National Park Service and champion of Mount Rainier National Park, the Muir Snowfield and Camp Muir are among the most visited places on the mountain. Camp Muir is the launchpad for the popular Disappointment Cleaver summit route, as well as other lines to the summit on the southern faces of the peak. Traffic is heavy on the snowfield and at the camp, which is a place of celebration when the summit is achieved and a place of reckoning when an accident occurs.

The Muir Snowfield crops up again and again in mountain's fatality records, not only for summiters, but also for skiers, snowshoers, and hikers content to explore lower on the volcano. Easy access is central to its prominence: The dead glacier stretches from above the tourist hub of Paradise to the historic high camp, and also serves as a challenging day hike destination.

The term *snowfield* implies something gentler than a glacier, and the Muir Snowfield doesn't boast the more significant crevasse dangers of Rainier's larger ice flows. But it's an ice field nonetheless and, like the rest of the high ground, is susceptible to sudden and hellish weather and snow conditions, including whiteouts. In storms the route-finding challenges amp up. Take a wrong turn and backcountry travelers may find themselves suddenly confronted by forbidding cliffs and perilous drops onto the Paradise or Nisqually Glaciers. Get unlucky in a longer event, and they may end up having to hunker down in a snow cave staving off hypothermia. Anticipating both potential hazards, everyone who ventures onto the snowfield should carry what they need to bivouac and should be skilled navigators with both map and compass and GPS units.

One of the earliest deaths recorded in the park occurred on the Muir Snowfield. Professor Edgar McClure, from the University of Oregon, died in late July 1897 after falling at what is now known as McClure Rock, above Paradise near the toe of the snowfield. His demise was the first recorded for a summiter in what had yet to become a national park.

McClure's loss, according to the June 1937 edition of Mount Rainier's *Nature Notes*, "did not dim this man's scientific achievement in making a barometric determination of the elevation of Mt. Rainier. With the utmost care and accuracy McClure set about his work, which was carried out while on the 1897 outing of the Mazama Club, of Portland." Using McClure's measurements, the peak's height was pegged at 14,528 feet—remarkable accuracy given the circumstances and tools of the time. As determined by modern methods, Mount Rainier's height is 14,410 feet.

In a more recent event—one that highlights the danger of drifting off-route on the snowfield—Douglas Vercoe, 34, and two friends were climbing toward Camp Muir on the first leg of a May 1983 summit attempt. The three were on skis, but according to a report in the *American Alpine Journal*, Vercoe was "less experienced" than his teammates and struggled with his no-wax equipment on the climb. As the weather worsened and the snowfield steepened, the team began to switchback uphill, which eased the ascent for the ill-fated climber.

But lessening the pitch did not change the outcome. "Because of the wind there was a tendency to traverse farther to the east, with the wind at their backs, than they probably normally would have," the *AAJ* reports. Vercoe was breaking trail when he yelled, then disappeared over a cornice. His teammates, hampered by poor visibility and difficult terrain, did their best to locate him before setting up a camp. Another team carried the news of the accident to rangers at Camp Muir. When the weather cleared—"Camp Muir was visible from the camp site," the report notes—a search ensued, but Vercoe could not be found.

Gibraltar Ledges

Though avalanches and crevasses arguably pose the most obvious hazards to climbers on Mount Rainier, rockfall is another common threat. The volcanic underpinnings of the mountain give rise to this particular hazard; the new rock is "friable," prone to fracturing and breaking loose due to freeze and thaw, seepage of rainwater, and just plain gravity. The Gibraltar Ledges route, popular in the early days of mountaineering on Rainier, was notorious for its rockfall danger even in perfect conditions. As mountaineer and climbing historian Dee Molenaar notes in *The*

Challenge of Rainier, "The route was precarious, especially when the heat of an afternoon's sun—or any warmth or sunshine, for that matter—softened the snow and melted the ice that congealed rock to mountain."

In July 1924, on a summit attempt via the Gibraltar route, the lead guide, veteran Swiss mountaineer Hans Fuhrer, did all he could to ensure the safety of his fellow climbers. An earthquake rendered those efforts moot. In the temblor's aftermath, Sidney Cole, of Sacramento, California, was hit by rockfall and suffered a skull fracture that killed him.

According to a report in Cole's fatality file, Fuhrer "heard the sound of descending rock and called hurriedly to the party to get under a protecting ledge of rock just above them. All members of the party except Cole reached safety, but a large boulder struck Cole a glancing blow on the right side of his head and caused a fracture at the base of the skull." Cole was transported to the hospital, where "everything possible was done to save his life."

The incessant rockfall danger eventually led to Gibraltar's fall from favor. In June 1938 a climber reported that about two hundred feet of the south face of the route had been demolished in a slide that took out a narrow but necessary ledge. The ledge had always been pummeled "by rock and icicle slides during the heat of the day," according to one park service report; now the slide "left a sheer face several hundred feet high which was impossible to pass."

The park service, along with guides with the Rainier National Park Company, surveyed a new route, which crossed the Cowlitz Glacier, passed through Cadaver Gap, and led up the Ingraham Glacier to the Emmons Glacier, thence to the summit. While the new route was longer and "more tedious" than the Gibraltar route, it was deemed less hazardous and became the route of choice for climbers going forward.

That didn't stop aspiring summiters from attempting variations on the Gibraltar route in the years to come, or stop lives from being lost along the way. In June 2005 Mike Beery, 29, was climbing with fellow firefighter Ryan Tillman when he slipped in the Gibraltar Chute, tumbling approximately nine hundred feet down the steep slope, according to the park service record. While rangers attempted to reach Beery from below, his partner, an emergency medical technician, climbed down to the injured man and commenced CPR. He worked on his companion for hours before the rangers arrived. In the end, no one could revive him.

An article about Beery's death in the *Seattle Times* quotes a park official who called the route by which the two were attempting to reach Columbia Crest "a perennial snowfield and debris chute for loose rocks from above" and a "moderately difficult climb." The article also notes that the two had been training for several months—and that Beery, a resident of the seaside town of Port Angeles who left behind a wife and two children, was a "big-hearted" man with an adventurous spirit.

Disappointment Cleaver

Given its current status as the primary line to Mount Rainier's summit, it's no surprise that a number of climbers have perished on the Disappointment Cleaver/Ingraham Glacier route. However, and once again, it's important to remember that most climbers who've taken on the challenge have reached the summit safely, or have turned around and retreated without mishap.

The "trail" takes climbers past (or through) places with names that appear again and again in the literature, including the ominous Cadaver Gap, so called because the bodies of Forrest Greathouse and Edwin Wetzel were deposited there prior to their removal from the mountain. Disappointment Cleaver, according to one story in the park's record of place names, represents "the point at which climbers who are feeling good about how far they've come up the mountain suddenly start to feel fatigue and nausea, and realize how far they remain from the summit."

The stories that follow describe the circumstances that resulted in a fatality on the route; the various levels of detail reflect how much information could be gleaned from media coverage and accessible park records of the events. They are presented in chronological order.

Among the first to die on a summit attempt via the Disappointment Cleaver was twenty-year-old William Haupert. A student from Pennsylvania, Haupert died in September 1957 after a snow bridge at thirteen thousand feet, above the cleaver itself, collapsed. According to a front-page story in the *Philadelphia Inquirer*, Haupert was part of a nine-person guided climb. He and another man, presumably his rope partner, plunged into a crevasse after the collapse. Haupert's neck was broken in the fall.

Twenty-four-year-old Michael Ferry was killed in a crevasse fall near the cleaver in August 1971. He was a member of a five-man party descending the Ingraham Glacier route. A report in the *American Alpine Journal* notes crampons were not being used at the time of the accident, and that Ferry was pulled off belay, then slid into a sixty-five-foot crevasse. The cause of death is recorded as a fractured skull.

Two climbers, Shirli Voight and Guillermi Mendoza, perished of exposure on the Disappointment Cleaver route in September 1978. Both were experienced mountaineers, according to a report in the *American Alpine Journal*: Voight, 30, was from Denver, Colorado, and director of the Colorado Mountaineering Club's mountaineering school; Mendoza, 28, was from Saltillo, Mexico, and a climbing instructor with the Mexican Mountaineering School. The journal report states the two, who were found buried in snow at about 13,300 feet, ignored the advice of other climbers on the mountain and "attempted to continue on through cold, punishing weather instead of holing up against a snowstorm that descended on them." The National Park Service also notes Mendoza suffered injury in a fall; in another *AAJ* report, Voight is described as having tried to protect the injured Mendoza by digging a trench and shielding him from the elements with her body.

Patrick Hill, 26, and Douglas Velder, 19, died in a fall from the Disappointment Cleaver route in September 1983. The park record simply states that two soldiers from Fort Lewis were "ill-prepared" for the trek ahead. The *American Alpine Journal* notes the climbers were roped together for their ascent, as is common practice, but that their kit was otherwise woefully insufficient. They were outfitted in "blue jeans and military ponchos with no packs. Neither had an ice ax. One carried a hand-held flashlight. Footwear consisted of tennis shoes inside rubber overboots, with crampons strapped on loosely."

Another team, which was descending the route after having been turned back from their summit attempt by poor weather, witnessed Hill and Velder fall about 250 feet down the mountain. The party scrambled to help the two men, with one member descending to Camp Muir to notify authorities while the others stayed on-site to administer first aid. Despite their efforts, Hill perished of his injuries on the mountain, and Velder died after being transported to the hospital.

Karl Feichtmeir, 38, and his climbing partner fell into a crevasse at 12,800 feet on the Disappointment Cleaver route in September 1991. Feichtmeir was killed; his partner was injured but survived. Newspaper accounts note Feichtmeir was an experienced mountaineer and telemark skier, but that this was his first attempted ascent of Rainier.

Nicholas Giromini, 25, of Petaluma, California, died in October 1997 after he took a 500- to 800-foot fall from about 10,700 feet on the Upper Cowlitz Glacier. Giromini and his partner, another Petaluma man, had nearly reached the safety of Camp Muir, according to accounts of the tragedy, but had wandered off-route in blizzard conditions and become separated. The survivor made his way to the camp safely and reported his partner missing. Giromini apparently found his way back onto the route, but then slipped and fell to his death. His body was found about seven hundred feet above the safety of the camp. He was not wearing crampons when he was found, but a park spokesperson noted that, given he'd just come off a rocky section, it wouldn't have been uncommon for the climber to have taken off his crampons. That Giromini didn't put them back on, however, could have been a factor in his fall.

In June 2002 Benjamin Hernstedt, 25, of Oregon, and Jeff Dupuis, 21, of New York, lost their lives in a fall on the Ingraham Glacier while on descent. According to a report in the *American Alpine Journal*, the two were discovered missing in the aftermath of another accident that took place on the same route, in which three climbers slid down the glacier and into a crevasse. Once those climbers were rescued, attention turned to finding Hernstedt and Dupuis, who hadn't returned to their tent after their summit bid.

The source for the *AAJ* report was climbing ranger Mike Gauthier, who described conditions on the peak at the time of the accidents: "The weather had been poor for numerous days before June 5, preventing many climbers from summiting. When the weather finally cleared on June 5, climbers started going for it. This weather window was enticing but such weather can also be accompanied by very firm snow/icy conditions, which can make for great climbing (i.e. cramponing) but can also be particularly unforgiving in the event of a fall."

Such a fall took out the three climbers who were rescued before Hernstedt and Dupuis were discovered missing, and also may have led to the demise of the two young men. Their bodies were recovered by helicopter from the base of an ice cliff on the Ingraham at about 12,400 feet, "entangled in rope."

A *Los Angeles Times* article on the tragedy reported that the two had not climbed the peak before. The article also notes that eight days prior to the fatal accident, a couple intending to marry atop the peak, along with their minister-guide, fell into a crevasse, but were fortunately rescued by rangers and guides.

Ed Hommer's death by rockfall while ascending the Disappointment Cleaver route in September 2002 brought an amazing life and a string of pioneering first ascents to an early end. A bilateral amputee, Hommer perished on Rainier while training for a second bid to reach the roof of the world, the summit of Mount Everest.

The forty-six-year-old climber was a veteran mountaineer, an experienced pilot, and an advocate for amputees. He lost his lower legs to frostbite after crashing his small plane on Denali's Kahiltna Glacier in 1981; he and a passenger survived a five-day storm on that formidable Alaskan peak before their rescue, while the two other people on the plane lost their lives.

Following that accident, Hommer battled depression and alcoholism, but pulled himself clear of both to become the first bilateral transtibial amputee to summit Denali, and also the first bilateral amputee to be cleared as a commercial airline pilot. A resident of Minnesota and the father of three children, Hommer established the High Exposure Foundation, dedicated to helping amputees in the United States and Nepal acquire prosthetics and return to the activities they previously enjoyed.

Hommer's first attempt to climb Mount Everest using specially designed prosthetics was thwarted several thousand feet below the summit by adverse weather conditions. After this defeat, Hommer told a reporter that "the mountain ultimately decides who succeeds, who fails, who goes home and who doesn't." Everest was the focus, both of the comment and Hommer's aspirations, but ultimately Rainier would be the decision maker.

Liberty Ridge and the North Face

Those with more ambition, who want to do really the finest route on the mountain, will climb Liberty Ridge. There's no route that's more straight and elegant and beautiful.
        —CLIMBER JIM WICKWIRE REFLECTING ON THE LOSS OF
        THREE CLIMBERS IN MAY 2002, FROM THE *SEATTLE TIMES*

Liberty Ridge is among the most desirable and difficult routes on Mount Rainier. It's described as elegant and challenging—a test piece for tougher climbs on higher peaks. It's also among the most dangerous.

Because the ridge features more technical climbing than other lines on the volcano, it attracts ambitious climbers whether they are prepared or not, both in terms of experience and equipment. The route also landed on bucket lists following its inclusion in *Fifty Classic Climbs in North America*, compiled by Steve Roper and Allen Steck and first published in 1979 by the Sierra Club.

The Emmons-Winthrop route represents a less difficult challenge on the north side of the peak, and is often used as the descent after a Liberty Ridge climb. It's also an escape route for climbers who find themselves in difficult straits on other lines. But that doesn't translate to safety. Steep and often slick, the Emmons-Winthrop has seen a number of fatalities.

As above, these accidents are described in chronological order, and their relative length reflects only the chosen sources, not the magnitude of the losses.

In June 1968, respected alpinist Patrick Chamay died of high-altitude pulmonary edema on the Liberty Ridge route. His obituary in the *American Alpine Journal* notes that the climber, an employee of Boeing, became enamored of mountaineering in the Cascades and quickly became one of the best in the region. "Few men in this world of daily cares die pursuing something they love," the *AAJ* brief notes. "Pat died in the mountains, which was his world; and on Mount Rainier, which he did love."

In July 1969 Mark Kupperberg, 25, and David Stevens, 28, both climbing with a large party guided by the Seattle Mountaineers, were killed in a crevasse fall on the Winthrop Glacier. An American Alpine Club report on the accident notes the climbers were on descent and that conditions were icy—Kupperberg and other climbers in the group were having trouble keeping their footing on the glacier. Kupperberg was the last person on his rope team when he took his final fall, pitching Stevens and another climber, sixteen-year-old Chris Marshall, into a thousand-foot slide. The two men who lost their lives fell 125 feet into a crevasse and were buried by snow and ice. The third climber on the rope, Marshall, was airlifted off the mountain and survived.

Summit climber Dean Klapper was descending the Emmons Glacier in July 1977 when his glissade, which started at about thirteen thousand feet, became a thousand-foot slide into a crevasse. He died after breaking his neck.

Climbers Doug Fowler and Bruce Mooney were killed in a fall on Liberty Ridge in May 1981, a month before the avalanche that claimed the lives of eleven climbers—the worst accident in American mountaineering history. Mooney, 20, and Fowler, 21, were both Tacoma residents. Associated Press reports note that the bodies of the two men were located via aerial reconnaissance and plucked from the mountain by helicopter after a pair of rangers ascended to their location on the Liberty Wall from the Carbon Glacier.

In the month following the devastating avalanche deaths, another climber lost his life on Liberty Ridge. Peter Brookes died of undisclosed causes in July 1981 after he became separated from his partner; his body was recovered two days after his disappearance.

Twenty-five-year-old Christopher Blight died on descent in May 1983, after summiting via the Liberty Ridge with a team of six from the Mountaineers. Blight perished while attempting to assist a teammate who'd fallen into a crevasse. He was unroped when he came to her aid and fell into the same crevasse. With the assistance of another team, his body was retrieved from the abyss.

Turkish national Fuat Dikmen, 28, of Madison, Wisconsin, was killed on Liberty Ridge during a solo summit attempt in October 1984. His body was recovered in May 1985.

In the accident that claimed the lives of Don Wiltberger and Dr. John Weis, both 31, video illuminates some of the challenges the two faced on their ascent of Liberty Ridge in May 1987.

According to news reports, the film that was discovered after the accident showed the two men enjoying their approach hike to the route, admiring a waterfall and gorgeous mountain views under sunny skies. The climbing took a toll nonetheless, prompting the climbers to take a rest day. On the fourth day of the ascent, the weather turned. A "fierce windstorm" settled onto the ridge, and the footage documents the men "breathing hard and complaining of icy footing" as they continued to climb.

It's not known whether Wiltberger and Weis reached the summit, but they set up camp below the crater rim, at thirteen thousand feet, in a heavy storm that buried their tent under three feet of snow. According to a report in the *American Alpine Journal*, the men smothered beneath the snowpack, perhaps in their sleep. Their bodies were recovered after more than a week, and one of the rescuers, according to the *AAJ* report, "had to be evacuated due to a case of acute mountain sickness."

The two men hailed from Olympia, Washington, and had attempted the ridge route twice before and failed, Weis's younger brother, Bill, told reporters in the wake of the deaths. And while it was hard to watch the video, the surviving brother also found some solace there, noting it was "great to see how incredibly uplifting it was for them, how they were doing what they loved to do."

Climbers Craig Adkison, 37, Greg Remmick, 32, and team leader David Kellokoski, 30, were reported overdue from their summit attempt via the Liberty Ridge by Adkison's wife, Lori, on May 15, 1988. The bodies of the men were recovered from the route five days later. Conflicting accounts obscure the reason(s) for the accident that claimed their lives, however, and the mystery fueled what one report called a "media event" surrounding the incident.

"There is no way to know just what caused the fall that resulted in the deaths of the three climbers," a report in the *American Alpine Journal* states. "It may have been a slip, an avalanche, or rockfall. Nor do we know for certain what time or day the accident occurred or whether the climbers were ascending or descending."

The climbers apparently had good weather up until what is assumed to be their summit day, when one of Rainier's notorious cloud caps developed, enveloping the upper ridges in storm. When the men were found, they were geared up for the conditions; they also had suffered traumatic injuries consistent with a fall. The park record states that team leader Kellokoski fell one to two thousand feet. The contradictions are in the details: The park's account differs from that of the *AAJ* in noting the climbers died on descent, and that Adkison was airlifted off the mountain before perishing.

A UPI report quotes a park source as saying the three likely were struck by an avalanche, given that the bodies were found "amid a mass of frozen chunks of snow." It also was reported that while Adkison had climbed Rainier before, via the Emmons Glacier, and Kellokoski and Remmick were experienced rock climbers, having scaled challenging big walls in Yosemite, none had extensive climbing experience on snow and ice.

Coverage of the recovery of the climbers' remains by the Associated Press from "an avalanche chute at the 10,000-foot level" includes a vivid description of a helicopter "equipped with a grappling hook" catching the rope that connected the climbers and lifting them off the slope. The AP report also quotes a park spokesperson lamenting the event might attract more "thrill seekers" to the dangerous route.

Two men from Lake Tahoe, California, died while attempting the Liberty Ridge route in May 1989. Richard Mooney, 33, and Peter Derdowski, 26, had hitched up with another team of two climbers from Tahoe for the approach, forming a loose alliance; the four began together, but then split into two rope teams as they gained altitude. They camped together on the evening before the summit bid, but Mooney and Derdowski, according to the survivors, didn't eat or drink much that night. The next day the two teams set off at the same time, but as distance stretched between them, the stronger team lost contact with Mooney and Derdowski.

When high winds began to buffet the mountain, the surviving team bivouacked below the Liberty Cap. One of the men, Larry Duin, told the *Reno Gazette-Journal* that "the winds nearly pinned us down. We found shelter in a crevasse, dug a cave and got in our tent." The next morning, as Duin and his partner, Steve Newell, resumed their climb, they came across the frozen remains of Mooney, who had perished of hypothermia at about fourteen thousand feet. Derdowski, however, was nowhere.

A three-day search ensued, involving forty-five rangers and volunteers, as well as search dogs and three helicopters, according to an American Alpine Club report. Derdowski was found at the base of the Liberty Wall; he had perished in a fall of about five thousand feet.

Scott Porter, 32, and Karl Ahrens, 35, died in August 1995 after falling 2,400 feet down the Emmons Glacier, coming to rest on the Winthrop Glacier. Their rope mate, Brian Nelson, sustained a brain injury in the fall but survived. The climbers had claimed the summit and were on the descent when the slip occurred. Conditions near the top of the mountain, according to one report, were "akin to walking on a wet ice cube."

On May 29, 2002, three people lost their lives while ascending the Liberty Ridge route. Keeta Owens, 21, and two companions, German nationals Cornelius Beilharz, 26, and Grit Kleinschmidt, 26, perished in whiteout conditions while attempting to bivouac below the Liberty Cap. Only one man from the summit team, Andreas Kurth, survived.

Owens died after falling on a 19-degree slope at nearly 13,400 feet, according to the park record, and the body of Kleinschmidt was discovered in a "shallow depression" at about 13,100 feet; the park believes she succumbed to hypothermia. Beilharz also died in a fall. The deaths were attributed to freezing weather and high winds, which enveloped the climbers on their descent, shredded the team's tents, and caused their snow caves to collapse.

Exactly what happened high on the mountain that day, one park official reflected, may never be known. But articles about the accident from the *Seattle Times*, posted on the Oregon Mountaineering Association website, describe unstable conditions and also offer insights from mountaineering rangers into what befell the four climbers.

A "Northwest mix of rain, snow and clear skies" was in play on Rainier as the four-person team—among 256 climbers on the peak at the time—headed toward the summit. Those conditions were forecast to deteriorate, but not everyone got, or paid heed to, the message, including Owens and her companions.

The team attained Liberty Cap, ascending a route that Rainier's lead climbing ranger, Mike Gauthier, noted "requires climbing savvy," but conditions forced the mountaineers to retreat before they reached the summit proper. The team also apparently veered off-course on the descent; they intended to head down the Emmons Glacier, the survivor told investigators, but found themselves, in fading daylight, on "a steep slope on the south side of Liberty Cap."

That's where the teammates bivvied, and that's where the winds shredded their tents. That's also where, according to reports, details get sketchy. Snow caves were dug and collapsed, climbers lost track of each other . . . fell . . . froze.

Reflecting on the accident and tragic outcome, ranger Gauthier told reporters that he "didn't detect any error, major bad decision or screw-up." The climbers didn't strike him as "novices." But for these climbers, experience was no guarantee against bad weather and bad luck.

In June 2004 forty-year-old Jonathan Cahill, a firefighter who lived in nearby Orting, died after he fell about two hundred feet from the climbing route on Liberty Ridge. The accident occurred at an elevation of about 11,300 feet. His climbing companion, a thirty-three-year-old firefighter from Bellevue, was rescued and airlifted off the mountain after the accident. Newspaper accounts of Cahill's death note he had climbed the peak at least twenty-five times previously. In one report, a colleague called Cahill a "110 percent kind of guy" who was athletic and "straightforward." He left behind a wife and four children. The park service fatality report lists the climber's name as Peter Cahill.

Luke Casady and partner Ansel Vizcaya, a pair of "experienced climbers" from Montana, were killed in an avalanche on Liberty Ridge during a ski/summit attempt in June 2004. The two were high on the mountain when a fierce summer storm blew in, described by ranger Mike Gauthier in an *American Alpine Journal* report as bringing both heavy snowfall and high winds to the upper mountain. "This was an uncomfortable night for climbers everywhere on Mount Rainier," Gauthier wrote, adding that snow and wind "destroyed several tents at Camp Muir."

The winds deposited a dangerous snow load on the mountain's leeward slopes, including the slope below which Casady and Vizcaya, both twenty-nine years old, are assumed to have bivouacked. In the storm's wake, a large slab avalanche broke loose and slammed into the climbers, presumably while they were breaking camp (the two weren't roped up when their bodies were found). The slide swept them off the ridge and down onto the Carbon Glacier.

"The avalanche most likely encompassed them and the entire upper route; everything was pushed down the 4,000-foot Liberty Wall to the

Carbon Glacier," Gauthier noted in the report. "Neither climber could have survived the fall."

Spotted from the air, Casady's remains were recovered at about nine thousand feet. He left behind a wife and young child. Vizcaya, a widely traveled botanist and a seasonal employee of nearby North Cascades National Park, wasn't found until a month later, after summer sun had melted away the snow that blanketed him.

On descent from the summit via the Emmons Glacier in late July 2010, the last person in a rope team of four lost his footing. In the hundred-foot chain-reaction slide that followed, each member of the group slid into a thirty-five-foot-deep crevasse at thirteen thousand feet. They were unable to self-arrest.

Lee Adams, a resident of Seattle and a well-loved instructor with the Washington Alpine Club, plunged deep into the rift with one of his teammates; the other two climbers landed higher up, on a ledge. The fifty-two-year-old climber, who had summited Mount Rainier previously and was remembered as an enthusiastic and accomplished climber in a report by the *Seattle Times*, was killed in the fall.

"Mr. Adams was a very competent and experienced climber who tried with all his strength to stop the fall of his team," Rainier climbing ranger Nick Hall noted in an *American Alpine Journal* report on the incident. "But his experience and strength alone were not enough to stop his teammates and himself from taking this ultimately fatal fall."

One of his students from the Washington Alpine Club told the *Seattle Times* she had encountered Adams on the mountain prior to his death. She shared with him the idea that "if you keep up a certain level of fitness into your 50s, you'll keep charging into your 80s." Adams responded by shouting, " 'Woo hoo, I'm good, I'm going to be climbing'. . . He always responded to life like that, in such an excited fashion."

Climber Robert Plankers was exhausted and hypothermic when he disappeared from his camp at 13,800 feet on Liberty Ridge in June 2011. It had been an exceptionally cold and snowy season, and even in early summer the mountain was still blanketed in snow and hammered by storms.

Rescuers were forced to bivouac for a night as they attempted to reach the spot where Plankers, 60, had been anchored to the mountain while his companions sought assistance for the ailing man.

An experienced climber from Olympia, Washington, who had five Rainier summits under his belt, Plankers became disabled by exhaustion, hypothermia, and possibly frostbite as he and his teammates made their way toward the summit, according to an *American Alpine Journal* report. His partners anchored him high on the mountain with shelter, food, and a stove while they descended for help, but Plankers was gone by the time that help arrived. Rangers found a two-thousand-foot slide path that careened down the mountainside, which "indicated intermittent airborne periods and ended at an icefall below Liberty Wall." Though Plankers's remains were not recovered, the fall undoubtedly took his life.

In June 2015 rangers were notified by phone that a party of three climbers had become separated at about 14,200 feet in a storm, and that one of the climbers, twenty-five-year-old Kyle Bufis, had gone missing. The group had been descending from the summit area via the Emmons-Winthrop Glaciers when Bufis disappeared. The climber's father, Jeff Bufis, told reporters that the three-man team had encountered whiteout conditions on Liberty Saddle and taken refuge in a crevasse to wait out the storm. When they discovered they'd left their stove "at another stop about 55 feet up the mountain," Kyle, who his father describes as an experienced climber, volunteered to retrieve it. He never returned.

When the weather cleared, a rescue was initiated. Bufis's body was spotted from the air and recovered the following day. The park record notes Bufis was climbing unroped and died of exposure.

CHAPTER 7

Remembering the Summiters

You can walk up sometimes, roped, with proper equipment but in shorts, but all it takes is one storm to come in—and this has happened many times—to kill people within half an hour of a road system. It has killed children on what seems like a gentle slope. It's something that can become very angry. It looks so lovely and so beautiful, and yet it can be a devil that shows pity on no one.
— MOUNT RAINIER NATIONAL PARK SPOKESPERSON CY HENTGES, AS QUOTED BY THE ASSOCIATED PRESS FOLLOWING THE DEATHS OF THREE CLIMBERS ON LIBERTY RIDGE IN 1988

The stories that follow don't fall neatly into chapters about crevasses, or going solo, or a popular route. And, as noted previously, the records of some mountaineering accidents are detailed, while for others details are sparse. For this reason—as well as the fact that fleshing out each story at length would result in a tome of biblical length—some of the entries that follow are brief.

But no matter the level of detail, the story of each of these fallen mountaineers provides insight into the types of accidents that occur on Mount Rainier's various and less-traveled summit routes, as well as into the responses to those events, and may offer some insight into the person at the heart of the tragedy. They are listed in chronological order.

In August 1911 Legh Osborn Garrett disappeared on a solo summit attempt via the Success Cleaver. Mount Rainier historian and climber

Dee Molenaar records that a search party, while unable to locate the young man, found tracks made by his "canvas tennis shoes."

A fall on a summit attempt doesn't have to be major to kill a mountaineer. Climber Gilbert Ordway, an attorney from Boston, Massachusetts, was descending the Cowlitz Cleaver in August 1915 when he took what could be considered, in light of some of the lengthy falls recorded on the volcano, a minor spill.

According to a letter written by Mount Rainier National Park supervisor D. L. Raeburn, the accident happened when Gilbert's "alpine staff" slipped, allowing him to "tumble forward to the trail below, a drop of about 15 feet. He struck his head just back of his left ear, rendering him unconscious, in which state he remained until his death." The group's guide, Harry Greer, descended swiftly from the scene to Paradise to secure help for the injured man. He then returned to care for the rest of the summit party, members of which he noted were "in a slightly nervous state," and which he wanted to secure "in a safe place." Regret permeates the letter Greer wrote about the incident: "You can sincerely believe that I am very sorry that this catastrophe has occurred and I hope that it will never again befall me to make another report like this one."

While bad weather and bad luck play significant roles in fatalities on summit attempts, at least one climber appears to have lost his life simply by relaxing. In July 1931, during a break on a summit attempt, Robert Zinn apparently reclined onto the ice, slipped, and took a mile-long slide down the slope above the Nisqually ice cliff into a crevasse. He was unroped at the time. His brother, Kenneth, tried to stop him and began a long slide too, but he was able to self-arrest using his alpenstock, a pole with an iron tip that was, at the time, a poor equivalent to the modern ice ax. Both Robert and Kenneth, sons of the Reverend John F. Zinn of Portland, Oregon, were members of a thirteen-person Mazama climbing club party.

Climber C. T. Bressler, a professor of geology at Western Washington College in Bellingham, was doing research on the summit when he reportedly died of high-altitude pulmonary edema (HAPE) in September 1959. Newspaper accounts of the death list the cause as a heart attack, but the park record attributes Bressler's demise to this severe form of altitude sickness, which results in a suffocating buildup of fluid in the lungs and can only be cured by descending to a lower altitude.

Two other men died in an effort to provide oxygen to the stricken summiter. Harold Horn, a pilot with the Washington Civil Air Patrol, and his passenger, Charles Carman, were killed when their small plane crashed while attempting to drop supplies; the overturned aircraft was found four hundred feet below the crater rim. An entry in the "In the Air" chapter details what amounts to a triple tragedy.

Milton Armstrong disappeared from Camp Muir in September 1968 while attempting to reach the summit. The sixty-four-year-old climber's car was noticed abandoned in the parking lot at Paradise; his pack was found unclaimed at Camp Muir, with a note saying he'd return to pick it up. He never did. Search and rescue couldn't locate him in the days following his disappearance; his body was eventually recovered from Cowlitz Cleaver. The National Park Service lists the cause of death as "unknown," but other sources say exposure was likely the culprit.

A party of five ascending the Curtis Ridge route in June 1969 was beset by rockfall at 11,700 feet. One of the climbers was struck "a glancing blow" by the falling rock, which was enough to send him and his two rope-mates tumbling. Their fall was arrested when George Dockery, 37, was "caught on a small rock outcropping." Dockery was killed in the accident; the other climbers survived. An extensive and complicated search and rescue ensued, with helicopters airlifting manpower to precarious and notoriously dangerous aspects on the mountain. "The Rainier north side ridges, and especially Curtis, have traditionally been considered rescue nightmares due to the long approach and steep snow and ice slopes," reads an account of the rescue in the *American Alpine Journal*. "The key to this effective rescue was utilization of highly competent high altitude climbers from four rescue units and the Park Service. . . . Coordinated chopper and ground movement expedited the speed of a rescue that otherwise might have been impossible."

David Taylor, a twenty-three-year-old park ranger from Wooster, Ohio, was caught in an avalanche near Success Cleaver in November 1974 while climbing with partner and fellow ranger Carl Fabiani. Newspaper reports describe the ordeal as recounted by Fabiani: The two had been turned around below the summit by accumulations of fresh snow and severe avalanche conditions and were on the descent, unroped, in bad weather, when they became separated. Fabiani tried to locate his partner, was unsuccessful, and then sought shelter from the storm overnight. He made a two-day solo descent to seek help. The park service attributed Taylor's death to the avalanche; his body was not recovered.

Rockfall on the central Mowich Face claimed the life of Mark Jackson, 17, on a summit attempt in August 1975. The victim, who suffered a head injury, and two others were caught in the cascade of stone.

In February 1977 Jack Wilkins, 55, a reporter for the *Seattle Post-Intelligencer*, died while glissading on Pyramid Glacier. The park service notes the summiter slid and tumbled a quarter-mile before coming to rest, and died of head and chest trauma. A report in the *New York Times*, however, quoted a park service spokesman as saying Wilkins "stumbled while doing camp chores and plunged 900 feet down the steep slope of Success Cleaver." He was a member of the Tacoma Mountain Rescue Council and both covered and participated in a number of mountain rescues, according to the report.

Mary Gnehm, 47, was on a guided climb with Rainier Mountaineering Inc. in September 1977 when one of the four climbers she shared a rope with slipped and failed to self-arrest. While the guide and other team members attempted to stop the slide, momentum carried the climbers more than a thousand feet down the mountain, according to a report in the *American Alpine Journal*. When the rope finally hitched up on a serac on the Ingraham Glacier, the climbers came to rest. Gnehm was killed in the 1,400-foot slide; two other climbers were injured.

Michael McNerthney, 17, of Tacoma, was killed in December 1977 when he was buried in an avalanche on descent from the summit. He was pulled from the avalanche debris alive, according to a newspaper report, but later died at a Puyallup hospital. The slide covered a two-hundred-yard-square area on the southwest face of Panorama Point and buried McNerthney under three feet of debris.

Todd Davis, 24, a commercial fisherman from Sitka, Alaska, was killed in May 1978 when a slab avalanche struck his climbing party and swept him and his two companions about two thousand feet down the mountain. The team was attempting to summit via the Fuhrer Finger route and began the slide at about 12,500 feet. Davis's partners, David Jones of Ward Cove, Alaska, and David Beckter, of Everett, Washington, spent a couple of hours trying to dig their teammate out of the avalanche debris, then retreated to Paradise for help.

The Davis team wasn't the only one dealing with adverse avalanche conditions on the mountain at the time. An article in the Sitka *Daily Sentinel* quotes park service officials who explained that, within the previous twenty-four hours, two other climbing parties—eight climbers in all—were swept off the Cowlitz Glacier in a snow slide. One of the teams included veteran Rainier guide Lou Whittaker and his son, who were swept more than six hundred feet down the glacier. The other team went for a shorter ride of twenty to thirty feet. Injuries among the other climbers were relatively minor, but included a possible broken ankle. Climbers were warned not to climb until avalanche danger on the peak, where heavy winds had deposited dangerous accumulations of snow in gullies and east-facing slopes, subsided.

Twenty-seven-year-old Dale Click was killed in September 1979 when he slid twenty-five feet into a crevasse on the Inter Glacier. The park record states he perished of hypothermia. A report in the *American Alpine Journal* notes Click, who was unroped, "carried his team's climbing equipment with him when he tumbled into the crevasse" and that his partner, Tom McKee, stymied by a lack of gear, was unable to come to Click's aid. Five hours passed before a rescue team arrived at the scene, and by that time Click had perished.

Attempts to recover the fallen man's remains were hampered by a severe storm that dumped eight feet of snow on the peak. A team on a charity climb, including a disc jockey broadcasting their ascent, was trapped in the same storm. A report from the Associated Press describes that team's struggle to survive, which included their near suffocation when their tent was smothered in deep snow. When the tent collapsed, the climbers took shelter in a crevasse "bigger than a basketball gymnasium." Those climbers survived.

In February 1992 Gregory Terry, 27, and Jeff Vallee, 26, were caught in an avalanche and killed while ascending via the Fuhrer Finger and Wilson Glacier. An obituary for Terry, published in the *Chicago Tribune*, noted he worked for REI, the outdoor retailer based in Seattle and founded by Jim Whittaker, who began his mountaineering career on Mount Rainier. Another newspaper account calls both men "experienced Seattle climbers." The bodies were recovered at about 8,400 feet about a week after they went missing, when one of their boots was spotted from the air.

In October 2004 Aaron Koester, 21, and Matt Little, 23, both residents of Monroe, Washington, abandoned plans for a summit attempt due to a late start, and opted to practice their climbing techniques on the Ingraham Glacier instead. The two were preparing for an attempt on Denali in Alaska.

The climbers were at about 11,700 feet when they were caught in a slab avalanche and swept back into the "cavernous crevasse" they were attempting to cross. When the ramp collapsed, the sliding snow carried them 150 feet into the icy rift, burying both men. Little was able to extricate himself, but Koester, a volunteer firefighter, was buried beneath the avalanche debris and was dead by the time his partner reached him.

In early July 2010 Eric Lewis, 57, unclipped from the rope that connected him to his climbing partners and disappeared. The team of three was climbing the Gibraltar Ledges route in severe weather and was at about 13,600 feet, nearing the summit, when Lewis disappeared. His companions searched for the missing man—the most experienced mountaineer in the group—but were unable to locate him, according to an *American Alpine Journal* report.

The two survivors descended to Camp Muir and reported the incident to rangers. In the hours and days that followed, more than forty people participated in a search-and-rescue effort that turned up the climber's pack, as well as evidence of a snow cave. But Lewis was never found and is presumed dead.

Tucker Taffe died on a summit attempt on May 10, 2011, falling into a crevasse at 13,200 feet on the Nisqually Glacier. He was part of a party of four that had approached the summit via the Fuhrer Finger, then proceeded on skis on the upper Nisqually Glacier. According to the park service record, Taffe fell seventy-five feet into the crevasse, and his teammates were unable to pull him out. By the time a guide arrived at the scene, about three and a half hours after the fall, Taffe had expired. Rescuers were flown to the summit and descended to the accident site, and Taffe was pulled from the crevasse that afternoon. A newspaper account of the accident notes the thirty-three-year-old victim was employed at the Alta ski area in Utah's Wasatch Mountains and was "regarded as an 'expert' skier."

In January 2012 four people disappeared on the mountain in a winter storm, including a pair of summiters. Seol Hee Jin, 52, a Korean national, disappeared and has not been found, despite an exhaustive search at the site where the remains of his companion and another climber were discovered. Eunsork Yang, also 52 and called Eric in news reports, a resident of Springfield, Oregon, was found at 8,200 feet on the Paradise Glacier in September 2012.

Part 2: Elsewhere in the Park

At this point we left the canyon, climbing out of it by a steep zigzag up the old lateral moraine of the glacier. . . . Still ascending, we passed for a mile or two through a forest of mixed growth, mainly silver fir, Patton spruce, and mountain pine, and then came to the charming park region, at an elevation of about five thousand feet above sea level. Here the vast continuous woods at length begin to give way . . . leaving smooth, spacious parks, with here and there separate groups of trees standing out in the midst of the openings like islands in a lake. Every one of these parks, great and small, is a garden filled knee-deep with fresh, lovely flowers of every hue, the most luxuriant and the most extravagantly beautiful of all the alpine gardens I ever beheld in all my mountain-top wanderings.
—FROM *AN ASCENT OF MOUNT RAINIER*, BY JOHN MUIR

In Mount Rainier National Park, for obvious reasons, the focus is on the peak, a magnet for action and drama. But the park is a big place, encompassing about 369 square miles. Lesser summits, grand forests, legendary hiking trails, roaring rivers and creeks, and spectacular cascades all lie within its borders. These features—including the wildflower gardens John Muir found so enchanting—constitute additional magnets for adventurers and explorers. Some have also been, on occasion, the sites of tragedy and death.

CHAPTER 8

On the Trail

AN EXPANSIVE WEB OF FOOTPATHS SPLAYS ACROSS THE FLANKS OF Mount Rainier. More than 260 miles of trail are maintained within the park, and a plethora of informal climbing and cross-country routes add to the possibilities for hikers, skiers, and mountaineers. The formal trails see their heaviest use in the summer months, when the bulk of the park's visitors—more than 1.4 million in 2017—arrive. A healthy portion of that number venture off into the woods.

Perhaps best known is the Wonderland Trail, a ninety-three-mile path that circumnavigates the peak's lower slopes. Walking the Wonderland Trail doesn't involve gaining Rainier's summit, but for thru-hikers the elevation gained and lost—sometimes more than three thousand feet in a day as they climb over ridges and drop through drainages—is hefty. Thru-hikers also must contend with whatever weather the mountain tosses their way, including torrential rain, biting wind, and thick snow.

But these adventurous distance walkers see aspects of Rainier that most day-trippers cannot: remote subalpine meadows abloom with wildflowers, thick stands of evergreens, and perhaps glimpses of wildlife that eschews the places most crowded with humans, like bobcats, black bear, marmots, and mountain goats.

Long-distance hikers don't have to traverse the Wonderland Trail to experience the wonders of Rainier's backcountry. Other routes stretch miles, reaching secluded destinations far removed from the hubbub of Paradise and Sunrise in summertime. Even the popular, shorter, interpretive routes in the park's front country, which provide perfect outings for families with small children, can be satisfying for the more experienced hiker seeking a crash course in Rainier's natural world. These can be as short as a third of a mile, and lead to a handful of the spectacular waterfalls, groves, and wildflower meadows the park is famous for. Venture more than a mile, and you may find yourself alone in a wildland, even if you are still within whistling distance of a major highway or visitor center.

Given the abundance of trails and the variety of users, it's no surprise that, on occasion, a hiker walks off-route and becomes lost. Most often these wanderers are found again alive, usually colder and wiser for the experience. Sometimes, however, hikers are lost forever.

Sifting through the park's fatality records, it becomes apparent that many of the hikers who have perished on Rainier's trails suffered heart attacks attributed to overexertion. Such an event on a day hike is impossible to predict, and while the loss is profound for family, friends, and even potential rescuers, often little more can be gleaned from public records than the deceased's name and sketchy details. I've listed these victims in the "Of Natural Causes" chapter.

This chapter focuses on those hikers who met their ends on the trail of less natural causes.

Where She Loved to Be

When outdoors writer Karen Sykes set out on a hike with her partner in June 2014, she certainly did not intend it to be her last. She'd notched hundreds—likely thousands—of miles on her hiking stick, and Mount Rainier was one of her haunts. She was a lover of wilderness, a poet with an artist's eye, and an experienced walker in the woods.

As is so often the case when a person dies alone, what exactly happened on the trail that day is unknown. The respected and well-loved seventy-year-old Seattle resident was on a work-inspired reconnaissance mission in the Owyhigh Lakes area, looking for wildflowers to photograph for a story she planned to write. She and partner Robert Morthorst had hiked about four miles up the trail toward the lakes when Morthorst opted to stop. A park official told the *Los Angeles Times* that snowmelt had rendered routes throughout the park treacherous, including the track to Owyhigh, and that Morthorst was loath to continue given the conditions.

Sykes carried on, armed with her camera and enough supplies to sustain her overnight, should that become necessary. She was not the kind of hiker to be turned away by difficult trails, or even by lack of a trail. In the introduction to her guidebook *Hidden Hikes in Western Washington*, Sykes identifies her audience as walkers with both "a sense of adventure" and the requisite route-finding skills to get out there and back again when footpaths disappear or cross-country travel is preferred. She was that kind of walker herself.

On this occasion, she didn't get there and back again. When Sykes failed to return to the trailhead and Morthorst realized something had to be wrong, he retreated to his vehicle to let officials know she was missing. While his report was relayed to search-and-rescue, Morthorst waited, doubtless hoping Sykes was merely overdue—delayed, perhaps, to catch the perfect light on the perfect bloom—and would come walking out at any moment.

Her remains were discovered after a three-day search-and-rescue effort that involved teams on the ground and in the air. She was spotted by a helicopter crew, her body lying in what's described as steep, rugged terrain near Boundary Creek. The coroner would note that Sykes had heart disease, which may have contributed to her death, but hypothermia was credited with claiming her.

Sykes built her career in the outdoors. In addition to guidebooks, she wrote stories for magazines and newspapers, maintained a blog, and wrote poetry. Morthorst collected her verse in a book published posthumously. Her daughter told the *Times* that she hoped her mother would be "revered for the writer and lover of nature she was and the beautiful ways she represented Seattle and the Northwest in her photography and writing."

Sykes's last blog post captures her personality and reverence for nature. Describing the Lime Kiln Trail just a few weeks before she passed, Sykes wrote, "Though I'm not young I still enjoy the challenge of rugged trails, obscure trails, abandoned trails and looking for artifacts even if the price is a losing battle with Devil's Club, salmonberry, rotting stumps and nettles. Sometimes it just feels good to tussle with Mother Nature; it builds character." The photos she posted to Flickr from the hike document not only the place, but also the artist's eye for color and the passion she carried for her subjects.

While at some point during those days in June Sykes lost her life on the mountain, another experienced hiker endured a similar ordeal and survived, according to one park ranger. The story goes that this backcountry veteran broke his ankle on his solo adventure, but was able to summon help with a SPOT device—a satellite GPS tracker. The park launched a search-and-rescue effort upon receipt of the distress signal and was able to rescue the disabled hiker. Given that Sykes had the experience and temperament of a survivor, and carried the equipment to sustain herself overnight, it's possible that if she had possessed such a device, she might have been rescued before the elements claimed her. Does this make her negligent? No; it's just that wanderers have new resources that, should they chose to carry them, could be life-saving.

The Loner

It's a common refrain in national parks and elsewhere: Don't hike alone. It's also inevitable that people will end up solo on the trail.

In some instances, hikers find themselves on their own by design. Sometimes, it's by circumstance. Perhaps they've fallen behind their group, or they've ventured out ahead and lost sight of those in the rear. Perhaps they've taken a wrong turn while their party was in front or behind. For these folks, the discovery that they are alone might be terrifying, and certainly warrants a reminder that any group should move no faster than the slowest hiker is able and that, should someone become exhausted or disabled, he or she should never be left behind.

Those who relish the solo hike—and I count myself among them— find the walking restorative and contemplative, a temptation impossible to resist. Most of us wander out and back successfully. Most of us have packed wisely, carrying enough food, water, and equipment to ensure that if we become lost or stranded, we can take care of ourselves until help arrives. We've told someone where we're going and when we expect to be back, so that if we don't return as planned, someone will come looking for us. And we've (hopefully) got enough experience to make wise decisions when the weather changes, or when we encounter a wild animal, or when the terrain gets too tough to manage, or when we lose our bearings, or when some physical limitation—exhaustion or injury—manifests itself.

Then there are those who blunder into the wild solo on purpose but painfully unprepared. Most somehow make it back safely, but they end up packing out much more than they packed in, whether it's a healthy respect for the mental and physical challenges of the trail, the decision to never do that again, or a glimpse into a world they'd like to know better. They also, hopefully, recognize that the next time they head out on their own, they at least need to wear better shoes and carry more water.

Darcy Quick tended toward the prepared hiker end of the going-it-alone spectrum. Quick, 22, was a recent college graduate and employed in the park with the Guest Services concession, as well as with a Christian ministry. In a *Chicago Tribune* article, family members remembered her as a lover of the Pacific Northwest with an adequate level of outdoors experience. She hiked and camped, but was not "hard-core."

Quick had been working in the park for about three weeks when she set out for Comet Falls in June 2006. She carried a day pack and let her roommate know her plans. Her body was found near the base of the falls, a popular destination off the Paradise Road between Longmire and Paradise. She had apparently fallen, but because she was alone, the exact circumstances surrounding her death can never be known.

Another park employee, Julie Fillo, 20, of St. Louis, Missouri, disappeared on a solo hike in the Indian Bar area in June 1977. The young woman was remembered as an experienced hiker, and she'd set off on her overnight hike amply prepared, with enough extra clothing and food to survive several days alone in the woods. Seven years later, the remains of the summer intern—her bones, hiking gear, and a pen inscribed "Fillo Sales and Engineering Co.," the name of her father's business, according to an obituary—were found by hikers at the base of a ledge near the Cowlitz Chimneys. Again, the exact details are a mystery, and the park record lists her cause of death as "unknown."

Marvin Skillman also had experience going solo when he ventured into Rainier's backcountry in November 1978. He had "fallen in love" with the mountain while in the service, and was amply experienced as both a hiker and a backpacker. But the thirty-four-year-old resident of

Anderson, Indiana, didn't come back from his adventure on the Paul Peak Trail. His remains were found by hikers the following March, and his dental records were requested to confirm his identity. According to a newspaper account of Skillman's demise, FBI investigators found no evidence of foul play, and "one theory holds that the hiker may have been caught in a severe snowstorm in the mountains and exhausted himself while trying to find shelter." Cause of death, according to the park record? Exposure.

At the other end of the spectrum—but only in terms of backcountry savvy—was the tragedy of noted writer and editor Joseph Lee Wood Jr., who was likely unprepared for conditions when he set out on his last day hike. Wood, who was in the Pacific Northwest for a journalism conference, disappeared while exploring the Van Trump Trail on July 8, 1999. That morning, according to a report in the *Observer*, the writer was asking tough questions of then-presidential candidate Bill Bradley over breakfast; that afternoon he was birding on Rainier's Rampart Ridge. And that was the last anyone saw of him.

Wood, 34, had reportedly purchased a windbreaker while in Seattle, but that would not have been much protection against the "second-heaviest snowfall on record on Mt. Rainier," which settled on park and peak in the days following his birding expedition. He also wasn't reported missing for six days, which substantially impacted anyone's ability to help him—or even find him—if he was injured or lost. When he didn't return to his home base in New York, his partner hired a private investigator to track him down; that's how it was discovered he'd headed off onto the mountain, according to the *Observer* report.

The *Observer* paints a portrait of a powerful and memorable writer who had "shaped a career for himself as a black cultural critic in the lily-white precincts of New York's publishing worlds . . . [and] one of a half-dozen black editors to be found in the book business." Wood explored the ideas of racial equality and black culture in his work, but was also interested in travel writing and the natural world. Those passions drew him to Mount Rainier National Park.

While on the mountain Wood encountered a fellow hiker and reported on the birds he'd seen as he climbed into the snow at about

4,800 feet—"stellar's jay, scrub jay, and western tanager," reads the list in the *Observer*. The hiker warned the writer about a flimsy snow bridge up ahead, and Wood replied that he'd be turning around soon. A park official, describing what would prove to be fruitless search-and-rescue efforts, told the *Observer* that if Wood had fallen through the snow bridge and been swept downstream under the snow, his remains likely wouldn't be recovered until the snow melted later in the year. That hasn't come to pass, and the location of Woods's final repose remains a mystery.

Another solo hiker, the son of a park volunteer, fell to his death on a hike on Eagle Peak in June 2007. Jeff Graves, a forty-seven-year-old father and husband, was following a trail that climbs about three thousand feet in about three and a half miles, and that was snow-covered above the five-thousand-foot level. Graves left the trail proper on his descent, then fell two hundred feet to his death. He was, according to a newspaper account, adequately dressed for the conditions and carrying a day pack; another article notes that, given foggy weather conditions, he might have missed a switchback and wandered into difficult terrain prior to his fall. It's also noted that trails in the park were in need of extensive repairs in the wake of damaging winter storms in 2006. His body was spotted by helicopter and recovered after a three-day search. For the record, the Minnesota man is called Brian Graves on the park's fatality list.

Finally, hiker Devin Ossman, a forty-five-year-old musician from Mukilteo, Washington, was alone when he died of exposure on the Kautz Creek Trail in March 2008. He had, according to newspaper accounts, headed out for a daylong excursion, and his wife reported him missing when he didn't return that evening. He was found the following day, about two miles from the trailhead. Ossman, a performer and composer who was well connected to the artistic community on Whidbey Island, erred on the side of the unprepared, having embarked on his journey wearing what rangers called "pretty light clothing to be up in the mountains this time of year, especially in wet and cold conditions." Searchers followed his track up the trail to 4,200 feet, then traced him back down to 3,000 feet, where his remains were discovered. A park spokesperson noted that it appeared Ossman was "stumbling and falling" near the end of his walk, and that disorientation and a lack of coordination are hallmarks of hypo-thermia, which was determined to be his cause of death.

The Unforgiving Muir

It's called a "dead" glacier, and the fatal accidents that take place there, year after year, add depth to that designation.

The dangers of exploring the Muir Snowfield, one of the most acces-sible alpine features on Mount Rainier, are both mitigated and exac-erbated by its popularity. Not only is it the jumping-off point for the bulk of aspiring summiters, usually under the supervision of experienced guides, but it's also a popular day-hiking destination. Since all kinds climb there—mountaineers, skiers, snowshoers, hikers—all kinds can run into trouble there.

Day-trippers are, arguably, the most prone to being oblivious to potential hazards on the snowfield. Some set off woefully unprepared, in sneakers and shorts, lulled into a sense of security by fair weather and a sometimes deceptive perspective on distance and elevation gain as the route is surveyed from the parking lot at Paradise. It can look like an easy walk-up to the untrained eye. Most hikers make it to Camp Muir and back no problem; others bail when it becomes evident that, yeah, sneakers were a bad idea.

But a few don't make it back at all. Such was the case for fifty-one-year-old John Repka, who set off on a day hike across the snowfield with his recovery group in May 1999. The experienced climber—he'd sum-mited Mount Rainier on a previous occasion—and his companions were headed for Camp Muir, but Repka became ill during the hike; he was vomiting, according to the park's search-and-rescue report. He fell behind his companions while descending the snowfield in whiteout conditions, but before his group lost contact with him, one person reported inform-ing the ailing hiker that he was drifting too far west on the snowfield and possibly was off-route.

His teammates would later tell rescuers they thought Repka was right behind them as they continued down, but he didn't make it to the park-ing lot. They established radio contact with Repka; at first he told them he thought he was near Panorama Point, but later relayed that he didn't know where he was. Then he went radio-silent.

The search-and-rescue effort that followed lasted more than a week, but was hampered by bad weather and difficult terrain, and eventually was called off. Repka's body was recovered the following September, after being sighted by a helicopter pilot on a routine flight. He was found in an icefall at about eight thousand feet on the Paradise Glacier, tucked into his bivy sack, and he still had his pack, ice ax, and radio nearby. The cause of death was exposure, despite the body's precarious location.

The lessons to be learned from Repka's death, according to rangers, include not abandoning teammates to fend for themselves, and not counting on electronic devices, such as radios, as a guarantee of safety. While self-sufficiency on the mountain is critical—and Repka had the basics—the safety of the group is integral to success on high ground.

The lessons to be learned from two experienced mountaineers who disappeared while climbing to Camp Muir in November 1999 are less obvious because the circumstances are unknown. Chris Hartonas, 40, and Raymond Vakili, 48, had obtained permits to practice technical mountaineering skills above Camp Muir, and set off on this mission with a companion in unremarkable weather. An *American Alpine Journal* account describes Hartonas as "an avid park visitor and mountain climber, known by many on the Park Service staff for his frequent ascents to Camp Muir, particularly under adverse weather conditions."

Neither Hartonas nor Vakili would make it to the camp, nor back to Paradise. No trace of them would be found, despite an extensive search encompassing the Muir Snowfield and beyond.

"Without clues, it's difficult to speculate what exactly happened to the men. It's perplexing when two experienced, cautious and mature climbers just disappear," Rainier climbing ranger Mike Gauthier wrote for the *AAJ*. "They were well equipped and Hartonas was very familiar with the area. Both men have a history of good decision making in the mountains and neither had a reputation for 'pushing it.'"

Frank VanLeynseele, who accompanied the two hikers on the approach to Camp Muir, later lamented his decision to turn around. VanLeynseele knew he was slowing the others down, so he retreated to Paradise while

Hartonas and Vakili continued upward into oblivion. Reflecting on the consequences of the choices he and his partners made on that fateful day, VanLeynseele told the *Seattle Times*, "I regret that I was not with them. If they were in a difficult situation, maybe I could have helped."

The fury of the weather caught up with another pair of hikers on the snowfield in May 2005. Timothy Stark, a fifty-seven-year-old airline pilot, and his nephew, Greg Stark, 27, employed with the University of Washington, planned to hike from Paradise to Camp Muir, where they were prepared to spend the night. But the storm that descended as they were hiking up proved deadly. According to a report in the *Seattle Post-Intelligencer*, conditions were so bad at Camp Muir that the wind was blowing snow "through cracks in the walls."

Ranger Mike Gauthier, who also "walk[ed] into the storm," reported that the two Starks "weren't dressed for the deteriorating conditions. They wore cotton clothing, and cotton sucks heat from the body when it becomes wet and cold, exacerbating the chance that hypothermia will set in." Otherwise their equipment was adequate: They carried sleeping bags, a tent, and other gear for an overnight stay.

The wicked conditions and crowded accommodations at Camp Muir prompted the two to attempt to retreat from the high ground, according to an accident report in the *American Alpine Journal*. But they never made it back. In the whiteout, they wandered off-route, onto the edge of the Paradise Glacier. There, pinned down by what Gauthier called "epic conditions," the Starks ended up trying, and failing, to set up a camp.

When their bodies were discovered in the aftermath of the storm, according to the *Post-Intelligencer*, uncle and nephew were "about 100 yards apart on the Paradise Glacier east of the Muir Snowfield, about 200 yards from one of the most popular climbing trails in the park." They were both sitting in the snow, their headlamps switched on; the light on Tim's had gone out, but Greg's continued to glow faintly.

Hypothermia was pegged as the culprit in the deaths, but the ferocity of the storm was a major contributing factor. Other parties also were stranded on the mountain by weather conditions that weekend. For the Starks, the difficulties posed by the storm were exacerbated by their level of preparedness. In a storm, as the *AAJ* report explains, "things that are normally easy become challenging and challenging tasks become exhausting."

"One may be tempted to make a pronouncement regarding what the Starks should have done or pick out mistakes that should have been avoided," Gauthier wrote in the *AAJ* report. "What is hard to grasp is the ease with which each small error snowballs, eventually creating an untenable situation."

Not to mention that Rainier, as Gauthier told the newspaper, "can be a rough place when the weather turns south."

Another whiteout storm, this one brewing 70-mile-per-hour winds, pinned down three day-hikers on the snowfield near Camp Muir in June 2008. As they hunkered in a trench hollowed into the snow at 8,500 feet, Eduard Burceag, a software engineer and experienced mountaineer, used his body to help protect his wife, Mariana, from the freezing conditions. "He basically sacrificed his life for his wife," Rainier climbing ranger David Gottlieb told the *Seattle Post-Intelligencer*, explaining that Burceag and the third hiker, David Vlad, another experienced mountaineer, had sandwiched Mariana between them, with Burceag on the bottom. "Imagine you're laying in the snow. It drains you."

Vlad eventually left his partners and climbed to Camp Muir, where he alerted rangers to the emergency. Rescuers were able to get all of the hikers up to the camp despite the blizzard conditions, but Burceag did not survive, and Mariana suffered frostbite.

Sacrifice in the defense of loved ones—this time the children—also claimed the life of fifty-one-year-old James Reddick in June 1968.

It started as an adventure with family and friends. Reddick and his two children, along with another man and his daughter, set out from Paradise in clear weather, planning to climb to Camp Muir, spend the night, and descend the following day.

The plans went awry with the weather. According to a report in the *American Alpine Journal*, a "thin cloud cap" began to form on the peak, and the Reddick group was advised by other climbers to turn around, as they weren't prepared for the conditions the cloud foreshadowed. When the storm descended in earnest, bringing whiteout conditions, high winds, and temperatures that dropped below freezing, Reddick's companion, identified as Mr. Sundquist, and his daughter retreated. Reddick and his two children remained on the mountain, eventually taking shelter in a trench he dug into the Muir Snowfield.

The party was reported missing by Reddick's wife the following day, but a rescue effort couldn't be launched because of the storm. Reddick expired at some point during the two-day ordeal, but his children survived. Though his decision to remain on the mountain as the weather deteriorated proved a fatal mistake, the father is credited with saving his children's lives using his body to shield them from the cold and wind.

Louis Landry, a thirty-seven-year old Puyallup resident, was another victim of furious weather on the snowfield. In December 2014 he was snowshoeing solo, headed for Camp Muir, when a blizzard settled in, resulting in what a newspaper account called "formidable conditions" on the mountain. Landry hooked up with a pair of fellow backcountry travelers also seeking shelter from the storm, and the three snowshoers attempted a bivouac near Panorama Point. But falling ice crushed their tent, and the three were forced to retreat toward Paradise in a whiteout. Landry became separated from his companions on the descent. The next day, the two who descended safely reported the lone snowshoer missing, but rescuers could only conduct a "hasty" and unsuccessful search that afternoon, with no success. Landry's body was discovered the following day near the headwaters of Edith Creek.

Twenty-three-year-old Lowell Linn was a victim of both deteriorating weather and inexperience on the snowfield. The young man was on a snowshoe hike in November 1957 with partner Harry Holcomb, a more experienced winter traveler, and the goal was Anvil Rock. But Linn became discouraged before the destination was reached and decided to retreat. He shared his apples with his partner, then turned to make the descent alone, while his partner continued. Holcomb made it to about nine thousand feet before he too turned around, acquiescing to the deteriorating weather. When Holcomb arrived back at the base, he discovered Linn had not come down. A search-and-rescue operation ensued, but strong wind and snow—twenty inches—forced them to abandon the effort. Linn was never found; he's "missing and presumed dead," according to the park record.

Finally, Michelle Trojanowski, 30, and Mark Vucich, 37, disappeared in January 2015 on what was assumed to be a winter camping trip near Camp Muir, though subsequent investigation indicated the two were actually following another pair of climbers toward the summit of Mount Rainier. Those two climbers perished in stormy weather on their attempt; Trojanowski and Vucich lost their lives to the storm as well. Trojanowski's body was found on September 6 at 8,200 feet, "hanging over the edge of a large crevasse on Paradise Glacier southeast of Anvil Rock," by one account. Vucich's body had been found at eight thousand feet on the Muir Snowfield a month earlier. The park lists cause of death for both as hypothermia.

When the Facts Don't Tell the Story

Sadie Jordan died after tumbling 120 feet off a trail into Van Trump Creek in July 1924. She was hiking with her new husband when the fatal accident occurred. Her body was discovered above Christine Falls.

That's all that could be proven at the time.

But weirdness was evident from the start. Mr. and Mrs. F. W. Hill encountered it when they met Sadie's husband, J. A. Jordan, at the trail-head. He was sitting quietly. The couple and the husband exchanged pleasantries, then Mrs. Hill asked Jordan what he was doing there. He replied that he was "watching the river." He had lost his wife, he explained, and he expected her to come floating down.

This unexpected response prompted the Hills to press further, and as they talked, Jordan revealed that he'd actually been asked by rangers to stay put while they searched for a sign of his wife, who had gone missing on a hike. The Hills would later note that Jordan "appeared to be extremely calm under the circumstances."

Those circumstances, the forty-seven-year-old Jordan later told rangers, involved a romantic sojourn to Mount Rainier National Park from the newlywed couple's home in Long Beach, California. The husband described an idyllic start to the pair's park trip. They went fishing in Louise Lake, and they met another couple and spent time getting to know them. Sadie revealed that she didn't like hiking and was easily tired, but Jordan convinced her to take a walk up the trail alongside Van Trump Creek anyway. The two climbed above the falls, a scenic tiered spill spanned by an equally charming arching stone bridge just off the Paradise Road.

But Sadie, true to her word (at least according to Mr. Jordan), didn't enjoy the hike. He told investigators that she complained about ugly scenery and about how her heart was thumping in her chest. Later, he would claim that his forty-eight-year-old bride suffered from heart ailments, dizziness, and "bilious attacks," and that mosquitos "make her awfully sick." She stopped by the stream to rest, Jordan explained, but she urged him to continue walking, to enjoy himself.

Jordan told rangers he didn't go far, stopping when he encountered a slide. There he smoked a cigarette, then returned to where he'd left his wife to slow her racing heart.

But she was gone.

Jordan testified that he called for her, walked up and down the trail searching for her, and then returned to his automobile, thinking she may have headed back. When he got to the vehicle he met other park visitors, who were having car trouble. Assuming his wife was hiding from him as some kind of joke, he was not yet worried, and took the time to solder a battery wire for the stranded motorists. When he returned to the streamside where he'd left Sadie and called again, there was still no reply.

At this point the husband was "puzzled and became frightened," according to records in Sadie Jordan's fatality file. He sought the aid of rangers, who eventually located the woman's remains in the creek.

It wasn't long before Jordan's story began to unravel. It turned out Sadie was the third Jordan wife to perish in a "fatal accident [after] being married only a short while" to the man. He admitted to multiple marriages: one to Bess, who secured a divorce; the next to Minnie, though apparently he didn't wait long enough to marry Minnie after Bess, as he was imprisoned in Leavenworth for polygamy at that point. In interviews, he also mentioned marrying a woman whose name he didn't remember in Sterling, Colorado; she was, according to Jordan, a prostitute, and died in Mexico. He spent years associated with a woman named Edith, who called herself Edith Jordan, but to whom he claimed he never was married. The files also mention another potential wife, a Jessie M. Jordan. He would eventually confess to seven bigamous marriages.

More to the point, Jordan had taken out a $2,000 life insurance policy on his most recent wife shortly before the trip. Sadie Jordan's handbag and garter purse were not recovered. Jordan said she had $100 in her possession at the time of the accident, of which $25 was recovered. She also wore glasses; those too were not recovered.

In a letter dated August 21, 1924, superintendent O. A. Tomlinson wrote: "I have read Jordan's statement with a great deal of interest. Jordan certainly is a very clever individual and has made a rather strong appeal for sympathy. This would indicate that he is preparing for a defense along the 'modern lines' which seem to be so popular nowadays, i.e., that of mental irresponsibility for criminal acts. With such a record behind him it would be pretty hard to believe that the Mrs. Jordan who met her death in this park fell over that cliff accidentally."

Sadie Jordan's fatality file contains a record of interviews with her husband conducted by investigators. The image conjured by the document is one of a Sam Spade–style interrogation.

> *Q: Jordan, you know what we think about the case, don't you. You killed that woman and you know it. We are going to prove it.*
> *A: I know you gentlemen think I killed her, but I certainly didn't. No, no, I could never have harmed Sadie . . .*
>
> *Q: You have a lot of sins to repent for don't you think?*
> *A: Yes, I know I have.*

Jordan escaped murder charges. In a letter to Tomlinson, J. S. Yancy, Long Beach's chief of police, wrote: "I am frank to say, Superintendent, that although we are convinced in our own minds that there are grave doubts regarding the truthfulness of Jordan's story as to how his wife met her death in your park, there are no grounds on which we could charge him with murder. A charge of Bigamy has been placed against the man."

"God alone knows how or why Sadie was taken—I don't," Jordan wrote in a long statement about the incident that remains part of his wife's fatality file. "The picture I have of her standing in the trail, hat in hand, calling to me above, 'You'll make it in low,' will be my comforter. I have confessed my sins as far as I know and have not one regret for the treatment of other women. A man can't do these things alone, but the women are never punished—it's the man every time. There is no malice in my heart for a living soul. All my life I looked for companionship with love. At last I found it, for a short time only to lose it. Fate—Just Fate. This is the truth and the only defense I have."

The Need to Know

In December 2011 fifty-four-year-old Brian Grobois, a psychiatrist from New Rochelle, New York, took a snowshoe hike along Stevens Creek not far from Paradise. He was, according to newspaper and magazine accounts, fulfilling a dream: He'd always wanted to explore Mount Rainier. The park record relates that somewhere along the line, Grobois lost his way in cold, unfamiliar territory; dropped into a drainage next to the creek at about five thousand feet; and expired there of exposure.

The story is not unusual. Though Grobois is remembered as an experienced outdoorsman, experienced outdoorsmen have repeatedly found themselves overwhelmed by conditions on Mount Rainier in winter. For the doctor to become disoriented in a place that was new to him, and to succumb to weather conditions of a type he'd likely never experienced before, is tragic but not necessarily news.

But what transpired in the wake of Grobois's death raised questions about what can be determined about cause of death when a person perishes alone in the mountains—and questions about who needs to know.

The issues that set the Grobois accident apart revolve around conflicts between his Jewish faith and the medical examiner's duty to conduct an autopsy. As an Associate Press story explains, while "Jewish law requires a fast burial and no autopsy," Pierce County's medical examiner had unanswered questions, and pressed for further investigation.

The circumstances surrounding Grobois's demise certainly point toward hypothermia as cause of death. The weather was brutal, plunging into the subzero range, and a park spokesperson told the AP that Grobois was not outfitted for an overnight bivouac in such conditions. The park concluded he'd wandered off-route, sat down to rest, and was claimed by the frigid conditions.

That was all the Grobois family needed to know. They wanted to take their loved one home, to honor him in traditional fashion. Autopsy is forbidden by Jewish law unless public health and safety are in jeopardy, and the family felt that wasn't the case in Grobois's death.

The Washington state medical examiner, however, is charged by state law to identify cause of death, and he had questions—questions that could only be answered by autopsy. Did heart disease play a role? Was there a fall? Dr. Thomas Clark's skepticism of the hypothermia hypothesis was based on the fact that there were no witnesses, and that Grobois's body was "covered in bruises, inconsistent with a finding that he wandered lost, fell asleep and died."

Though the family objected, Dr. Clark petitioned the courts for the right to fulfill his mandate. The religious implications were "very real" for Grobois's family, Dr. Clark acknowledged, but he told the AP those concerns were "in conflict with Washington law and our charge to accurately determine deaths, and I can't make everybody happy."

The battle ended up in the courts, where a judge upheld the family's wishes, and Clark acquiesced. Grobois was buried in Jerusalem; his death certificate lists "cause and manner of death as 'undetermined.'"

Remembering the Hikers

While the details of some hikers' deaths are sketchy, and a few contain only what the park's fatality list records, they nonetheless offer some insights into whether the walker was prepared or unprepared, lucky or unlucky. Here are their short but important stories, presented in chronological order.

While hiking in Stevens Canyon in August 1936, Peter Sater was killed by rockfall.

In July 1937 eighteen-year-old John Farris fell while hiking on Mount Wow. His fall carried him under a snowfield into a stream and, having been knocked unconscious, young Farris drowned there. An enrollee in the Civilian Conservation Corps, Farris had become separated from his four companions and was taking a different route back to camp when the accident occurred. According to the park's superintendent, a search party recovered his body later that evening.

In June 1960, according to the park record, fourteen-year-old Brian Crecelius was glissading in the Edith Creek Basin when he lost control, slid over a cliff and a waterfall, and was killed. Newspaper accounts tell a different tale: In these stories, young Crecelius was hiking up from Paradise to meet his brother, who had climbed to about ten thousand feet, when he slipped, fell into a crevasse, and was buried under snow and ice. His father discovered his young son's tracks, which descended about fifty yards before "signs of a slide" were found.

Elmer Post and his nephew, David Post, fell into a crevasse on the Paradise Glacier in September 1967 while hiking down from Camp Muir in foul weather. Elmer's cause of death is listed as hypothermia and David's as traumatic injuries; both are also noted in the park record as having died of exposure. An *American Alpine Journal* description of the incident notes that while the men and their two climbing partners initially fell into the crevasse, three opted to stay in the icy cleft to shelter from the storm. The third man survived a long, cold night by pacing at the base of the crevasse. The fourth man was able to make his way down to Paradise, navigating through the storm by following a telephone line and creek drainage downslope to the main trail and safety.

Navy lieutenant Martin Quinn, stationed on the USS *Enterprise*, was hiking with a friend and fellow naval officer near the Ipsut Creek Campground in August 1968 when the two decided to venture cross-country over loose, rocky terrain. Accounts of the accident note that the twenty-three-year-old native of Connecticut was unroped and climbing a chute on Mother Mountain when he lost his footing and fell more than two hundred feet down a talus slope to his death. Rescuers observed the men were "totally inexperienced and inadequately equipped [to] climb terrain that would tax the ability of experienced men equipped with ropes and associated equipment."

Thirteen-year-old Bruce Wahler became separated from his brothers while hiking in the Spray/Seattle Park area in September 1970. He succumbed to hypothermia.

Phillip Englund, a twenty-year-old from Minneapolis, Minnesota, was vacationing with friends in the park when he disappeared while hiking in August 1972. He'd apparently become separated from his companions while on the trail to Barrier Peak; the park superintendent told a Minneapolis newspaper that he may have been trying to take a shortcut to meet up with the others when he lost his footing on a patch of heather and fell. His remains were recovered from a rockslide in the Owyhigh Lakes area.

Eugene Sullivan fell while hiking with two others near Panorama Point in September 1973.

In October 1978 forty-nine-year-old poet and writer Joan Webber was killed in the Sluiskin Mountains after being hit by a rock dislodged by another climber; the impact caused her to fall fifty feet to her death. A notice about the hiker's death that appeared in the *Seattle Times* identified her as a much younger woman; that, the writer of another remembrance explained, was due to Webber's "essence," which exuded "youth, vigor, vitality, energy." The report notes that the accident occurred at about 6,800 feet on Papoose Peak.

In November 1997 solo hiker Chet Hanson, 27, disappeared while hiking on the Deer Creek Trail toward Owyhigh Lakes. A four-day search turned up no sign of the man, who reportedly was wearing light clothing and was unprepared for the freezing temperatures prevalent on the mountain at the time he disappeared. He is presumed dead.

In November 2004 Vasily Kozorezov, 16, was hiking with his brothers and cousins across rugged terrain on Eagle Peak in the scenic Tatoosh Range when he fell two hundred feet and died upon impact with the boulders below. The group was hiking off-trail, and newspaper accounts note it took fifteen hours to recover the youth's body from the inhospitable terrain.

According to the park record, Timothy Swift was a frequent visitor to Mount Rainier and often took "long overnight backpacking trips" in the park. He was reported missing in November 2008, and his body was recovered the following May near Spray Falls.

In July 2014 Edwin Birch, 64, and his son set out to tick off another leg in their section hike of the Wonderland Trail. The father, a resident of Tacoma, Washington, departed from Box Canyon after dropping his son off at the White River trailhead to walk the same stretch of trail in the opposite direction. The section the two planned to traverse is nineteen miles in length, a tough distance on a path notorious for its taxing ups and downs. The two met up at the halfway point, north of Indian Bar camp in Ohanapecosh Park; at that point, in midafternoon, according to the son, his father seemed well, if a bit tired.

The son completed his hike at about midnight and climbed into the car at the Box Canyon trailhead to return to the White River trailhead, where he planned to pick up his father. But Edwin Birch never arrived at the rendezvous. A search was initiated the following day, with ten people walking the trail and a helicopter searching from the air. No sign of the missing man was found. It wasn't until more than a year later, in August 2015, that his remains were located, near the Frying Pan Glacier and the highest point on the Wonderland route, at 6,800 feet. The cause of death was undetermined.

In September 2015, Timothy Hagan, 62, of Bellevue, Washington, fell while descending from the Sluiskin Mountains toward Crescent Lake. According to newspaper reports, Hagan was an experienced mountaineer, having climbed major peaks in Mexico and Ecuador. He and his companions were far from help when the accident occurred; an article by the Associated Press notes that Hagan's friends "hiked more than 13 miles to report the accident." District ranger Geoff Walker, along with other park personnel, planned to recover Hagan's body by helicopter, but bad weather put those plans on hold. When a weather window opened the following day, Hagan's remains were retrieved.

Burt Meyer and three friends set out to climb in the Tatoosh Range, which offers wonderful views of Mount Rainier, in July 2017. As they neared the summit of their destination, Meyer, a seventy-five-year-old musician from Olympia, Washington, opted to leave the main Eagle Peak Trail—and his companions—to hike cross-country. Exactly what transpired next is unclear because the hiker was alone when the accident occurred, a park spokeswoman told the *Seattle Times*, but he either fell in a rockfall area or was struck by rockfall, which the other hikers heard and reported to the park service. The search-and-rescue operation involved using the National Park Service's "exclusive use" helicopter, which dropped a pair of rangers to the accident site so they could prepare Meyer's remains for recovery. In an obituary for Meyer, a friend remembered him as "Mr. Music. . . . He was really a beloved person and a fabulous musician."

CHAPTER 9

On a Climb

THE MOST DRAMATIC WAY TO DIE IN MOUNT RAINIER NATIONAL PARK is on a climb, but not all climbs take place on the namesake peak. Smaller summits appeal to mountaineers as well, and can pose similar challenges and hazards.

Like Rainier, lesser peaks in the park are composed of volcanic rock, much of which can be described as "friable." This means pieces can break free at any point, sometimes pulled from the matrix by a human hand, sometimes separating as the snow and ice holding the rock in place melts away, sometimes flaking off due to gravity and time. In addition to the dangers of rockfall, smaller peaks are subject to sketchy weather, some of it created by the big mountain itself.

Most of those who die on less popular climbs don't get the same kind of press that summiters of Rainier do, but that doesn't mean there aren't lessons to be learned from them, or that the losses are less profound for their companions, family, and friends. Their stories are compelling for these reasons, and serve as cautionary tales for those who think less high translates to less dangerous.

Crumbling Rock

Solid as a rock. Hard as a rock. Bedrock. These iconic statements of geologic imagery conjure confidence. Even if you drop the idioms, the word "rock" still imparts impermeability and foundational stability.

But any experienced climber knows that not all rock is created equal. And the devastating outcomes of attempts on lesser peaks in the park point out just how breakable and unreliable Rainier's volcanic rock can be.

In August 1924 Paul Moser fell while climbing 6,917-foot Unicorn Peak in the saw-toothed Tatoosh Range. Moser was no stranger to mountains or to service in national parks, according to superintendent O. A. Tomlinson, who noted that the twenty-five-year-old native of Switzerland had worked in Yosemite before seeking employment at Mount Rainier. Moser's fatality file contains letters from the eager young man, who assured the park's chief that he was an ideal candidate. "Wish to say that I am not afraid of hard work or hardships and that I am fully determined to make useful work in the great out-of-doors my life's task," Moser wrote. He was willing to start with grunt labor, including road construction, but he really wanted to be a ranger.

At the time of his death, Moser had yet to be hired as a park employee, but was working as an assistant guide with the Rainier National Park Company, then the park's concessioner. According to notes in the park's archives, Moser was off-duty and climbing with a fellow assistant guide named Joseph Griggs (also off-duty) when the accident occurred.

Griggs detailed the accident in an account that's part of the fatality file. The party faced some minor technical difficulties on their ascent, as well as crumbling rock and route-finding challenges. Right before the accident occurred, "Moser took off his shoes to get better purchase on the 'hobs' in a chimney the two were attempting to ascend." He climbed on Griggs's shoulder to negotiate a tough spot.

Then the rock gave way. When he first pitched off the route, the fall was relatively short—about twelve feet. But the stunned Moser didn't stop there; he tumbled another several hundred feet down the mountain and sustained injuries that left him "broken, bruised and mangled." Griggs ran down the mountain to Moser's aid but he knew, given the magnitude and distance of the fall, that his pal was dead.

A few years earlier, another climber fell victim to a similar failure of the substrate. In August 1919 a member of a Mazama climbing party on a camping excursion lost his life on Little Tahoma Peak, an iconic 11,139-foot pyramidal summit on the east side of Rainier framed by the Emmons, Ingraham, and Fryingpan Glaciers. Jack Meredith, a twenty-four-year-old veteran of the Great War and a resident of Portland, Oregon, had gone with a companion to retrieve a camera that had been left on the peak earlier in the trip. On the descent, the rock ledge beneath the young man's feet crumbled and he fell fifty feet, then rolled five hundred more feet to the bottom of a crevasse and was "instantly killed," according to park archival records.

Crumbling rock also played a role in the August 1977 death of a man climbing Faraway Rock. Above Louise Lake not far from Stevens Canyon Road, Seattle's William Hershey, 19, and his companion, another nineteen-year-old from Tacoma, Washington, had climbed to the high point and were on the descent when Hershey slipped on a ledge. To stop his slide, Hershey grabbed onto some rocks, only to have them give way. He fell two hundred feet onto more rocks below, and died after suffering massive head injuries.

Other Victims of the Tatoosh

This arcing crest of jagged summits rises to the south of Paradise, a clutch of children hugging the skirts of the mother mountain. The peaks are beautiful and appealing: Climbers aren't faced with the massive glacial crevasses and altitude-related illnesses that present themselves on towering Rainier, but must approach with skill and caution. And, when they reach an apex, the world rolls away beneath their feet.

Still, the peaks of the Tatoosh—Pinnacle, Unicorn, Plummer, Eagle—have claimed their share of lives.

One of the park's earliest fatalities was that of Charlot Hunt, a resident of Tama, Iowa, who perished on a climb of Pinnacle Peak in August 1912. She was part of a YMCA party of eighteen people, one of ten girls on the adventure.

"The ascent was made in perfect safety with no indication of nervousness from any one," reads a letter in the park's archives from H. R. Carter, physical director of the YMCA Tacoma. "She [Charlot] stood in apparent safety on a secure ledge of rock which afforded perfect footing. The vast depth sheering off below her feet, seemed to completely unnerve her, the effect probably causing a fit of dizziness, for she leaned forward then toppled over, striking on her head about twenty feet below, bounding and rolling from there a distance of perhaps 800 feet down the slope. With four other men I hurried to the spot where she lay but life was extinct before we reached her."

In July 1970 Eric Weigel, an eighteen-year-old associate guide with Rainier Mountaineering Inc. (RMI), fell to his death on a solo climb of Pinnacle Peak. The young man had chosen to climb alone on his day off; his intended partner had gone off climbing with another RMI guide.

In his *Memoirs of a Mountain Guide*, RMI founder and legendary guide Lou Whittaker recalled his panic when he heard about the accident. Joe Kennedy Jr., son of Ethel and Bobby Kennedy, was a summer intern with RMI that year, and Whittaker knew Kennedy's climbing mentor had taken him to Pinnacle Peak to practice climbing techniques. Whittaker sprinted up toward the site, which deposited him on a rockslide. As he ascended, he lamented the wisdom of route choice:

"It was about an 800-foot vertical cliff, with a steep rockslide and boulders as big as cars. Not the best site to climb on. We have some granite on Rainier, but since the mountain is a volcanic peak, most of the rock is igneous. It's unstable, creating what I call 'portable handholds.'"

Whittaker found his guide among the boulders at the base of the cliff. It wasn't Kennedy, but any sense of relief was quickly overcome by a sense of loss. "I was shook up," Whittaker wrote. "We rarely lose a guide. When we do, I feel as though I've lost a child."

Unlike Weigel, climber Andre Genereux, 26, was not alone when he set off to climb Unicorn Peak. He and his partner, Edwin Murray, were best friends from Michigan and arrived in Mount Rainier National Park in July 1988 intending to do some rock climbing, not peak bagging. But after attending a class with RMI, Genereux, who was described in one account of his accident as having an impatient nature, was keen to climb Rainier. Guides advised against this, cautioning that the two young men were unprepared for the conditions and terrain. The two took that advice, deciding instead to climb Unicorn Peak. They acquired the appropriate permits and additional equipment before setting off on their adventure.

Once on the peak, according to Murray, whose recollections are recorded in an *American Alpine Journal* report, the two encountered issues with route-finding. Genereux finally thought he'd found an easy way up, but the rock he was ascending gave way, and one of the freed pieces struck him in the head. The rockfall then tore the climber from the mountainside. Though Murray attempted to catch his friend, Genereux fell past him, airborne for about eighty feet, before he struck the scree slope below and perished.

Going Remote

While the peaks of the Tatoosh Range are closely hitched to Mount Rainier, others are farther flung. Naches Peak is a stony high point on the far eastern edge of the park, near Chinook Pass and within striking distance of the famed Pacific Crest Trail. Rising nearly 6,300 feet and accessible by a popular 3.5-mile loop hike with great views of Rainier, it presents a tempting target. But a popular trail to a moderate summit doesn't necessarily translate to a safe and easy ascent.

In August 1951 seventeen-year-old Joann Ramey was climbing Naches Peak with teenaged friends, and was on the descent when she opted to take a "short-cut down a steep slope toward some rock cliffs," an *American Alpine Journal* record of the accident reports. Wearing sandals and proceeding against the advice of more experienced companions, Ramey slipped and tumbled two hundred feet into jumbled rock below. Commenting on the victim's lack of training and inadequate footwear, the *AAJ* advised local guides to actively pursue the education of outdoorsminded youth in proper mountaineering techniques.

Fifty-two-year-old Jeremy Anderson also encountered crumbling rock on his climb of Naches Peak, causing him to fall off a cliff to his death in October 1987, according to the park record.

On the opposite side of the park, off Westside Road and closest to the Nisqually entrance, Mount Wow rises to almost 6,100 feet. It presents a rolling profile, streaked with rock bands and slopes that support stands of evergreen. About four miles of hiking from the end of Westside Road leads to Lake George, on the mountain's northwest flank; the lookout on Gobblers Knob affords views of Mount Rainier when the weather permits. Reaching the summit of Mount Wow requires cross-country navigation and some climbing skills, as no maintained track leads to the top. Twenty-two-year-old Mark Wolstoncroft was on a solo climb of this challenging peak in June 1973 when he suffered a fatal fall.

In September 2013 George Merriam set off for the summit of Pyramid Peak, which rises to nearly seven thousand feet on Mount Rainier's southwest flank. The sixty-six-year-old resident of Lakewood, Washington, didn't return as planned from his day hike, and his worried wife reported him missing. A hasty search-and-rescue effort was launched the evening of his disappearance, but was postponed when darkness fell. His remains were spotted the next morning during an aerial reconnaissance, about two hundred feet below the trail, in what the park characterized as "steep terrain." Poor weather precluded his recovery by helicopter, so a large crew of people spent seven hours retrieving his remains overland.

Remembering the Climbers
The accidents that befell these two climbers lie on the fringes of neat categories and aren't detailed in the park record. Anne Bavette died after falling on her descent from the summit of Pinnacle Peak in the Tatoosh Range in October 1993. For Harold Siess, a twenty-six-year-old lieutenant in the US Air Force, ascending a peak apparently wasn't the goal, but he died in what the park deems a climbing accident. According to the record, in June 1983 Siess lost his life after tumbling 250 feet onto a talus slope at Ricksecker Point, just off the Paradise Road.

CHAPTER 10

In the Air

IN THE SIMPLEST AND MOST OBVIOUS WAYS, WEATHER IS THE PRIMARY cause of plane crashes on Mount Rainier. The peak's size and proximity to the Pacific coastline lend it a special—and deadly—ability to amplify the weather systems that regularly sweep in off the ocean. Given its propensity for generating its own severe storms, typically foreshadowed by the cloud cap that gives pause to aspiring summiters, pilots must exercise special care when navigating around the mountain.

Topography is also at play: Mount Rainier towers thousands of feet above the ridges and summits immediately surrounding it. And still, amazingly, the massive peak is great at playing hide-and-seek. In foul weather, with the sky low and gray, pilots must rely on their instrumentation to tell them where it is, and must gauge their altitude and position accordingly. Any miscalculation of weather or flight path can be, and has been, devastating.

"The Highest Headstone"
Weather was the primary driver in the deaths of thirty-two marines who lost their lives when their transport plane collided with the mountain on December 10, 1946. The crash remains the deadliest on Mount Rainier, and was the deadliest to have occurred in the United States at the time. Its repercussions are lasting. The South Tahoma Glacier, where the wreckage of the plane and the bodies of its passengers are entombed, has remained off-limits, set aside as hallowed ground in honor of the marines. And to this day people gather at the mountain to honor the dead soldiers.

In his superintendent's reports following the accident, John C. Preston notes that weather in the park through the first half of December "was severe, with heavy snowfall and rain causing washouts and flood conditions on the lowlands. On December 11, a record of 6.13 inches of precipitation was recorded at headquarters for the previous 24-hour period." The marines, who were headed home for leave, flew directly into that maelstrom.

The Curtis R5C transport plane (called a Curtis Commando) was one of six that left San Diego that day, bound for the naval station in Sand Point in Seattle. All six aircraft hit the bad weather as they flew north from Portland, Oregon. Given the conditions, four of the pilots opted to turn around and wait out the storm in Portland. The fifth plane was able to forge ahead to a safe landing at the Sand Point station.

The ill-fated plane, piloted by Major Robert Reilly, also continued north toward its planned destination. The pilot was using instrumentation to stay on what he assumed was a safe course, as visibility was nil. He was also making course corrections to account for the 70-mile-per-hour winds that were buffeting the Commando. An investigation into the crash would reveal that, despite those corrections and because he was flying at an altitude of about 9,000 feet, Reilly ended up steering the plane onto a collision course with the 14,410-foot peak.

But this was something the major wasn't aware of at the time. According to a report in the *Chicago Tribune*, in his final radio communication with a ranger station in Toledo, Washington, just prior to the crash, Reilly stated "that he was about 30 minutes south of [the station] and under normal circumstance." In fact, he was northeast of the town on the Cowlitz River. Other reports note the pilot said he was going to attempt to climb above the clouds and out of conditions that were causing ice to form on the wings of the aircraft.

Because he was so far off course, and because of his speed—author Bruce Barcott notes, in *The Measure of a Mountain: Beauty and Terror on Mount Rainier*, that the plane was traveling at approximately 195 miles per hour—Reilly likely had no idea what was coming until it was upon him. It's also likely that none of the passengers knew either, and that no one suffered. They were killed instantly on impact.

The initial focus of the search was the Cowlitz River drainage, but that shifted to the park with reports that a plane had been heard at Longmire and Paradise on the evening of the Commando's disappearance. The weather continued to be uncooperative, however, failing to clear for five days following the crash and stonewalling rescue efforts. In that time five feet of snow buried any sign of the plane and further complicated not only the rescue operations, but also the chances for potential crash survivors to remain among the living.

But neither snow nor waning hope stopped the park, the army, the navy, the coast guard, and a host of civilians, including a Boy Scout troop from Seattle, from launching a concerted search when the weather cleared on December 16. Rescuers scoured the mountain by land and by air for signs of the missing transport and its passengers.

The search received widespread press coverage. During the initial recovery effort, the park's assistant chief ranger, Bill Butler, who would later play a pivotal role in determining what happened to the plane and its passengers, slipped "while negotiating a steep, icy slope" on the peak, the superintendent noted, and injured one of his ribs. Butler's heroic efforts in the search and eventual discovery of the plane's wreckage caught the attention of *Time* magazine, which featured him in an article on the crash. The ranger also received several awards for valor: In one image in the park's archives, a somber, upright man in uniform receives a commendation on the forested lower slopes of the mountain.

Because no one knew exactly where the plane had gone down, and because winter held Rainier in its dark, icy grip, the army and coast guard units pulled out of the park on December 18 and began to search for the wreckage elsewhere in the region. After two more weeks of scanning the territory, plagued by bad weather and knowing that chances of survival for the servicemen were now virtually nonexistent, the rescue effort was called off. It would resume again once the summer sun melted the winter snow, only then as a recovery effort.

As expected, come July, the wreckage of the transport was revealed. Ranger Butler was on his day off, climbing on the Success Cleaver, which separates the South Tahoma Glacier from the Success Glacier on the southwest face of the mountain, when he spotted it—the flash of metal in the sun. He knew what this meant, and took the lead in unraveling the mystery of the now-found plane and its passengers. Butler spearheaded a series of reconnaissance missions to the crash site over the ensuing month, hoping to devise a safe and effective way to find and retrieve the remains of the marines and return them to their families for burial.

But conditions on the glacier, even in summer, were formidable. One account notes Butler's worry about the collapse of snow bridges that provided access to the site as the season progressed, and the appearance of new crevasses along the route. Barcott's account includes this description of what rescuers faced on the glacier:

"The bergschrund of the South Tahoma Glacier, where ice peels away from the 4,000-foot headwall, is one of the most dangerous spots on the mountain. Ice holding the cracked rock of the headwall together melts in the late morning, sending a shower of boulders onto the glacier. Most arrive at killing speed."

Barcott also quotes a former marine lieutenant, Bruce Meyers, who told the writer, "It was like an artillery barrage. . . . As the rock came down the larger pieces broke up and turned into shrapnel. It was as close as you could come to an artillery barrage in civilian life."

A picture from the scene, showing fragments of the fuselage jutting from a towering block of ice, illustrates the stunning scale of the mountain's glacial architecture, the force with which the plane struck the mountain, and the insurmountable obstacles faced by the living men attempting to recover the deceased. The caption reads: "Two large portions of Marine Plane suspended in the glacier ice some 40 feet below the surface in a large crevasse of the South Tahoma Glacier."

Still, a month after the initial discovery, Butler and the other mountaineers were able to locate the nose of the plane and the remains of the eleven men "tangled inside." Later in August, Butler and his team returned to the crash zone, where another fourteen men, "most encased in ice, and a considerable amount of the broken plane, were discovered wedged in a crevasse."

In the end, the steep glacial terrain would prove too hazardous for recovery efforts to continue. The decision was made to call it off, and to forbid travel on the South Tahoma Glacier in honor of the men entombed there.

A ceremony honoring the lost marines has been held at Mount Rainier every year since the crash. As each of the thirty-two names are read, a bell is tolled. An honor guard fires a salute, and a rose is placed at a commemorative memorial site. (The original memorial is at Round Pass on Westside Road, within view of the crash site; a new memorial was placed in nearby Enumclaw in 1999, after flood damage forced closure of Westside Road. The closure made the memorial accessible only by foot, rendering it a hardship for aging family members and friends to reach the site.)

The people attending the memorial with firsthand connections to the men—those whose lives were touched by them—grow fewer as time passes. At the 2014 service, captured in a local newscast, one of the speakers called Mount Rainier "the highest headstone," a monumental marker for those lost in the crash for all time.

Those who perished on the mountain on that December day were Private Duane Abbott of Minneapolis, Minnesota; Private Robert Anderson of Raymondville, Texas; Private Joe Bainter of Canton, Missouri; Master Sergeant Charles Criswell of San Diego, California; Major Robert Reilly of Memphis, Texas (pilot); Lieutenant Colonel Alben Robertson of Santa Ana Heights, California; Private Leslie Simmons Jr. of Kalama, Washington; Private Harry Skinner of Confluence, Pennsylvania; Master Sergeant Wallace Slonina (Wallace Slonin in the park record) of Rochester, New York; Private Lawrence Smith of Lincoln, Nebraska; Private Buddy Snelling of Columbus, Ohio; Private Bobby Stafford of Texarcana, Texas; Private William St. Clair of Los Angeles, California; Private Walter Stewart of Austin, Texas; Private John Stone of Los Angeles, California; Private Albert Stubblefield of Bakersfield, California; Private William Sullivan of Ardmore, Oklahoma; Private Chester Taube of Fresno, California; Private Harry Thompson Jr. of Kansas City, Kansas; Private Duane Thornton of Biola, California; Private Keith Tisch of Marne, Michigan; Private Eldon Todd of Fort Collins, Colorado; Private Richard Trego of Denver, Colorado; Private Charles Truby of Anthony, Kansas; Private Harry Turner of Monroe, Oregon; Private Ernesto Valdovin of Tucson, Arizona; Private Gene Vremsak of Calexico, California; Private William

Wadden of Cedar Rapids, Iowa; Private Donald Walker of Hoquiam, Washington; Private Gilbert Watkins of Tucson, Arizona; Private Duane White of Ottawa, Kansas; and Private Louis Whitten of Oklahoma City, Oklahoma.

Other Military Losses

Plane crashes on Mount Rainier claimed other servicemen in the years following the marine transport tragedy. Five men perished when their DC-6, on a cargo flight originating in Seattle, crashed on the South Mowich Glacier in April 1965. The DC-6 collided with the mountain at the 10,200-foot level, according to a report on the Aviation Safety Network, which cites the probable cause as "the improper correlation of the aircraft position with respect to obstructing terrain while continuing the flight on a VFR [visual flight rules] flight plan in instrument weather conditions." In other words, the weather was bad, and the pilot was unable to correlate his position with the position of the massive peak.

Captain Alvin Petry, as well as William Newland, James Middleton, Walter Bryant, and Carl Baker, lost their lives in the accident.

An account of the D-6's final flight in *Death, Daring, and Disaster: Search and Rescue in the National Parks* notes that, when asked his position relative to Mount Rainier, Petry did not respond. That wasn't cause for worry at the time: "It was assumed that the plane had flown behind the mountain where radio and radar could not pick it up," author Charles "Butch" Farabee Jr. wrote. It wasn't until the plane didn't land at its destination, an air force base in Utah, that a search-and-rescue mission was launched.

Even though the mountain was shrouded in cloud cover and rescuers were buffeted by "squirrely" winds, the wreckage was located by aircraft. But the plane and its victims could not be reached until the following day, when a "crack three-man climbing team" was lowered onto the glacier to recover the remains.

Another airborne military accident occurred in April 1968. Colonel Wilfred Crutchfield, 50, and Major Ivan O'Dell, 45, were en route from Mather Air Force Base near Sacramento, California, to McChord Air Force Base in Tacoma, where they were stationed, when contact was lost with their T-33 jet trainer. The park record notes that the aircraft received "faulty directions" prior to the accident; weather was also a factor, as Mount Rainier was swathed in a snowstorm. The wreckage was located at about 10,500 feet on the Wapowety Cleaver the day following the crash, though the plane was initially reported to have gone down near Randle, just southwest of the park boundary.

As is often the case, recovery efforts were hampered by both poor weather—rescuers reported that "rough flying conditions stymied search efforts by smaller Civil Air Patrol planes" in the aftermath of the accident, according to a local newspaper—and what the park service considered to be "almost inaccessible terrain" at the crash site. Two park rangers were finally lowered to the wreckage from a helicopter, and were able to carry the dead fliers to the hovering craft so they could be airlifted away.

In March 1983 five navy men died in the crash of an Air Force C-1 on the mountain. The victims—all assigned to the USS *Constellation*, which was in dry dock in Bremerton, Washington, at the time—were on a "routine instrument training flight" when the accident occurred, according to the Associated Press. The wreckage was discovered scattered at about ten thousand feet on snow and ice. The AP article states the plane crashed on the Tahoma Glacier; the park record lists the accident site as the Success Glacier. Both ice fields are on the southwest face of the volcano. Severe weather, including a wind chill factor that dropped temperatures to twenty degrees below zero, hampered recovery efforts.

Lieutenant Commander Donald Olson of Eugene, Oregon; Commander William Hayes of Viper, Kentucky; Commander Ivan Choi of Redlands, California; Lieutenant Commander William Mortison of San Diego, California; and Petty Officer Third Class Richard Rocker of North Syracuse, New York, were killed in the accident.

Rescue from the Air
Aircraft are commonly employed in rescue and recovery efforts on Mount Rainier. Weather permitting, helicopters and their pilots are particularly adept at mountain rescues, able to pluck the survivors of climbing accidents and other mishaps off a mountainside and then transport victims to hospitals with all necessary speed. The use of helicopters for search and

rescue removes the onus from rescuers on the ground, who might otherwise be forced to negotiate sketchy terrain—rivers in flood, avalanche chutes, glaciers riddled with crevasses—to reach those they seek to help.

Planes have less utility in terms of dropping rescuers onto glaciers or retrieving victims from ridgetops, but fixed-wing aircraft are useful for reconnaissance, helping to pinpoint the locations of lost hikers, climbers, and the wreckage of other aircraft gone down in bad weather. Small planes are also employed for air drops of supplies, including food, water, and medicine, to people who may be stranded on a peak.

That's what fliers Harold Horn, 40, pilot and member of the Washington Civil Air Patrol, and Charles Carman, 29, were attempting to do in September 1959 when their plane crashed near the summit of Mount Rainier. The two were on a "mercy flight" for a forty-five-year-old scientist suspected of suffering a heart attack, likely brought on by high-altitude pulmonary edema (HAPE), on Columbia Crest. They planned to drop oxygen for the victim, who was visiting a research team studying the mountain's geology on the summit when he was stricken. The best treatment for HAPE—or a heart ailment, for that matter—is descent, but that was impossible under the circumstances. The next best hope for Dr. C. T. Bressler, a professor from the Western Washington College of Education, was the aid carried aboard the small plane. Those supplies, along with Horn and Carman, were lost when the aircraft, which was flying at night, crashed about four hundred feet below the summit. The wreckage was discovered upside down near the lip of the crater.

Rescuers attempting to reach the fliers, as well as Bressler, were hampered by the continuing bad weather—one storm pinned a pair of men attempting to reach the summit in a "shallow crevasse" overnight, according to one account. When inclement conditions persisted on the peak, efforts to recover the bodies were suspended, and the decision was made to leave the two airmen where they lay.

Bressler was another victim of those tragic September events, succumbing to his affliction the day after the crash. His remains were brought down overland from the summit by his fellow scientists/climbers. In *Death, Daring, and Disaster*, author Farabee notes the researcher had considerable experience in the field and was well liked by his peers.

Farabee also records that the park had initially denied the geology team permission for a summit camp, but that that decision was "overturned by uninformed desk-bound Washington bureaucrats 3,000 miles away," and quotes one ranger as believing the events constituted "a classic example of political interference costing 3 lives."

Of Cowboys, Car Dealers, and Sightseers

Five men, four of them cowboys on their way to Penticton, British Columbia, to compete in one of the rodeos leading up to the famed Calgary Stampede, perished when their small plane slammed into the south face of Mount Rainier in July 1990. A park spokesman told the *Seattle Times* the plane "augured into the Kautz Glacier at the 12,500-foot level."

Weather played a role in the demise of those onboard the Cessna—a storm front was moving in and recovery teams encountered rainy conditions low on the mountain and high winds near the crash site, according to accounts of the accident—but exactly what the conditions were for the pilot could have been different. According to the *Times* article, climbers had reported clear skies above eleven thousand feet.

The veracity of information provided by the Federal Aviation Administration (FAA) to the pilot was also cited as a factor. According to the *Times*, pilot Harry Card was flying by sight (visual flight rules), which meant he should have been able to see the peak. But when air traffic controllers asked if he could see Rainier, the pilot replied no, "that he was going to pass by it . . . go around it." The FAA controllers saw something different on their instrumentation, and at the time communication with the plane was lost, they were trying to steer Card and his passengers clear of the danger.

In the wake of the accident, the family of one of the cowboys, thirty-one-year-old David Smith, of College Place, Washington, filed a wrongful death suit against the FAA for not issuing a safety alert prior to the crash. Smith left behind a wife and young son and was remembered as "a champion calf roper." Also killed were Card, 50, a veteran pilot from Oregon; cowboy Mike Curran, 25, of Oregon; and two competitors from Texas, Randy Dierlam, 29, and David Bowen, 28.

Three auto dealers—Bill Steitz, Kenneth Fry, and Kenneth Bride—were killed in January 1972 when their plane crashed into the Cowlitz Glacier at seven thousand feet. The men were en route to Seattle from Pasco, Washington, where they had been attending business meetings. Steitz, of Fresno, California, was the pilot and was last heard from when he asked air traffic controllers about weather conditions in Seattle. He was told they were "unfavorable," according to a report in the *Seattle Post-Intelligencer*, but "the plane flew on."

A six-day search failed to locate the wreckage in the aftermath of the crash, and the fate of the three men was a mystery until remnants from the accident, including human remains and "airplane parts that included the plane's identification number," were found by rangers in September 1992. The bulk of the wreckage, along with the bodies of the long-lost men, were later discovered by a former climbing ranger who was hiking on the glacier in September 2001. The park's aviation coordinator described the wreckage as shattered, as if someone had dropped a mug into a kitchen sink.

Ronald McDonald, 53, and Randall Bates, 42, perished when their small plane, a Piper single-engine aircraft, crashed into Rainier's summit crater at 14,200 feet in January 1990. It's believed the two men from Tacoma, Washington, were sightseeing; no flight plan was filed and no destination recorded. The plane's emergency locator beacon tipped rescuers from the national park as to the crash location. The bodies of McDonald and Bates were airlifted from the summit the following day.

Bette Filley, author of the *Big Fact Book About Mount Rainier*, adds an interesting footnote to this story. While leading an attempt on the summit a month later, a guide encountered the remnants of the plane. A couple of years later, the guide returned to the crater and ventured into the steam caves there, discovering the wreckage "suspended in the ceiling of the cave as if it were in a flight museum. It had taken two years to melt through 30 feet of ice."

Summit Flyer Survivor

It should be noted that, remarkably, at least one flyer has been able to park his plane on Rainier's airy summit and survive.

In April 1951 air force lieutenant John W. Hodgkin landed his single-engine Piper Cub, equipped with skis for touching down on snow and ice, on the crater rim. After taking pictures to document his daring-do, however, he was unable to get the plane started again. "A pilot since 1926, Hodgkin somehow hadn't planned on frozen spark plugs," wrote author Butch Farabee in his account of the incident. Hodgkin ended up spending a cold night alone on the mountain; meantime, a rescue effort was mobilized. By the time rangers reached the crater rim, Hodgkin had rescued himself; he pushed the plane over the edge and glided to a safe landing on frozen Mowich Lake.

Remembering Those Who Fell from the Sky

These short stories of lost aviators were gleaned mostly from the park record, and are presented in chronological order.

Noland O'Neil perished in a plane crash in an undisclosed location in the park in April 1944.

Helmut Kupfer and Julianne Jonnes died in a plane crash near Grand Park in August 1966. Jonnes died on impact; Kupfer was evacuated but died a short time later.

Rendle Moore, 35, of Long Beach, California, and Chris McKay, 24, of Kent, Washington, were killed when their small plane collided with Backbone Ridge in August 1973. The park record notes the two were presumed missing in the Columbia Gorge; newspaper accounts of the accident make note of an extensive search that was unsuccessful and eventually called off. The remnants of the plane, which was piloted by Moore, were discovered on the ridge in early September.

Two couples, Gordon and Louise Barry and Robert and Violet Henry, were killed when their Mooney Mark 20, piloted by Gordon Barry, crashed into Pyramid Peak in September 1973.

William Saul, 54, was flying at night and off-course when he slammed into the Willis Wall in March 1988.

Randall Lane and Phillip Cruise lost their lives when their Piper Cherokee hit a tree inside the northern boundary of the park, in the Lost Creek drainage, in March 2001. According to the park record, the plane struck the tree about forty feet off the ground.

CHAPTER 11

On the Job

SCATTERED IN THE PAGES OF THE PARK'S FATALITY FILES ARE A HAND-
ful of stories of young men whose lives were cut short while they were
assigned to Mount Rainier National Park working with the Civilian
Conservation Corps (CCC), a New Deal program that provided much-
needed employment during the Great Depression. Three other men—
also not technically park employees—lost their lives near the turn of the
twentieth century while employed as miners on the mountain. Any scars
left by these decades-old deaths don't have a direct impact on the lives of
the people currently working at Mount Rainier National Park, though
every life lost casts a long shadow.

That's not the case, however, with three more recent tragedies. In
1995 two climbing rangers were killed in the line of duty. In 2012 a ranger
was shot and killed while staffing a roadblock on the road to Paradise. A
second ranger lost his life that year during a rescue operation high on the
mountain. Memories of these colleagues and their sacrifices are still vivid,
and the losses still deeply felt.

The CCC and Storbo

Of the young people who lost their lives while working with the CCC,
several were killed in vehicle accidents, one lost his life in an explosion,
one had a fatal reaction after being stung by wasps, and one drowned on
his day off. For some there are details; for others not much can be gleaned.
Their deaths are described in the chapters that follow. The park's record
also includes a CCC camp "superintendent," H. E. O'Neill, who passed
away of a heart attack at Camp Tahoma (aka Camp No. 1 and Camp

O'Neill) on June 15, 1934; the camp's assistant superintendent, A. H. Cox, replaced his former boss.

Among the earliest to lose their lives in the park were three employees of the Mount Rainier Mining Company, also known as the Storbo (sometimes spelled Starbo) mining operation. Owned and operated by Peter Storbo of Enumclaw, the mine was located on the northeast face of the mountain in Glacier Basin and was formed at the turn of the twentieth century to extract copper from the flanks of the peak. The park record doesn't include a lot of information: The date of death is New Year's Day 1907; the cause of death is listed as an avalanche. Nils Brown, a man named Cresent (as per the fatality list; his first name is not recorded), and a boy with the surname Prestline (whose first name is also not recorded) expired from "traumatic injuries" upon being buried in the slide.

It seems likely that these three are the same individuals who "had their lives snapped out in a lonely cabin in Glacier basin at the head of the White river, three months ago," according to an article in the April 7, 1907, issue of Walla Walla's *Evening Statesman*. The story lists the deceased as "Ernest Shaler, aged 40, of Buckley; Nels Brown, aged 28, of Seattle; and Alfred Preslin, of Norman, near Everett, aged 15," and reports that the cabin in which they were found "was a mass of ruins covered with snow and ice."

The coroner who examined the bodies and the scene speculated that the cabin "was wrecked by a terrific windstorm while the inmates were asleep and then covered with a snow slip. The bodies were in a perfect state of preservation, being frozen stiff." The date of the event was narrowed to January because of the quantity of supplies that remained untouched in the cabin. The three workers had been dispatched to the site in early fall of the previous year to complete "development work" for the copper mining operation in the area, and had been outfitted with food and necessities to make it through winter.

Sean Ryan and Philip Otis

The passage of time has tamped the pain left by the loss of climbing rangers Sean Ryan and Philip Otis, who died on a rescue mission on August

12, 1995. But their story still resonates as a reminder of the dangers that confront every ranger on every mountain rescue.

The two were seasonal rangers, working on the north side of the mountain out of Camp Schurman, when they were alerted to an accident high on the Emmons Glacier. A climber had broken his ankle on descent from the summit and was unable to continue under his own power. His two companions climbed up and over the summit crater, then down to Camp Muir to report the incident, leaving the injured climber alone, but well provisioned, near the mountaintop.

Climbing rangers at Camp Muir were unable to launch a rescue immediately, according to an accident report in the *American Alpine Journal*, so the rangers at Camp Schurman were dispatched: Ryan, twenty-three years old with eleven Rainier summits under his belt; Otis, who had only climbed Rainier once; and Luke Reinsma of Seattle Mountain Rescue, who had more experience but was feeling tired and ill. They loaded up with gear for themselves and for the victim and his companions, including sleeping bags, tents, and first-aid equipment, knowing they'd have to bivouac high on the peak with the injured climber given the evening start, and thinking that the hurt man's companions had remained with their partner.

Reinsma's malaise caught up with him as he climbed. He was slowing the two younger rangers down, so after consultation, he decided to return to Camp Schurman. By then the rescuers also had learned that only the injured climber was on the peak, so Ryan and Otis offloaded some of their gear for Reinsma to carry back, then continued upslope, into the darkness. The *AAJ* report notes that Ryan and Otis "were enthusiastic, eager to get on with the climb up to the injured climber at 13,400 feet."

Hints at trouble began with a call from Ryan indicating they'd reached 12,900 feet, but that one of them (it would turn out to be Otis) was having trouble with a crampon. An investigation into the incident revealed the twenty-two-year-old climber was using crampons that didn't fit his boots and were likely borrowed from stored gear kept in the Schurman camp. He'd attempted to secure the ill-fitted and perhaps broken equipment to his footwear with duct tape and athletic tape.

That was the last time anyone heard from either Ryan or Otis. When rangers from Camp Muir arrived on the scene, they found the stranded climber safe where he'd been left, "in good condition and out of the wind, with adequate clothing, food and fuel." There was no sign of the two rangers. A helicopter was dispatched to airlift the injured man off the mountain; after he'd been transported to the hospital, the chopper returned to look for the missing.

It was a search with a wrenching outcome.

Their bodies were sighted at about 12,000 feet. Otis's ice ax and a part of his crampon were discovered at about 13,200 feet. While exactly what transpired can't be known, the evidence included "slide marks" and the ax with its tip buried in the snow. Whatever the cause, the result was that two of the park's own slid about 1,200 feet down the Emmons Glacier to their deaths.

Sean Ryan's sister Ashley wrote a poignant essay that was published in the *Seattle Times* ten years after the accident. She had come back to the mountain looking for answers; she wondered if her brother's death, and that of Phil Otis, could have been avoided. "Deaths on Mount Rainier are nothing new—an average of two to three climbers are lost each year," she wrote. "Hundreds of families across the world have suffered the whims of this unforgiving peak."

But there were problems to be addressed. She had dinner with then–Rainier climbing ranger Mike Gauthier, who was aboard the Chinook that removed the bodies from the mountain. She wrote that Gauthier "had been Sean's climbing partner, mentor and friend.... He introduced Sean to glacier climbing and mountaineering, and took him on his first ascent of Rainier. Gauthier encouraged Sean to become a climbing ranger, and he feels deeply responsible for his death."

Gauthier told her about shortcomings in how "the park's ranger and rescue programs were run, from hiring criteria and training to rescue management." He was working to rectify those inadequacies: In the years following the deaths, the park toughened its hiring requirements for climbing rangers; improved training programs; instituted mandatory climbing fees, the proceeds of which help fund rescue training and the purchasing of equipment; and "revamped" its search-and-rescue procedures.

Ashley Ryan walked away from Mount Rainier with answers, with misgivings, and with a better sense of what her brother—and others like him—cherished about Rainier. When, on the second day of her visit, the mountain came out, "all I could do was stare in wonder at its beauty, and feel its draw, its magic," she wrote. "I felt myself wanting to go higher, and higher, and higher. Many times, I have thought Sean was foolish to do what he did, to take such risks. Now, I thought he would have been a fool not to."

Margaret Anderson

In a portrait that once graced the bottom of Mount Rainier's homepage, Margaret Anderson offers viewers a sweet smile. She stands in front of an American flag, outfitted in the hallmarks of her employment as a ranger: flat-brimmed hat, gray and green uniform, National Park Service patch. Her vitality shines as brightly as her badge.

Click on the image, and an outline of her life and death are laid out. She was thirty-four years old. She was the mother of two young daughters, and the wife of a fellow park ranger. Her career in law enforcement with the National Park Service included assignments at Bryce Canyon National Park in Utah and at Chesapeake and Ohio Canal National Historical Parks in Maryland. She and her husband, Eric, both started working at Mount Rainier in 2008.

On New Year's Day in 2012, Margaret Anderson was responding to a call about a vehicle that had failed to stop at a chain-up checkpoint, where park officials confirm visitors have put chains on their tires to safely negotiate snowy and/or icy roadways. When she intercepted the driver, Benjamin Barnes, he shot and killed her.

Newspaper accounts of the circumstances of her murder describe a senseless act with disturbing and unknowable origins. If Anderson had been a climber on the peak, her killer was the equivalent of a freak storm that burst upon her with fury and without warning.

Benjamin Barnes is portrayed as a twenty-four-year-old lost soul. A picture in a *Seattle Times* article describing his background shows a clean-cut, straight-faced young man hefting an automatic weapon in each hand. Barnes was a veteran who had served in Iraq but was discharged following "an arrest for driving under the influence and illegal transportation of a private weapon." He had recently broken up with his girlfriend, the mother of his daughter; the relationship was allegedly abusive, and she took custody of the child. He was distraught over the suicide of a friend. He was homeless and unemployed. And he was about to commit murder.

Earlier on that day, not long before his encounter with Ranger Anderson, Barnes was reportedly involved in another shooting incident, one in which four people were injured. Now he was, according to the *Times*, "running for the mountains, the place a friend says he felt most at home."

After Barnes blew through the chain-up checkpoint near the park entrance, Rainier's law enforcement rangers sprang into action. Anderson was at Paradise. According to an in-depth account of the incident in *Outside* magazine, she had driven a short distance down from the winter visitor hub and parked her vehicle across the two-lane Paradise Road to stop the driver, who was being pursued by another ranger. She was the roadblock. The goal was to ensure Barnes wouldn't get into trouble higher up on the slick mountain road.

But Barnes *was* trouble. When he encountered Anderson, he stopped his car, grabbed an assault rifle, and opened fire, mortally wounding the ranger. Then he terrorized the park—he was an unknown shooter with an automatic weapon and a military background. He also fired on other law enforcement personnel, though they were uninjured. The armed standoff and the uncertainty of Barnes's intentions forced the visitor center at Paradise into lockdown and prevented help from reaching the wounded Anderson for more than an hour. She passed away in her vehicle before rescuers could reach her.

Barnes met a different end. He fled into the woods, and a massive manhunt ensued. Four to five feet of snow blanketed the ground, which both hindered the search and enabled law enforcement to track the killer. Barnes's trail led to the glacier-fed Paradise River. Given the season, his pursuers knew the young man would have a hard time surviving the freezing temperatures of the long winter's night without proper gear, much less after making a frigid river crossing. And he didn't. His body was discovered the next day in the river near Narada Falls. Though the park record lists the cause of death as unknown, other accounts say he drowned in the waterway, and that as predicted, exposure played a role in his death.

Commenting on the loss of Anderson in the immediate aftermath of her murder, park spokesperson Lee Taylor noted that the young mother was "on the job not for money or for glory but out of a love for wild places and the national parks. . . . She was a person with a quick smile, a very gentle person, a very competent ranger. This gunman took the life of somebody who had a great deal to live for and was making great contributions to society by being a national park ranger."

The formal account on the park's website notes the honors Anderson received after her death. Her sacrifice was recognized in a memorial service "widely attended by National Park Service employees and members of the law enforcement and fire service communities from all over the United States and Canada, dignitaries, and the general public." She was commended by the Washington State Senate. The post office in Eatonville, where she lived with her family during her time at Rainier, was renamed in her memory.

The tribute is thoughtful, subdued, and prominent, as is Anderson's legacy in the collective memory of the park. Mention her name among her colleagues, and the mood shifts. It's not exactly sadness that suddenly prevails, but more a wistfulness. She is still present.

Nicholas Hall

The park posted the following on the five-year anniversary of climbing ranger Nick Hall's death:

> On June 21, 2012, the country lost a true hero when Climbing Ranger Nick Hall fell to his death during an upper mountain rescue on the Emmons Glacier. Nick was devoted to the ranger's call to serve and save. He had a passion for wilderness and possessed strength and courage that inspired those who knew him. He lived his life embracing his passion for skiing and climbing mountains. Nick died doing what he loved—saving lives during a highly technical rescue under difficult and unforgiving conditions. Join us in paying tribute to Nick—friend, co-worker, and devoted ranger. Rest in peace, Nick.

The death of Nicholas Hall came hard on the heels of Margaret Anderson's killing. His photo appeared alongside hers on the park's homepage. The image captures the ranger taking a break, framed by bluebird skies and the cliffs of the mountain he worked and loved.

Hall's background reads like an almanac for the outdoors professional. The park's memorial describes the ranger, a native of Maine, as "a quiet youth who drew his energy from nature. Inspired and motivated by the outdoors, he lived his life embracing his passion for skiing and climbing mountains." He served in the US Marine Corps, and graduated from the Recreation and Outdoor Education Environmental Studies program at Western State College in Colorado. He worked as a ski patroller at Lake Tahoe, California, and in Washington; as a river ranger; on a fishing boat in Alaska; and as a climbing ranger with the US Forest Service before landing at Mount Rainier.

Hall was one of several climbing rangers and independent climbers who came to the aid of a party of four that had taken a long, potentially fatal fall on the upper Emmons Glacier. The climbers, all from Texas, had summited and were inching their way down the steep, frozen face when the last person on the rope slipped. Like stitches pulled from fabric, the mountaineers skittered downslope. Their slide was arrested when one of the climbers, Noelle Smith, plunged into a crevasse. She was their anchor.

As the climbers assessed their situation and began to do what they could to self-rescue, one called rangers to report the incident and request assistance. A climbing guide who was on the mountain at the time witnessed the fall, and also went to the Texans' aid. The rescue was under way.

Each of the fallen climbers had incurred substantial injuries—one had severe head trauma, another had a broken leg. The wounds were significant enough that the victims would need to be airlifted off the mountain. Hall was flown to the scene aboard a Chinook helicopter that had been dispatched from McChord Air Force Base in Tacoma. The plan was to secure the injured climbers in litters and hoist them, one after the other, into the aircraft, then fly them to a local hospital. The rescuers etched a platform into the exposed, steeply pitched, and icy slope so they could "package" the injured for the hoists.

However, dropping an empty litter from the hovering aircraft proved tricky. The slope was buffeted by wind, and turbulence from the helicopter's rotors made catching and securing the basket difficult. Still, the first climber was successfully lifted into the craft. When the empty litter was lowered again, Hall struggled to catch and secure it. He finally succeeded, unhitched it, and settled it on the mountainside, but when it began to slip downhill, the climbing ranger lost his footing and began to slide with it. He wasn't anchored, and he'd put down his ice tool so he could better maneuver the rescue apparatus. As he slid, witnesses watched Hall try to self-arrest, try to jam the teeth of his crampons into the slope. But he couldn't get purchase. And there was no way those watching could help.

The climbing ranger came to rest on the glacier about 2,400 feet below; the helicopter crew that had flown him to the rescue peeled away from the accident site to track him down. A fellow ranger was lowered from the craft to his aid. Asked if an evacuation was urgent, Hall's colleague responded that it was not. There was no sign of life.

Three of the four climbers were successfully evacuated that evening. Tricky winds and impending darkness forced a couple of rangers and the least-injured Texan to spend the night high on the peak; they descended the next day. Hall's body remained on the mountain that night as well; he was brought down when conditions permitted.

The climbers who were rescued that day spoke with the *Houston Chronicle*. In the aftermath, one man told the paper that he still wonders why he survived. "One of the things that kills me—knowing that Nick was somebody's friend, that he was somebody's son, that he was somebody's brother. How do you say, 'Thank you and I'm sorry' to the family? If we had not been on the mountain that day, their son would still be here."

But Nick was doing his job; he loved his work, and was aware of the hazards. "Mountains, like Mount Rainier, are inherently wild places," park superintendent Randy King explained in the park's remembrance of Hall; he'd been guided to the summit years earlier by the fallen ranger. "Risk and risk management are a component in the climbing experience. Rangers like Nick work hard every day to help climbers make good decisions on the mountain, to stay safe, to go home again."

CHAPTER 12

On the Water

The most dramatic stories of death by water in Mount Rainier National Park involve tumbling over waterfalls or being carried away by swift water . . . but that's not the only way it comes down.

In Ella Kolbinson's case, she simply went under. The accident occurred in August 1923, when Kolbinson and her friend, Lucile Sandner, both waitresses at the Paradise Inn, headed up to Reflection Lake to enjoy their day off. The two young women swam out into the frigid water, paddling thirty to forty feet from shore before turning around to swim back.

Then Ella went down. According to Kolbinson's fatality file, Lucile reported that she'd "heard the dead girl call out for help; that she tried to encourage her, but that the Kolbinson girl sank almost immediately and did not rise to the surface again." Lucile told investigators that "Ella got out beyond her depth [and] became excited,"—or panicked, as was more likely. Young Lucile headed back out to help her struggling friend, but the water was too deep.

Four men were on the scene and witnessed Ella's struggle, but declined to help. A "young medical student" then arrived, pulled the girl from the water, and tried to resuscitate her. Though the park record notes her death as a drowning, a letter from T. H. Martin, general manager of the Paradise Inn, mentions the suspicion that the young woman may have suffered a heart attack because her rescuer "could get no water from her lungs."

Kolbinson's is not the only death in Reflection Lake attributed to a possible heart attack. The cold water also was the suspected culprit in the death of a young man who perished there in August 1933.

Joseph Tobits, 24, and Benjamin Levine were both employed by the Civilian Conservation Corps (CCC); Tobits was from New York City, a "bank teller by profession," and "efficient and well liked," according to a letter from Preston Macy, assistant chief ranger for the park. Tobits and his companion hiked up to the lake from Camp Narada on a warm summer day, planning to swim and then walk back to camp. But once in the water, Tobits went under and didn't come back up. Levine and another CCC employee, William Hickey, dove in after their comrade, but couldn't locate him. Hickey then ran for help, but given that he had to travel about three miles to reach assistance, Tobits's fate was sealed. His body was recovered later that day.

In the investigation that followed, both Levine and Tobits were cleared from having undertaken their swim under the influence of liquor or "narcotics." Inexperience, however, was an issue. In his affidavit, which is part of Tobits's fatality file, Hickey mentioned that the young man "was not an expert swimmer, but had the ability to swim for a few feet."

A letter about the incident from superintendent O. A. Tomlinson points up the rarity of an event like the one that claimed Tobits's life. "The accident occurred directly in front of the Reflection Lake cabin, about fifty yards from shore, where thousands of persons have bathed each summer," Tomlinson wrote, "and although everyone was aware that a lake of that character would naturally be of great depth, it was considered relatively safe for any person exercising the normal amount of judgment customary in any other body of water where life-guards are not employed."

Tomlinson reflected on the circumstances surrounding the incident, noting that Tobits and Levine may have been overheated after their warm-weather hike: "It is probably that the shock of going into the cool water of the lake was too great a shock and resulted in heart failure." The fact that Tobits never surfaced or struggled supported this theory.

At the other end of the temperature gradient, Ohanapecosh Hot Springs also has claimed a couple of victims, including Katherine Donahoe. According to the superintendent's report for September 1938, Donahoe, a seventy-seven-year-old resident of Chehalis, Washington, went into the bathhouse at noon and was found dead about twenty minutes later, "her head submerged under fourteen inches of water." The coroner ruled the cause "accidental drowning." Another person—the park record lists the identity as "unknown"—also drowned in the hot springs in June 1939.

Over the Falls

By some counts, Mount Rainier National Park boasts more than 150 waterfalls within its boundaries. Fed by year-round snowmelt and bolstered by abundant rain, the falls are a major attraction for tourists, especially those cascades closest to the park's main thoroughfares.

One of the easiest to reach is the seventy-foot spill of Christine Falls, just off the Paradise Road. Narada Falls, where the Paradise River drops nearly two hundred feet, first draping over a rock face and then free-falling, is not far downslope from the visitor hub at Paradise. Comet Falls is another popular destination; its drop of nearly four hundred feet is one of the highest in the park, and its name is drawn from its stunning display—a narrow, tapering wash of water like that of a comet's tail.

When flush with high water, cascades are magnets for hikers and aficionados of watersports alike. A seasoned whitewater kayaker who had logged a number of challenging first descents on "unexplored canyon waterways" in the Northwest, William (Bill) Bowey was one of those enchanted by Rainier's rivers and streams. But the paddler, remembered by one mourning admirer as the "King of Steep Creeking," met his match on an "exploratory run" down Stevens Creek in July 2004. His body was recovered below Sylvia Falls, a whitewater churn funneled through a stair-step channel before making a frothy drop into what, in high water, is yet another maelstrom.

The park record notes uncertainty about whether Bowey slipped over the falls while scoping them out, or whether he attempted to run them. Whatever his intent, the forty-eight-year-old paddler left behind a legion of admiring followers who applauded his humbleness, his skill on the water, and his love for the rivers he ran. Bowey was credited with "[paving] the way for a new generation of boaters" by author and paddler Jeff Bennett, who was quoted in the *Seattle Post-Intelligencer*. Bowey was also a trailblazer: "Many of the runs he pioneered now attract kayakers from around the globe to this region for the opportunity to run spectacular Class V whitewater drops," the newspaper notes.

The paddler was a dedicated husband and father of two, as well as a teacher. In a remembrance posted on the Oregon Kayaking website, Jason Rackley wrote, "Bill was a legend, a larger-than-life paddler who was also a genuinely great guy, kind and generous to all." Though running rivers and creeks was his passion, and Bowey reportedly loved "regaling fellow boaters with river tales," another friend told the newspaper, "We all looked up to him for how well he balanced family and kayaking. . . . He would have given all the rivers back for those two kids."

While Bowey was an expert at reading water, and was trained to gauge the forces that would ultimately undo him, most of those who have lost their lives near Rainier's falls likely had no idea the danger they were in.

Sadly, children figure in the tally: In August 1970 two were swept into flows near waterfalls. Nine-year-old Susan Bullinger drowned in the Ohanapecosh River near Silver Falls, which is reached via a trail touted as a great option for a family outing. The park warns hikers to be wary near the river and falls, advising that although streamside rocks are "inviting to sit on," they are also slick and should be approached with "extreme caution." Young Susan was, according to a newspaper account, out on a hike with her family on a summer's afternoon and merely dangling her toes in the stream below the falls when she slipped into the river. Before anyone could rescue her, the strong current swept her away. Her body was recovered by a scuba diver.

In the same month, ten-year-old Eric Bruce drowned after he fell 150 feet over Christine Falls. The story goes that the boy ran ahead of his father and brothers on the trail, and then disappeared. Rescuers searched for the boy overnight; his body was eventually recovered from under a log at the falls.

Then there are those whose level of preparedness around waterways lies somewhere between the innocent child and the seasoned expert. An Associated Press article exploring an increase in deaths in the national park in 1977 notes that the dead included two people who had perished in auto accidents, three on climbs, four on hikes, and two who died in cascades: Margaret Maurer, an eighteen-year-old park employee from

Puyallup, Washington, who fell 250 feet over a fall on Dead Horse Creek in June, and sixteen-year-old Jacques Jackson, part of a group from Auburn Adventist Academy who drowned in the Ohanapecosh River after he slipped near Silver Falls in September.

(An aside: The AP article also notes that "park officials say they're puzzled by the increase" in fatalities, and visitor protection specialist Jack Ritenour observed, "We could play the numbers game and simply say the visitation is up so accidents are too." Not only had visitation increased 55 percent over the previous year, but the snowpack was light as well, which meant visitors were able to access the backcountry, and arguably more hazardous terrain, earlier in the season.)

It's tragically common in parks worldwide—and especially in those with spectacular waterfalls—for people to lose their lives attempting to get a better photograph. That's what happened to Roger Wagner, a resident of Florida who was visiting the park with his son in September 2011. The accident took place on the Comet Falls Trail, near the scenic bridge spanning Christine Falls, where Wagner, 59, tumbled over a forty-foot cliff. A newspaper account notes that, because the accident occurred late in the day, Wagner's remains could not be recovered immediately, and that overnight, his body was swept over the falls and came to rest in difficult terrain not far from the park road.

Down the River

Rivers are deceptive. When they swell with meltwater in spring, the dangers are obvious. Whitewater screams warnings and most people steer clear, except experts like kayaker Bill Bowey, who are drawn to the extreme thrill of running fast water.

But when the weather warms in summer and the flows appear to mellow, the lure of a gentle float downstream in a raft or inner tube, of skipping stones from the shallows, of fishing in an eddy, or simply cooling your heels in a pool after a long hike becomes irresistible. Caution may slip away. So too, unfortunately, may the unlucky swimmer or rafter.

Louis Santucci was just eighteen years old when he and four friends, all members of the Civilian Conservation Corps and slated to leave for home the following day, decided to go "bathing" in the Ohanapecosh River, according to a superintendent's report on the tragic event that claimed Santucci's life in June 1938. To safely access the stream, the young men rigged a rope, which was tied to a tree and then slung over a cliff into a deep pool. "Santucci lowered himself into the pool and for some unknown reason let go of the rope," the superintendent recorded. "He immediately sank and the under current carried him down the turbulent stream."

Santucci's friends attempted rescue, but the water was high and milky with runoff from the glaciers above. Additionally, the superintendent related, "Santucci had never learned to swim." A formal rescue was then launched, but the young man's body wasn't recovered until the next day, having been carried a quarter-mile downstream from the place where he'd slipped beneath the surface.

The White River has also claimed youthful victims. Six-year-old Nicholas Kuhnhausen was on a hike in July 1981 when he fell into the waterway and was "swept downstream," according to the park record. In August 2010 eleven-year-old Jason Russell was wading across the White when he lost his footing and was carried off by the current. The accident occurred off WA 410, from a camp near the Silver Spring Guard Station on the northern boundary of the park. The boy, from Puyallup, Washington, wasn't found immediately; swift water rescue and dive teams responded and conducted an exhaustive search, hoping against hope that the child had somehow made it to shore somewhere downstream and would be found alive.

A few years later, in August 2013, eight-year-old Ahamed Asiri (as per the park record; the name is spelled Ahmad in a newspaper account) fell into the Inter Fork of the White River near the White River Campground. The child, a visitor from Saudi Arabia, was playing on a log when the mishap occurred. The *News Tribune* reported that the boy's older brother jumped into the river to try to save him, and that rangers attempted to resuscitate him once he was pulled from the stream. He was flown by helicopter to a local hospital, but did not survive.

Lovers Lost

The tale of the lovers who drowned in Ipsut Creek in March 2007 still resonates within the park. On a turbulent spring day, Frances Annette Blakely, called Annette, attempted to cross the storm-fed stream on a log and slipped into the rushing water. As she was swept away, her husband, Robert Blakely, jumped in to save her. Husband and wife ended up pinned against deadfall by the creek's powerful flow—a force so strong they couldn't free themselves or save each other.

Ipsut Creek was the couple's favorite campground in the park, but a series of storms earlier in the year had rendered the site inaccessible by car, washing out the bridge that ordinarily afforded access and depositing clots of debris in the waterway. Flows in the Carbon River, which is fed by Ipsut Creek, were more than twice the norm, according to one newspaper account. Rangers had flagged the safest crossing, via logs, to and from the camp, but apparently the Blakelys didn't use that route—perhaps because they didn't see the flags. However, they definitely understood the danger. Given the high water, they had postponed leaving the camp for a day. In the end, that decision didn't make the crossing any safer.

An account of the accident in the *Olympian* recounts how, after the couple became "trapped in the creek's frigid, waist-deep rushing water by logs and other storm debris," a friend who was camping with the Puyallup couple went for help. But by the time rescuers arrived, Annette, 47, and Robert, 44, had succumbed to the forces of nature. Though the park record lists the causes of death as drowning, given that the creek was swollen with snowmelt, hypothermia may have played a role.

"He would have died to save her and she would have died to save him," the pair's twenty-four-year-old son, Chris Blakely, told the *Seattle Times* in the wake of the accident. "I think they would have rather died together than live if the other one couldn't."

Remembering Those Lost to the Water

Ferreting out the details of how drowning victims met their ends is complicated by the fact that often those victims were engaged in another activity—a hike, a climb, a ski trip—when the accident occurred. In a few cases, the details simply aren't part of the park or public record, as the brevity of some of the stories attest. They are listed in chronological order.

John Thompson died in July 1949 when he drowned in the Carbon River.

Kenneth Stetson drowned in Fan Lake in July 1958. A newspaper account notes that the twenty-year-old Seattle man, a summertime employee in the park, had ventured off for a swim alone. His body was recovered from ten feet of water.

In July 1968 air force sergeant Bruce MacDonald, a thirty-nine-year-old survival instructor, was on a reconnaissance mission in the park, scouting the Ohanapecosh River to determine its suitability for survival training exercises. He and a companion were pitched into the current when their raft overturned, a local newspaper reported. The other man in the raft was able to reach safe ground, but MacDonald was swept downstream. It's assumed that he drowned; his body, the park notes, was not recovered.

Deborah Wetherald was hiking on the Fourth of July in 1982 in the Edith Creek Basin when she slipped into a steep gully and then over a set of falls.

In July 1983 Martin Richey, 25, perished after falling into a box canyon while on a hike along the Cowlitz River.

Twenty-four-year-old Christopher Pennington attempted to cross the stream above Comet Falls in August 1986, but was swept over the precipice to his demise.

In June 1990 Vicen I. Pfost, 23, was on a hike when he fell into the Paradise River and drowned.

A thirty-five-year-old Wenatchee resident, Kristine Sitton, was hiking near Silver Falls in August 1991 when she slipped, fell into the

Ohanapecosh River, and was killed. Reports conflict about whether she went over the falls or not.

Adrian Arceo fell into the Ohanapecosh River while on a hike in October 1991. He was pulled out and evacuated to a hospital in Yakima, but died there, according to the park record.

William Olson disappeared from the Ipsut Creek Campground in July 1994 and was discovered drowned in the Carbon River nine days later.

CHAPTER 13

On the Road

GIVEN THE DISTRACTIONS, KEEPING YOUR EYES ON THE ROAD IN MOUNT Rainier National Park is a challenge even in the best conditions. Tumbling waterfalls, steep glacial valleys, swift-flowing rivers, ethereal forests . . . and then, if the mountain is out . . .

Traffic congestion, in these instances, can be a blessing. When you are stuck crawling along a park highway in an automotive conga line, taking a long look up toward the peak poses little danger to a driver or passenger. But when there are no crowds, the anticipation of a good hike, a summit bid, or a riverside picnic lunch may invite speed. Rounding a bend, Rainier may burst into view. But given the narrow, twisting nature of roadways within the park, in that instant even momentary inattention can invite disaster.

Another aggravating factor when it comes to safety on the park roads: snow and ice. Many roads close in winter, including the highway through Stevens Canyon beyond Paradise, the roads to Sunrise and White River, and the Mowich Lake Road. Even the "year-round" road from the Nisqually entrance to Paradise may be gated at Longmire—or even at the park entrance—due to slick pavement.

Adverse winter conditions and the dangers they present to drivers are nothing new to park officials. In February 1946 the superintendent commented on "quite a number of automobile accidents . . . most of them caused by carelessness, or icy roads." One of the accidents took place on January 2, when a fellow named V. J. McElderry destroyed a bus by driving it into the check-in booth at the Nisqually entrance. The driver was not injured in the crash, and was determined to have been either drunk or asleep at the wheel. He was fined for his carelessness.

While random acts of nature have resulted in some automobile deaths within the park's boundaries, most fatal accidents have been caused by distraction, bad decisions, or bad luck. In terms of bad decisions, speeding, driving without consideration for conditions, aggressive driving, and obliviousness have all resulted in fatalities on park roadways. The tragedy is that, for the most part, many of these deaths were avoidable.

Motorcars in the Park

As the turn of the twentieth century approached, Mount Rainier National Park was finding its identity as an American "pleasure park." Only about five hundred people visited in the summer season, making the trip on foot or by horseback. By 1893 James Longmire's "Mountain Road," running from Ashford to Longmire Springs, was open, though passage was "restricted to wagons whose axles could clear the dozens of stumps that still needed to be rooted out from between the parallel wheel ruts," according to the park's administrative history.

The first "automobilists" entered the park by special permit in 1908—Mount Rainier was the first national park to allow the newfangled conveyances, though other park superintendents would acquiesce to permitting motorcars in their sanctuaries within a few years. As was the case in all American national parks at the time, the arrival and ascendance of the automobile was transformative. Given the National Park Service mandate to both provide for protection of the natural resources within the parks and provide access so that people could enjoy those resources, Mount Rainier and its sister parks focused on building safe and scenic roadways as soon as funding was available. Today about 150 miles of roadway, paved and unpaved, run through the park, and in 2016 more than seven hundred thousand vehicles were logged passing through the various entrances.

The restrictions imposed on motorists in the early twentieth century seem onerous today: Only 117 permits were issued; the speed limit was 6 miles per hour; and autos were required to make way for horse teams pulling wagons and stages. By 1911, according to the park history, Rainier's "gatekeeper" was logging the arrival of people "by foot, horseback, wagon, bicycle, stage, and automobile—all of whom shared the same narrow, mountain road to Longmire Springs and beyond."

The point of these restrictions was to mitigate the dangers of travel on the twisting thoroughfares. At the time, the Paradise Road "featured innumerable blind curves and steep embankments and many narrow bridges." Such features are dictated by mountainous terrain and are what make the modern park highways so attractive, as well as potentially dangerous.

Snow, as noted above, was also an issue: In 1946 the superintendent reported that 166 inches of the white stuff had accumulated at Paradise. To make the roadway accessible, twenty sticks of dynamite were detonated every twenty to thirty feet along the route to loosen the snowpack enough for removal by the "Snogo," a snowplow with a blower used to clear roadways throughout the high country.

Pavement has long since replaced ruts and mud. Laying down asphalt, coupled with improvements in vehicle technology, has allowed drivers to explore the park more safely and comfortably, and has also enhanced the ability to gain speed, for better or worse. Though it's not stated directly in the park record, the fact that so many of those who've lost their lives in vehicle accidents in Rainier ended up leaving the roadway at a sharp curve, often plunging down an embankment, indicates drivers were either exceeding speed limits or driving faster than was safe given the conditions.

It's only logical that the number of traffic accidents within the park would grow as traffic counts increased over the years. That said, given the millions of vehicles that have safely traveled through Mount Rainier National Park, even in winter, the odds of a person dying in an accident are slim. Still, compared to other activities that have taken lives in Rainier, driving ranks high as a likely means to a devastating end.

In the Early Years

The earliest death by automobile in the park occurred in May 1918. Ruth Dory was riding in a car with a number of servicemen when the driver lost control near the park entrance, "presumably from some mechanical defect," according to the superintendent's report. The vehicle landed upside down with the passengers underneath; all were injured in the accident, but only Dory was killed.

A stenographer working in Portland, Oregon, the young woman was engaged to be married. Her fiancé was in the car and survived. In addition to the loss of Ruth, the fiancé "had traveling orders from the War Department" to report for duty, as World War I was under way. This request made the accident, and the demise of his loved one, "doubly hard on him," the superintendent noted.

Mrs. L. G. Vitous was behind the wheel in August 1925 when she swerved to avoid an oncoming car on the Dry Creek Bridge below Longmire. The bridge was only wide enough for one car to pass, and neither of the two converging vehicles made way for the other. Attempting to avoid a collision, according to the park's fatality files, Mrs. Vitous crashed over the bridge railing, and the car plunged into the creek bed fifteen feet below. She was killed, and three passengers were injured. The other car, according to the file, did not stop.

Another early accident occurred in September 1928. Hiski Tanttu, aka H. Stanley (the park superintendent notes that because his Finnish name was too hard to pronounce, the man adopted the pseudonym), a "well developed man" of about sixty-five years, was "absolutely crushed" in a steam shovel accident near Paradise. He'd tried to "climb on a loaded gravel truck while it was in motion and in doing so had taken hold of the trip lever which dumps the load," the superintendent recorded. This caused the lever to drop, "and he went down with it, and fell in front of the rear wheel." The park's assistant chief ranger, Preston Macy, details the injuries in an exhaustive, gruesome report: Stanley suffered severed lungs, crushed ribs, a nearly severed aorta, and crushed legs. The driver of the gravel truck, according to the file, was held blameless.

The Civilian Conservation Corps

The Civilian Conservation Corps (CCC) was a New Deal–era program instituted by president Franklin Delano Roosevelt's administration to employ young men during the Great Depression. The corps completed a number of construction projects within Mount Rainier National Park (and other national parks), including the building of park residences, campground amenities, and shelters in the backcountry. The crews, housed in six camps at various locations within the park starting in 1933, also helped with fire suppression, trail construction, road building and maintenance, and blister rust control within the forests. The park's administrative history notes that the crews became close-knit teams during the tenure of the program, and left a lasting, artful, and functional legacy.

Two young CCC workers, however, would lose their lives in automobile accidents while doing good works at Mount Rainier. One was Edward English, a twenty-three-year-old enrollee from Brooklyn, New York, who died in September 1938 on Westside Road when the dump truck he was riding in "climbed up a bank for ten feet and turned over." English was killed instantly. The driver, another CCC enrollee, suffered minor injuries, and two other CCC workers were also hurt in the accident. The workers were based out of the Tahoma Creek Camp and were collecting rock from St. Andrews Creek to be used in construction projects elsewhere in the park.

In his report on the accident, the park superintendent noted that it was the end of the work day when the crash occurred, and that the truck was traveling 45 or 50 miles per hour down a "6 percent grade out of gear" when the driver lost control. He also noted that the truck suffered $340 in damage.

Then, in 1939, John Janskowski, a nineteen-year-old CCC worker, was "killed instantly" when the dump truck he was riding in on the Carbon River Road, near Cataract Creek, rolled down a forty-foot embankment. The CCC camp leader, identified only as Crowell in the superintendent's report, was also in the cab and received minor injuries in the accident.

On Two Wheels

The vulnerability of motorcyclists in any collision was tragically borne out in a September 1993 accident that took place on what was described as a beautiful day for sightseeing in Mount Rainier National Park, with fair weather that drew in crowds of motorists.

The accident took place on WA 410 at the Deadwood Creek Bridge, which was being rebuilt at the time and was subject to one-way signalized traffic control. A posse of twenty to thirty riders, members of a local Harley-Davidson motorcycle club, had the green light to cross the span, and Robert and Mary Hyde were leading the pack as it passed over the creek. On the other side, the driver of what was described in the *Seattle Times* as "a small, old school bus that had been converted for use as a motorhome" came up on a line of cars stopped at the red light on the other side. In swerving to avoid rear-ending the autos, the bus driver ended up plowing into the oncoming cyclists.

The Hydes and their motorcycle were forced off the road and plunged three hundred feet down a steep slope. Neither husband nor wife, residents of Tacoma, survived. Robert was forty-six and the founder of the motorcycle club he was riding with, and his wife was forty-one; they left behind two daughters. Four other riders were injured in the accident, including a pair who suffered severe trauma, including head injuries.

In the wake of the accident, the families of the dead and injured motorcyclists filed a lawsuit seeking damages from the bus driver and the state and federal authorities responsible for setting up the traffic controls at the bridge construction site. Though the bus driver had passed signage indicating construction was under way a thousand feet ahead, the Associated Press quoted the Hyde daughters' attorney as noting that traffic was backed up for most of that distance: "This guy comes around a corner and bingo, there's 900 feet of cars in front of him." The lawsuit was settled for more than $2 million in 1997.

The Hydes aren't the only cyclists to have lost their lives in the park. In August 1985 Jackie Brown, 20, was a passenger on a motorcycle that went over an embankment in Stevens Canyon, and died in the accident. Pamela Johnson, 24, was killed while on a motorcycle in a head-on collision with a van at Kautz Creek in August 1990. In August 1994 Jerald Wentlandt lost control of his motorcycle on WA 123 about two miles south of Cayuse Pass, hit a rock wall, and was killed.

Two decades later, 2014 would prove a deadly year for a couple of men involved in separate motorcycle accidents. The first occurred in July, when Eric Hansen lost his life in a crash on winding Stevens Canyon Road. According to the park service, Hansen was westbound with his wife on the back of the bike when, on an S-curve about a mile west of the fee station, "the motorcycle traveled off the roadway and down an embankment that consisted of loose boulders."

Hansen's wife was able to crawl up the embankment and flag down help, and the accident location was ultimately broadcast on the park radio. Rescuers attempted to resuscitate Eric Hansen upon arrival at the scene, but this was "terminated per agency protocol after 45 [minutes]." Hansen's injured wife was airlifted to a nearby hospital.

The second accident occurred in September, again on Stevens Canyon Road. Thomas Casias, a sixty-four-year-old resident of Mesa, Arizona, was part of a group of motorcyclists traveling westbound when he lost control of his bike on a curve near milepost 17.5. Casias laid the bike down for some reason, then traveled off the roadway and down a "rocky slope," according to the park record. His comrades went directly to his aid, but were "unable to find the victim's pulse." Nor were the other motorcyclists able to determine what caused the accident, a park spokesman told a local newspaper.

When park personnel arrived, they performed CPR and also attempted to shock the man's heart back into rhythm with an automated external defibrillator (AED). Four cycles of shock were administered, to no avail, and Casias "was declared deceased."

Portrait of a Modern Mountain Accident

In June 2017 Patrick Stalder and his female passenger were negotiating the moist, wooded four-wheel terrain in the Evans Creek ORV (off-road vehicle) Park near Mowich Lake, just outside the park boundary, in a Jeep Wrangler when Stalder lost control and the vehicle began a thousand-foot tumble down a steep hillside. According to accounts of the accident in local newspapers, the passenger was tossed from the vehicle on the way down the slope, which was credited with saving her life, though she sustained injuries that landed her in critical condition at a local hospital. Stalder rode with the Jeep to the bottom of the hill and was killed.

One of first people on the scene was Ky Dewald, who spoke to the *News Tribune* about what he found when he arrived. Debris was scattered down the steep slope, which he descended "like a Slip 'n Slide." After determining the driver had died, Dewald sat with the survivor, trying to keep her awake and alive. He and friends wrapped her as best they could in blankets, but were unable to move her off the bed of the devil's club she had landed in. Devil's club, a spectacular shrub endemic to the understory of forests throughout the Pacific Northwest, has recognized medicinal attributes but is also studded with thorns.

The rescue of the survivor, who spent hours on the hillside before she could finally be transported to a medical facility, was a feat. "Paramedics splinted her leg and placed her in a metal basket, then rescue crews carried her 250 feet up the hill," the *News Tribune* reported. She reached the hospital seven hours after the accident occurred.

"We're all just shaking our heads," a Pierce County sheriff's spokesman told the paper. "This is something that nobody should have lived through."

Remembering Those Lost on the Road

The bulk of these accounts of vehicle accidents within Mount Rainier National Park, presented in chronological order, were culled from the park's fatality list, which was not forthcoming with details in most instances. Newspaper stories about the accidents, particularly for the middle of the twentieth century, are few and far between. Thus, regrettably, the bare-bones listings that follow, which capture the stories of at least some of those who have perished along the park highways. The details may be lost, but the people are not forgotten.

W. Bacon and Peter Espland died in a vehicular accident at an "unknown" location in November 1929.

Clifford Byland was in a vehicle accident in September 1931. He may have died in the crash, but the park notes that the records are "unclear."

In June 1934 Louis Foss lost his life in a car accident two miles inside the Nisqually entrance.

The superintendent's report from October 1938 notes the death of Peter Elich, 54, of Seattle, who was killed when his car blew a tire on the East Side Road. The fatal accident occurred about six miles north of the Ohanapecosh entrance.

An unknown person died in a vehicle accident in June 1939.

C. E. Ringenback died in a car crash in June 1951.

Three members of the Carpenter family—Harold, his wife, and his son Dennis—were killed in a car accident in July 1951.

In August 1951 Ralph Fisher and Lester Bloom lost their lives in separate vehicle accidents in the park; the park fatalities list contains no details about exact locations or causes of death.

Richard Olson died in April 1956 in a car crash at an unknown location.

William Purcell was killed when his car struck a boulder in the road on Chinook Pass in August 1956. A report in the *Port Angeles Evening News* describes how Purcell, 42, and two companions—army sergeant Kenneth Hendershot (the driver) and James Tom, whose age was "about 12"— plunged approximately two hundred feet over a cliff after striking the obstacle.

A passing motorist, Ray Harris, witnessed the accident and tried to flag down other drivers to stop and help, to no avail. Harris then drove forty-five miles to a telephone, where he called to inform park rangers of the accident.

"Hendershot, meantime, had crawled out of the wrecked car. He struggled up the cliff and finally stopped another motorist," the *Evening News* reported. Purcell and Tom had to be rescued by park rangers and were transported to a local hospital. The boy survived his injuries, but Purcell did not.

An unknown person was killed in a vehicle accident at an undisclosed location in October 1957.

A family tragedy was born of a birthday outing in the park in August 1959. Irvan Scalf, a World War II veteran turned logger, and relatives Coreen Goble and her brother, Emory, had ventured into the park on a "fishing and swimming jaunt" to celebrate Coreen's sixteenth birthday, according to a story in the Centralia *Daily Chronicle*. Seventeen-year-old Emory was behind the wheel when he lost control on gravel and plowed into a tree. He sustained minor injuries; his sister and the thirty-four-year-old Scalf were taken to a hospital in Enumclaw, where they passed away. The accident took place a couple of miles north of Ohanapecosh.

The three relatives were from the town of Randle, located just south-west of the park boundary on the Cowlitz River. Scalf left behind a griev-ing widow and three daughters, as well as other family members, and services with military honors were planned. The article makes no mention of survivors or services for Coreen Goble; the magnitude of the loss and the circumstances doubtless stunned the girl's family and friends.

Wayne Henry died in a vehicle accident in August 1960. A brief mention of his passing is contained in an article in the Centralia *Daily Chronicle* on the deaths of eight Washington residents over a single weekend. The report notes that Henry was thirty-six and a resident of Tumwater; it also states that he was killed after his car plunged over a 150-foot bank. Neither the *Chronicle* nor the park's fatality list provide the location of the accident.

In October 1962 fifty-five-year-old Nettie Carlberg of Portland, Oregon, was killed when her car skidded on a snowy WA 410 about two miles from the road's summit and plunged off a two-hundred-foot cliff, land-ing on the roadway below. "Old Man Winter popped out of his lair this weekend and took a brisk, icy stroll across the Cascade Mountain passes," the Centralia *Daily Chronicle* noted in a paragraph devoted to the passing of Mrs. Carlberg. In the wake of the storm, one pass was closed, while another was "troubled with slides and [wore] a white mantle."

Gayle Stevens was killed in an auto accident at an unknown location in the park in October 1962.

Percy Thorn died in a vehicle accident on Maternity Curve, located on the road to Paradise just above Longmire, in August 1963.

In November 1966 Richard Feldman died in a car accident; the location within the park is listed as unknown.

Charles Moore died in an automobile accident in October 1971. According to a local newspaper article, the forty-one-year-old resident of Tulsa, Oklahoma, was killed when his vehicle left the roadway and rolled over after striking an embankment. The National Park Service notes the accident took place one mile north of State Camp; the paper states it was thirty-five miles east of Enumclaw. The park record also notes that the victim had two aliases—Charles Moor and Charles Minor—and that he suffered a chest injury in the crash.

In June 1977 thirty-nine-year-old Moises Alvarez, of Napa, Idaho, drove his vehicle off a six-hundred-foot cliff at Windy Point on WA 410 and was killed. The park fatality list notes that Alvarez was driving drunk.

In 1977 twenty-one-year-old Craig Perky died of a pulmonary embolism at Madigan Hospital after a vehicle accident. A news report in the Port Angeles *Daily News* notes that Perky, a soldier from Fort Lewis, was injured in August and died of his injuries in September. The accident occurred seven miles into north Stevens Canyon.

In August 1980 five-year-old Marie Olinares was killed in a car accident on Stevens Canyon Road after she was ejected from the vehicle.

Robert Goodwin, 49, died in September 1987 when he lost control of his car and went over an embankment at Deadwood Creek.

In July 1988 sixty-four-year-old Merle Huibregtse lost control of his vehicle on WA 410 near Ghost Lake, crashed, and perished. The park record notes that he was intoxicated when the accident occurred.

Fred Ogden died of head injuries suffered in a car crash on WA 410 at Windy Point in July 1989.

The park's fatality record lists a pair of women, Laura Siebert and Margit Haugerudgraathen, who lost their lives on Stevens Canyon Road on separate dates in August 1991. Both deaths are attributed to hitting a rock wall (or rockfall) at the Ohana viewpoint.

In August 1995 Miwako Suzuki, 21, and Keisuke Masumori, 24, both residents of Japan, were killed when their vehicle overturned after running off the embankment on the Ghost Lake curve, north of Cayuse Pass on WA 410. Three other people in the car were injured when it careened off the roadway, according to one newspaper account. All were in their early twenties at the time of the crash, and three were Japanese students studying abroad in Seattle.

Donald Pettigrew, an eighty-four-year-old man who is noted to have suffered from dementia, died in a vehicle accident on WA 410 at Windy Point in November 1997. The conditions were snowy and icy, according to the park fatality list, and the vehicle was found forty feet down the embankment. A brief obituary in the *Great Falls Tribune* notes that Pettigrew was a native of Shelby in northern Montana, and that after graduating from Montana State University, he "worked as a salesman and electrician until World War II."

In September 2000 James Beslow and Scott McEachin were burned beyond recognition when their vehicle was engulfed in flames on the Ghost Lake curve, west of Cayuse Pass on WA 410.

Yuri Glavan was a passenger in a vehicle involved in an accident a mile from the Nisqually entrance to the park in November 2000. He died at St. Joseph Hospital in Tacoma.

In October 2004 Samuel Neimoyer, a forty-one-year-old project manager with a construction firm and a resident of Port Orchard, Washington, was ejected from his vehicle in a single-car accident at Windy Point on WA 410. The vehicle and victim weren't found until three weeks after the accident. He left behind a wife and two sons, and was remembered as being both active in his kids' sporting activities and fond of fishing in Alaska, according to an obituary published in the *Kitsap Sun*.

Dorothy Kennedy died in a vehicle accident at milepost 59 on WA 410 in June 2005; she was a passenger in the single-car incident.

CHAPTER 14

Snow and Ice

Winter settles on Mount Rainier National Park as early as October and can linger into June. It usually brings prodigious amounts of snow: The average seasonal total at Paradise is 643 inches, or 53.6 feet, and the record is a whopping 1,122 inches set in 1971–72—also a world record at the time. That snow often lingers in the park's mid-elevations, from five to eight thousand feet, into midsummer and is ever-present on Mount Rainier's airy elevations.

As for average winter temperatures, highs in the park hover just above freezing from December into April, and the lows drop into the single dig-its Fahrenheit, with the extremes slipping into negative numbers. Para-dise sits at about 5,400 feet in elevation; higher on the mountain or on surrounding peaks, where winds blow more fiercely and extreme altitude comes into play, those numbers regularly dip even lower.

Gusts of wind clocked at 70 miles per hour or more—strong enough to blow climbers off their feet, off their route, or even off the slopes—come into play in many accounts of accidents in storms on Rainier itself. With wind speed comes wind chill. Plug a 32-degree Fahrenheit temperature and a 30-mile-per-hour wind into the National Weather Service's wind chill calculator, and what a person feels is a bone-numbing 17.6 degrees.

Other factors come into play when considering the fatalities related to snow and ice described below. Consider that winter-like conditions are possible any time of year, given the latitude and elevation of the peak and park, as well as its proximity to the coastline. Consider that, regardless of the season, when storms brewed in the Pacific or the Gulf of Alaska swing into Washington state, the first big landmark they hit is Mount Rainier.

Accidents on snow and ice are a year-round phenomenon, given that winter is present year-round in the park.

Trouble in Paradise

Paradise is a place of staggering beauty in winter, even if storm clouds hide the big mountain and the spires of the Tatoosh Range. When the sun shines on a winter weekend, the parking lots are packed with visitors and the snowplay area is clotted with sleds and tubes and saucers. Packed trails branch into open bowls and thick trees, offering skiers access to pristine slopes and snowshoers access to quiet woodlands. The place hums with good times.

But it's not always fun and games. On a bluebird powder day Rainier's snow is friendly, but it becomes cement-like when whipped by wind, and warm temperatures followed by a freeze can solidify it like rock.

For winter recreationalists, most often it's the knees and ankles that suffer. In 1937 the park's superintendent, O. A. Tomlinson, recorded twenty-three injuries at Paradise in December, including seven sprains (knees, ankles, and feet); a puncture wound to the abdomen made by a ski pole; lacerations to the head, nose, and hands caused by sledding mishaps; three broken leg bones (likely ski injuries); and a broken nose. The numbers were even greater in March and April, totaling forty-three injuries. These included sprains and fractures of the lower legs and ankles and lacerations of the scalp, lips, and jaws, with a fractured rib and two injuries to skiers' eyelids thrown in. In February 1938 the number of injuries jumped to fifty.

In most cases the victim could be bandaged up and sent home, where he or she could heal and return for another play day later in the year. But in some cases, even the most innocent of winter activities has proven deadly.

Robert Linderman was sledding on an air mattress in the Edith Creek Basin in May 1973 when he hurtled over Myrtle Falls to his death. In February 1976 fourteen-year-old Robert Anderson suffered traumatic injury while tubing at the Paradise Valley Road entrance; he died at Madigan Hospital. And in July 2012 David Watson died while glissading with his son in Paradise Meadows.

The park describes an unusual series of events in Watson's case, which points up how changing conditions can radically alter the consequences of a simple activity. A crust that had formed on the snowpack failed as Watson slid across Edith Creek. Plunging into the waterway, he was swept downstream for about thirty feet and lodged under the snow there. Rangers and local guides executed "a highly complex rescue that was time critical, and hazardous," but Watson was found face-down in the water and lifeless. The cause of death was determined to be hypothermia.

The Paradise Glacier Ice Caves

They were gone by the 1990s, but for decades caverns of ice low on the Paradise Glacier were a major tourist attraction on Mount Rainier. The caves were a relatively easy hike from the tourist hub at Paradise, and because they were located on a dead portion of the glacier—a section that wasn't moving—they were also a relatively safe place to visit for those unfamiliar with travel on potentially crevassed snow or ice fields.

Historic photos of the caves—even those in black-and-white—illustrate a surreal environment. They show caverns ten feet high with ice cupped and polished all around, illuminated by shafts of sunlight that set the blues in the frozen snow aglow. In some images meltwater falls from the ceilings in cascades, and the bottoms of the caves are flushed by moving water whitened with glacial silt.

The ice caves were closed to tourist travel in the 1970s, as the lower Paradise Glacier receded and the danger of collapse increased. By the 1990s the lower glacier was gone, and so were the caves. But in earlier years they were explored and exploited, and were also the site of several fatal accidents.

The first occurred in September 1915. A letter from guide Harry Greer to park supervisor D. L. Raeburn, which is included in the dead man's fatality file, describes the events.

C. W. Ferguson was part of a touring party of seventeen, which included six members of his family, on the guided outing to the caves. The party stopped after traveling about a mile on Timber Line Ridge, where the folks at the front of the pack rested while those who lagged caught up.

Greer admonished those in the lead to stay put while he herded the group together, but Ferguson, his wife, and their two boys ignored the request.

The family entered into a tunnel in a snowdrift, which Greer estimated was 150 feet in length. The boys went all the way through, but the husband and wife stopped inside and Ferguson "went to picking at the snow overhead with his alpine staff." Such a staff is also called an alpenstock: This wooden pole, four to seven feet long, with metal spikes affixed to one end, was employed as a walking stick and also as "a third leg to prevent slipping."

"The snow broke and caved in upon him before he could move," Greer continued. "It was a big block 8 feet long, 8 feet wide, and 3.5 feet thick." Ferguson was killed instantly, but his wife survived.

Greer asserted that the accident was due to Ferguson's mistake, and noted that Ferguson's uncle agreed. "They should have stayed where I told them to wait," the guide wrote. "Altho I sincerely regret to have any accident in any of my parties, in a case of this kind where a person does not obey orders, the responsibility shifts from my shoulders and attach[es] itself to the disobeyer."

Another family tragedy associated with the Paradise Ice Caves occurred in July 1967. In this instance, the Louden family was returning from an excursion onto the Paradise Glacier to explore the caves and, according to a report in the *American Alpine Journal*, decided to take a shortcut across a snowfield. The father and son made the descent safely, though they "lost control" on the slick snow and fell over a "cascade" into a small stream. When mother Phyllis, 26, and daughters Kelly, 5, and Karen, 4, didn't follow, Mr. Louden reported them missing, and a search was launched.

The victims were eventually found in what the park termed a "snow moat." The *AAJ* report states the three "had apparently fallen over the same cascade and slid into the mouth of [a] snow cave. The cave was long and narrow and had several chambers. All were located between 40 and 100 feet from the small opening." A report in the *Indianapolis Star*, where members of Phyllis Louden's family resided, noted that young Kelly was "recovered from a pool in a 100-foot-long ice hole at the foot of the mountain."

Twenty-two-year-old Edith Anderson also lost her life on an excursion to the ice caves. She and her husband, along with a friend—all members of the National Speleology Society—had hiked up to the glacier to "study and photograph the caves," according to an Associated Press report. But they were caught in a sudden storm on the way back down to Paradise and forced to take shelter in a shallow cave they etched out of a snowbank using their axes and helmets.

The threesome ended up passing the night on the mountain, and the following morning the couple's friend "stumbled down from the makeshift cave to the ranger station at Paradise Valley" and alerted rangers to the emergency up the trail. The Andersons were rescued, but Edith succumbed to shock and exposure in the wake of the ordeal.

Skiing on the Edge

> *Skis hit the fall line. Earth jerked into motion. With the world rushing up and a flurry of arms and legs accelerating beside me, I felt like a snowball swept up in an avalanche. I tried to imagine what it was like in 1934, with over sixty skiers riding a wave of leather and hickory. Out of the corner of my eye, I could see climbers on the hiking trail suddenly look up, as if to mouth, "What on earth . . ."*
> —LEWIS SKOOG DESCRIBING A REENACTMENT OF MOUNT
> RAINIER'S CLASSIC SILVER SKIS RACE

By April 1940 the Silver Skis Race was hailed as the "classic event" of Mount Rainier National Park's long ski season. The four-and-a-half-mile race, which first took place in 1934, started at Camp Muir and followed a steep, meandering course down the Muir Snowfield, past Panorama Point, to finish at Paradise. Skiers traveled from around the world to participate in what was dubbed "America's Wildest Ski Race."

The magnitude of the race's impact on the park in the 1930s and '40s is captured in the comments of the park's superintendent, O. A. Tomlinson. In 1937 the event had to be cancelled because of storms. More than 6,200 people had gathered on the mountainside for the competition—a number that approached the record set in 1935 for the pre-Olympic trials (and which included superintendent Harry Liek of Mount McKinley National Park, who had participated in the first attempted ski ascent of Denali). Contestants, including veterans of the 1936 Olympic Games, were anxious to compete as well, so the cancellation resulted in "much disappointment among the spectators as well as among the skiers," Tomlinson wrote. A nifty solution was devised: Instead of racing, the professionals gave the crowd a different kind of show by doing "short slalom runs, jumping, and ski stunts."

"In fact, the exhibition was more spectacular and entertaining to the visitors than the Silver Skis Race would have been," the superintendent noted.

The challenges of the race were part of its appeal. The terrain was difficult and steep, the snow conditions were variable, and the competition was intense, with all racers on the slope at the same time (as opposed to the modern norm where one skier follows the next down the course). But despite the potential for disaster, park records indicate only twenty-five injuries and one fatality associated with the race, an accident rate that worked out to "only 1.77 per thousand skiers."

That fatality was Sigurd Hall, a popular and accomplished ski racer of Norwegian descent who died during the April 1940 event. Hall was "considered one of the Northwest's best skiers," and was a member of the Seattle Ski Club. The accident occurred when the skier became "confused and crashed into protruding rocks about one-half mile below the starting point at Camp Muir," Superintendent Tomlinson recorded. "Hall plunged headfirst onto the rocks and was killed instantly." An image in the park's archives shows the site of Hall's death, which Tomlinson notes lies just below "a rock ledge called 'Little Africa' by skiers."

Conditions for the race that day were not optimal, according to accounts of Hall's accident. Observers noted that the course was obscured by fog, which made route-finding difficult. Hall lost his way while traveling too swiftly—the Associated Press called it "express-train speed"—in icy conditions. "Straight-running the opening slope of the race over flare ice, Hall ran off the course, struck a snowbank and smashed headlong into an outcropping [of] rock at the 9,000-foot level of the mountain," the

AP reported. "He called for help but died soon after rescuers reached his side." He was twenty-five years old.

With Hall's death, the area's ski community lost an admired pioneer. In a biography of the skier, Lewis Skoog writes, "Less than a year before his death in the Silver Skis race, Hall made the first ski ascent of Mount Rainier, completing his quest to ascend or descend on skis every Cascade volcano from Mount Baker to Mount Hood. . . . As the top practitioner in both ski racing and ski mountaineering (simultaneously!), Sigurd Hall occupied a place in Northwest skiing history that may never be filled again."

Despite the tragedy, the Silver Skis Race continued into the late 1940s, taking a brief hiatus during World War II and, on occasion, suffering cancellation due to bad weather. The last Silver Skis competition on the mountain was in 1948, though a group of skiers enchanted by the idea, including its "geschmozzel," or simultaneous start, would stage a reenactment in 2005.

Other skiers have lost the trail—and their lives—on the open slopes above Paradise. These include twenty-six-year-old Mark Fogerty, who had, with two partners, successfully summited Mount Rainier and returned to Camp Muir in January 1991. The last leg of their adventure was descending from the camp to Paradise. Fogarty's teammates made the trek on foot but Fogarty opted to ski instead, and told his companions he'd be on the west side of the Muir Snowfield looking for better snow. He never made it to the base.

The following day, searchers "found Fogarty's ski tracks leading to a steep, icy slope at the 9,050-foot level, where they disappeared over a cliff into Nisqually Glacier canyon," the *AAJ* report states. His body was recovered from a snow slope a thousand feet below that point. An investigation revealed that Fogarty had drifted well off the advised descent route and onto a steep, icy slope, where he fell and slid over a cliff.

Reporting on another skier death on the mountain, a July 2001 *Seattle Post-Intelligencer* article begins this way: "For two years, Mount Rainier has held the body of William Tres Tietjen in its embrace. On Tuesday, the mountain returned him."

In June 1999 twenty-seven-year-old Tietjen went missing while snowboarding from Camp Muir to Paradise, according to the park record. A ranger observed that on the day of his disappearance, the Muir Snowfield was shrouded in cloud and whiteout conditions obscured the route. Rangers also told the newspaper that a snowboarder following the pitch of the slope without being familiar with the terrain, as was the case with Tietjen, would drop toward the Nisqually Glacier, not toward Paradise. "A snowboarder heading down to Paradise would have to bend east—almost as if going uphill—to avoid cliffs," the rangers explained.

Though heavy snowfall concealed the lost boarder's body for two years, when discovered it was, as suspected, at the base of a waterfall near the Nisqually Glacier at an elevation of 5,800 feet.

Tietjen's father told the paper the family had been mourning their only son since the disappearance, knowing that solo snowboard adventure had been the avid outdoorsman's last. "Frankly, I think it would have been wonderful if he remained as part of the mountain," he said.

Riding Shotgun Down the Avalanche

Avalanches aren't unpredictable. Slopes loaded with snow by windstorms, slopes that angle between thirty and forty-five degrees, slopes with weak layers in the snowpack—all of these conditions signal avalanche danger. Conditions that create unstable snowpack and severe avalanche danger are carefully monitored by state and local agencies, and warnings are issued when the danger creeps toward the extreme.

Experienced backcountry skiers, particularly those seeking to carve turns, generally have a working knowledge of how to avoid areas prone to avalanche. They carry shovels, avalanche beacons, and telescoping ski poles, all of which are crucial tools should one or more of their buddies be caught in a slide. Shovels are also useful for digging snow pits; by testing and knowing how to analyze the stability of the layers in the snowpack, backcountry travelers can predict whether a particular slope is safe to cross. But even if they employ all precautionary measures, backcountry skiers run an increased risk of being caught and killed in an avalanche simply because of what they're doing.

Such was the case for Richard Pearce, a twenty-eight-year-old architecture professor at the University of Washington. In February 1932 Pearce and six other men, all from Seattle, were skiing off the Paradise Road about two miles from the Paradise Inn when an avalanche swept the whole party down the hillside. The slide deposited all the skiers 30 to 150 feet below the roadway, and everyone was able to extricate themselves, even a man buried to his neck in snow.

Everyone, that is, but Pearce. His friends found the dead man near the bottom of the slide, according to Pearce's fatality file, with his skies "entangled in a small fir tree." They determined he had "made a diagonal run down the slope in the route of the snow slide hoping to outrun it, which he perhaps could have done had it not been for the tree which stopped his progress."

The outcome was happier for a young skier caught in a slide in February 1939. Richard Romaine was buried under four feet of snow after his companions, who were labeled "fourth-rate skiers under 20 years of age" in the park record, set off an avalanche near Louise Lake. His companions managed to stay on top of the slide and weren't injured, but Romaine's burial left him hypothermic and in shock. The slide took place at about 2:30 in the afternoon and rescue efforts took nearly four hours; it was about 6 p.m. when the young man was finally tobogganed out to Narada Falls and then taken to the hospital.

Unfortunately, fifty-year-old Arnold Manthey would not survive his avalanche encounter. In November 1975 Manthey and three other skiers were caught in a slide on Paradise Valley Road. An article in the Centralia *Daily Chronicle* notes that the four—Manthey; his son, Scott; and another father-son team, Les and Kent Sanford—were out in a period of high avalanche danger and were swept off the road by the slide. "We have fresh, wet snow on top of an icy crust," a park spokesperson told the paper, adding that the severe danger "led to a delay" in recovering Manthey's body. Scott Manthey and the other two skiers caught in the slide were able to dig themselves out and also freed the elder Manthey from beneath four to five feet of debris, but "could not revive him."

Snowshoers are not immune to triggering or being buried in snow slides and, like skiers, generally take care to confine their backcountry explorations to periods when avalanche danger is low. But when twenty-two-year-old Kirk Reiser and a friend attempted to snowshoe up to Camp Muir in December 2007, they were traveling in terrain that was steep enough to slide, and on a snowpack that had layers of instability built into it. The two snowshoers were turned back by rotten weather before they reached the camp; a park service report notes eleven inches of new snow accumulated on the day of the incident. On the descent, Reiser was overtaken by an avalanche; his body was found at the base of a ten-foot waterfall in the Edith Creek Basin, not far from Paradise.

Summer Walking on Winter Terrain

Accidents on snow and ice occur most often in winter, which may stretch into spring and early summer if the snowpack lingers. Incidents generally taper off as the weather warms and the snow melts, but that doesn't mean danger disappears come long summer days and heat waves.

Dorothy Haskell and her family experienced this awful truth in September 1917, when they took a fair-weather stroll on the Paradise Glacier. The outing ended in tragedy when the fourteen-year-old girl unexpectedly dropped into a crevasse and was killed.

The Tacoma teenager and her mother, father, and a family friend were day tripping from the Paradise Inn when the accident occurred. Dorothy was walking ahead of her father when she broke through a "crust" and dropped thirty-five feet into the crevasse. Her death was likely instantaneous.

The family's decision to take a walk on the glacier was criticized in reports by park rangers. "It seems impossible that the huge crevasses cutting into the ice at all angles were not sufficient warning to them that their particular route was dangerous," the park's supervisor wrote in a letter to the director of the National Park Service describing the incident. Haskell's fatality file also includes the commentary of ranger John Yorke, who was lowered into the crevasse to retrieve the teen. The party "was not equipped for ice or snow in any manner and the whole thing was foolhardy in the extreme," Yorke wrote.

In response to the criticisms, the survivors sent a heartfelt letter to the park, castigating rangers for their insensitivity. "You are used to the

Mountains; know the pitfalls and the extreme danger attending anyone's entrance upon one of the glaciers," the letter states. "The people at large are invited to visit the Park and know nothing whatever of its dangers until experience has taught them. And what a price, our experience last Sunday morning has cost us."

In another letter, attorney M. H. Palmer opined, "Many other people besides Dorothy have lost their lives on the glaciers, not from murderous or suicidal intent, but merely sheer ignorance that such a danger existed through the jaws of those terrible crevasses."

Though the park service didn't follow through on requests that "danger or prohibition signs in large glaring letters" be posted at timberline and in the hotels, some signage warning people of the "danger ahead" was installed on the glacier following the incident.

Remembering Those Lost to Snow and Ice

Not every winter recreationalist who died in the park was the victim of some terrible accident—nor can the circumstances always be detailed. But each of those who perished on skis or in avalanches is listed below, no matter how short their story.

Edward Bulgar overexerted himself while skiing in January 1934 and died the following day in the National Park Inn.

Skier John Northrop was killed in March 1936 when he was caught in an avalanche. The location was not disclosed on the park fatality list.

Myrtle Neyhart died in May 1948 when her car was buried in an avalanche at an unknown location.

Clare Combat died in August 1954 after an uncontrolled glissade— typically a controlled slide on snow—resulted in a fall into a crevasse on the Meany Crest.

John Aigers was skiing on Panorama Point in March 1969 when he was buried in an avalanche.

In April 1986 James Rodgers, 45, collapsed while skiing above Paradise and died.

Pamela Lee, 28, died after she and a partner set off an avalanche while skiing on Plummer Peak in March 1988.

James Kampe disappeared while skiing on the Muir Snowfield in October 1990 and is presumed dead.

On May 24, 1999, David Persson, a Swedish national living in British Columbia, fell 1,000 feet to his death after skiing "over the edge" on Liberty Ridge near the top of the Black Pyramid.

Stanley Quande, a fifty-four-year-old "experienced skier," ventured out of bounds from the Crystal Mountain ski resort and had entered the park when he was killed in an avalanche in February 2007.

In July 2017, a skier broke through a snow bridge spanning Pebble Creek below Camp Muir, and disappeared. The park conducted twenty-two searches on the ground and from the air trying to locate the missing man, and he was found more than a month later at the base of a waterfall. More than forty people were involved in the search-and-recovery efforts. The skier was not identified by name by the park service in its press releases, but an article in the *Tahoe Daily Tribune* identifies the victim as Dmitri Pajitnov, a thirty-year-old member of the ski patrol at Heavenly Valley resort in South Lake Tahoe. A website dedicated to the skier's memory notes he was a first-year medical student, a dedicated Burner, having attended the Burning Man festival seven times, an amateur lumberjack, and "[a]n incredible brother, son, cousin and friend."

Mark Naiman of Seattle, Washington, had reached Mount Rainier's summit in July 2017, and was skiing the Emmons Glacier on descent when he dropped 150 feet into a crevasse and perished. The skier was forty-two years old. The two other members of the summit party were able to descend safely despite what one newspaper report describes as "erratic winds and steep terrain" at the accident site, which prevented a rescue via helicopter.

CHAPTER 15

Of Natural Causes

IT HAPPENS ON THE TRAIL. IT HAPPENS IN THE CAMPGROUNDS. IT HAP-
pens in the lodges. It has even happened in the parking lots. Maybe there's
some inkling that something is wrong. Maybe it comes on without warning. But the heart stops, the breath stops, and life passes away. The same
thing that has taken a number of lives in Mount Rainier National Park
also takes place every day in hospital beds, in bedrooms, in backyards, and
in workplaces. It's tragic, but it's also natural.

We can't know for sure because the dead can't tell us, but from the
perspective of the living, dying in Mount Rainier of natural causes, like
a heart attack, sounds like a pretty good way to go. The folks who visit or
work in the park are there because they love the place. The longing for
wild country, beautiful vistas, and wandering in the woods has enchanted
them. To know a loved one breathed a last breath of mountain air scented
with evergreens and wildflowers may bring some consolation.

Consider the case of Gust Johnson. In September 1927 the sixty-five-
year-old park laborer settled under a small hemlock tree in the Longmire
Campground and passed away. He had three cents in his pocket when he
was found. His worldly possessions included candy bars, tobacco, clothing,
and $189.50 in several pocketbooks. Since the park was unable to contact
surviving relatives, it handled the funeral arrangements. There's no record
as to the nature of Johnson's memorial services, but other records detail
the settling of accounts: His funeral expenses totaled almost $200, but
Johnson was due $33 in government pay. When added to his pocketbook
funds, all was settled equitably.

Consider also the case of Peter Dyrendahl. In the hours before he collapsed in Paradise, the Seattle resident told his ski companions that he "never felt better in his life," according to a 1933 report made by Carl Tice, a Paradise Valley ranger. Dyrendahl, a salesman with the Mount King Ski Company, had spent the May morning and some of the afternoon skiing from Narada Falls to Paradise with friends. His two buddies reported that Dyrendahl went to get a camera at about 3 p.m. and collapsed as he was climbing back up to meet them. The friends called over to a pair of young women from Seattle, Ruth Porter and Ila Stevens, to help them confirm Dyrendahl had expired, and by the time rangers, including Tice, arrived on the scene, the skier "was unquestionably dead." His passing was unexpected and tragic, but Dyrendahl had been, by all accounts, a happy man in the last hours of his life.

And then there's Mrs. Frank Greer, wife of the park's district ranger, who died in January 1937 at Longmire of what can be assumed to be natural causes. In a superintendent's report Mrs. Greer, "one of the oldest residents of the park" was hailed for her hospitality. She arrived in Mount Rainier in 1916, and over the years had managed a small restaurant at the Nisqually entrance and a lunch counter at Glacier Bridge. The nature of her passing is not detailed, but it's clear from the tone that whatever the circumstances, her death was without controversy, and she was remembered fondly.

The theme carries through to a death in October 1999, when seventy-three-year-old Donald Campbell, a retired forest supervisor, died of a heart attack in the park. This was a man dedicated to the woods: He'd begun his career with the US Forest Service straight out of college and was appointed supervisor of the Okanogan National Forest in 1967. In 1970 he took on the leadership role in the Mount Baker–Snoqualmie National Forest, the largest in Oregon. In the spirit of the Forest Service's first head, Gifford Pinchot, who advocated for putting public lands to the highest and best use, Campbell "took it as a compliment when an audience member complained during a debate that he couldn't tell if Campbell was more in favor of the environment or logging," according to an obituary published in the *Los Angeles Times*. It's not difficult to imagine that his death in the park was a fitting end to a life lived in harmony with nature.

Resuscitation

Accounts of the deaths of heart attack victims on the park's fatality list, and those that are also chronicled in newspaper reports, often mention resuscitation efforts, some lasting for hours, and most of them futile.

In an era where many are trained in the techniques of cardiopulmonary resuscitation (CPR), it makes sense that such efforts should take place. But according to Dr. William Forgey, author of *Wilderness Medicine*, CPR in the wild is not likely to be effective. "Providing CPR to a heart attack victim who cannot be defibrillated within 4 minutes is a lost cause," Forgey writes. "The only significant reason for starting CPR, if the person becomes pulseless, is to placate the onlookers. Due to the virtual zero salvage rate, you are treating yourself and the others watching who, after perhaps half an hour, will consider that everything has been done that was possible. This may be a very important part of the emotional support required by individual group members as they reflect back upon the event."

"Not likely" is not definitive, however, and CPR certainly should be performed if someone suffers a heart attack on the trail or on a climb—or even in the parking lot of the National Park Inn at Longmire. But should you be required to administer life-saving techniques, and should your patient or loved one expire regardless, remember it's not because of anything you did . . . or didn't do. As the next couple of stories demonstrate, even professionals outfitted with an automated external defibrillator (AED) are often unable to resuscitate heart attack victims.

For example, in August 2015 Jack Kipp suffered a heart attack while hiking with members of his family on the Skyline Trail above Paradise. The sixty-three-year-old victim was about a tenth of a mile below Myrtle Falls when he was stricken, and the emergency call reporting the incident noted Kipp was having trouble breathing. A rescue effort involving rangers and volunteers on foot and an Airlift Northwest ALS helicopter was set in motion.

When rescuers reached the fallen man, they began CPR, and they also administered a pair of shocks using the AED. Kipp came around and was able to answer questions for a short time before he went into cardiac arrest a second time. Another shock didn't revive him, so the rescuers again began administering CPR. Kipp received an injection of epinephrine from a park anaphylaxis kit, administered by a "bystander" who happened to be a physician. The helicopter delivered flight nurses who rushed to the scene and were able to provide advanced life support, but they too were unable to resuscitate him. In all, CPR and other measures were given for more than an hour, but Kipp could not be revived.

An obituary published online includes this observation: "Jack's death was sudden and without any warning. There is some comfort in knowing that he was among friends, in a beautiful setting, and doing something he loved."

Efforts to resuscitate Craig Falk, who was hiking on the Naches Peak Loop Trail in August 2016, were also unsuccessful. The fifty-four-year-old Falk was, according to the park fatality list, on a hike with his fifteen-year-old son when he went into cardiac arrest. The report that came in to park rangers was that CPR was in progress, but did not start until about ten minutes following Falk's collapse. A family practice physician out of Yakima, Washington, arrived on the scene at that time, according to the record. The doctor determined Falk, who was estimated to weigh two hundred pounds, had a "very weak pulse when he first arrived." When Falk's pulse failed, the doctor started CPR, and worked on him for more than twenty minutes. By the time rangers arrived, efforts at resuscitation had ended. An AED was on hand, but it was too late to be effective. Falk's body was carried back to civilization on a litter and turned over to the country coroner.

Remembering Those Who Died of Natural Causes
The deaths listed below include victims of heart attacks as well as victims of other causes that could be classified as "natural," such as asthma attacks. The list also includes those whose cause of death is undetermined. In most cases, details could not be gleaned from the available park record or newspaper archives. The events are presented in chronological order.

Two people are listed in the park record as having succumbed to heart attacks in the park in the 1920s: Mrs. Charles Johnson in August 1925 and John Parker in 1927.

Harry Hagadorn died of a heart attack in May 1931.

John Berquist, 76, died following a hike in the park in July 1934; the death occurred in Paradise Valley Camp.

In July 1937 seventy-five-year-old Peter Olaf Holland perished at Ohanapecosh Hot Springs.

Elizabeth Wecker, 57, died at Longmire Campground in August 1937.

Tacoma resident Frank Messo, 38, suffered a heart attack after hiking near Narada Falls in February 1938. According to archival records, he was on the trail with his wife, daughter, sister, and friends when he succumbed. He was brought back to the Paradise Lodge, where the Rainier National Park Company doctor tried to revive him, but to no avail.

Jean Baunsgard of Tacoma collapsed while hiking on the Van Trump Trail near Comet Falls in July 1940. The fifty-four-year-old was "given artificial respiration" by her husband for two hours. She was carried down to Longmire, where a doctor declared her deceased; the cause was assumed to be a "coronary occlusion."

In August 1940 fifty-four-year-old T. B. Brockway, a resident of Yakima, Washington, suffered a heart attack after hiking. While the superintendent's report on Brockway's demise doesn't mention which trail he'd explored in his final hours, it does say he died in the Tipsoo Lake picnic area.

In August 1956 Russell Miller died of an asthma attack; the park reports he suffered from bronchial asthma, but doesn't disclose the location or circumstances surrounding his death.

Two women perished of heart attacks in July 1957, but the locations and circumstances surrounding the deaths of Catherine Crowther and Mary Sovereign are not elaborated in the park's fatality list.

Elmer Branch died of a heart attack in March 1960.

Thomas Pieper died of a cerebral hemorrhage in July 1964; the location is not disclosed on the park's fatality list.

Caroline Jenkins succumbed to an asthma attack at an unknown location in April 1966.

In August 1966 Clay Thompson suffered "coronary thrombosis" at a location listed as "unknown."

Melvin Barklow perished of "coronary thrombosis" in June 1967.

Having overexerted himself while hiking in Van Trump Park, John Hull suffered a heart attack in August 1967.

Walter Truesdale suffered a fatal heart attack in the Paradise Inn in September 1969.

David Woodward, who was with a scouting group near Berkeley Park, died of a heart attack in September 1969.

Seventy-five-year-old Florence Veall suffered a heart attack at the Paradise Inn in July 1975.

Infant Peter Lepard, just two months old, perished of crib death in the Longmire Campground in May 1978.

Rexford Norton suffered a heart attack at the Cougar Rock Campground in June 1978.

In August 1978 John Stenson suffered a fatal heart attack at the Pinnacle Peak saddle. The event was brought on, according to the park record, by exertion. He was evacuated from the park by aircraft.

Murray Falkin died of a heart attack on the Muir Snowfield in August 1981 while attempting to reach the summit of Mount Rainier. He was with his wife at the time of his death.

A heart attack claimed Warren Mullinnex, 56, at the Ohanapecosh Campground in July 1982.

Nancy Keaton died of a heart attack in July 1983; no location is provided on the park's fatality list.

In July 1983 Robert Jacob died in his camper at the Cougar Rock Campground; no cause of death per the park's fatality list.

Alfred Westburg had a heart attack in the Summerland area attributed to overexertion after backpacking, but the circumstances are unclear, as the fatality list notes "driving" as the activity at the time of his death. Westburg, who died in July 1984, was fifty-four years old.

Forty-three-year-old William Hutson collapsed in the upper parking lot at Paradise in June 1987 and was pronounced dead upon arrival at St. Peters Hospital.

In October 1988 Phyliss Newton, 71, suffered a heart attack while in a car on Maternity Curve. She was transported out of the park and died at Madigan Hospital outside Tacoma.

Lyle Longaker, 70, died of "natural causes" in the Ohanapecosh Campground in June 1990.

Kenneth Cardy, 64, was visiting the park from New Zealand when he collapsed and died while hiking on First Burroughs Mountain in the Sunrise area in September 1991. The cause of death, according to a newspaper account, was an "apparent heart attack."

James Ruby was cross-country skiing at Barn Flats in Paradise in March 1993 when he suffered a heart attack and collapsed; he was declared dead at the scene.

Robert Bartlett collapsed and died about an eighth of a mile up the Myrtle Falls Trail in June 1993.

Leroy Lamb suffered a heart attack and expired in his vehicle at the Ohanapecosh Visitor Center in July 1995.

Jeremy Zaccardi suffered a fatal asthma attack at 9,500 feet on the Emmons Glacier and died at the scene in July 1996.

Kent Swanson suffered a heart attack just above the Carbon River suspension bridge in March 2000. His son and a bystander performed CPR for an hour and a half before he was declared dead at the scene.

Lawrence Minard suffered a massive heart attack and died on the Disappointment Cleaver on a guided summit attempt in August 2001.

Dale Collins suffered a fatal heart attack in September 2001 at Frozen Lake. He was discovered unconscious. Rangers administered CPR and he was airlifted to a local hospital, but he could not be saved.

Marie McClafun suffered a fatal heart attack while hiking on the Sourdough Ridge Trail below Frozen Lake in September 2002.

Erica Smith died of an accidental overdose of albuterol while suffering an asthma attack in July 2003 at the Jackson Visitor Center. She expired on the way to the hospital.

Alvin Craver was found dead of a heart attack at about 5,800 feet on the Dewey Lake Trail in September 2003.

In July 2009 Dennis Newton hiked from Sunrise into Grand Park, where he experienced a heart attack. He died in the backcountry before his companions could summon help.

Hiker Richard Dawson suffered a heart attack and died at milepost 62 on WA 410 in August 2009.

His cause of death is listed as "pending" on the park's fatality list, but Michael Hendrickson was stricken at his residence in the Glacier Dorm, operated by GSI (Guest Services Inc., the park concessioner) at Paradise in June 2011. He received advanced life support as he was transported from the park.

Eighty-two-year-old Richard Hudson was found dead in the Paradise parking lot in September 2011.

In July 2013 David Toarmina suffered a fatal heart attack while hiking on the Skyline Trail near Paradise. Later that same month, Stan Sattelberg succumbed to a heart attack at the Jackson Visitor Center in Paradise.

In September 2013 Alan Burgestahler died of a suspected heart attack while asleep in the Cougar Rock Campground.

CHAPTER 16

Of Unnatural Causes

RANDOM AND UNLUCKY. THAT'S THE ONLY WAY TO DESCRIBE THE CIR-
cumstances that surround the first death reported on Mount Rainier, and
some of the other tragedies that have taken place in the park.

The details of E. H. Hudson's death, which occurred before the park
was a park, are recorded on an index card, the sole document contained
in his fatality file. Handwritten by an unnamed park naturalist following
an interview with Len Longmire, grandson of homesteader James Longmire, the story is short, poignant, and pragmatic. The dates of Hudson's
death vary; on the fatality list, his accident is documented as having taken
place on New Year's Day in 1893, but the card in the file records the year
as 1888.

Hudson was part of a hunting party that approached the Longmire
homestead via the Yelm Trail that winter and set up a camp in Longmire
Meadow. "On the last day as they were breaking camp," the naturalist
records, "Mr. Hudson dropped his derringer pistol from his vest pocket as
he was starting to put out the campfire." The pistol "exploded" and a bullet
discharged, hitting him in the throat.

Hudson's young son ran for Maude Longmire, who attempted to stop
the bleeding to no avail. The hunter died by the fire. His coffin was a
wooden bathtub, and because the ground was frozen, his remains were
stored in a shed for the duration of the cold season. When relatives failed
to claim his body in the spring, Hudson was buried beside the trail below
his camp.

Longmire also related how, in 1904, Eugene Ricksecker, who was
engineering the new "pleasure road" to Paradise, placed road stakes

through Hudson's gravesite. Fortunately, when road construction began in 1906, the alignment was moved to the south, and Hudson's resting place remained undisturbed.

"The grave is still there," the naturalist records Longmire as saying. "Our family put flowers on it for a number of years, and the American Legion fixed it up with [a] pipe headstone and wooden cross in the 1930s."

Unnatural and Uncertain

Information about the circumstances surrounding some deaths is even sketchier than that for E. H. Hudson. According to the park's fatality list, in February 1928 a nameless person died on Panther Creek. How? Why? It's impossible to know.

There's a bit more detail in other listings, but not enough to shed light on cause of death. For example, Joseph Murphy died in the park in August 1930, but the park records nothing further—not where he expired, not what he was doing. Google Joseph Murphy in 1930 in Mount Rainier, and nada; the results are hardly illuminating. The same holds true for Lewis Aycock, who perished in the park in July 1954 at an unnamed location of unknown causes.

Then there are the cases where maybe a person died . . . and maybe not. Two listings in the park record slot into this category. The first is a person with the surname of Hepworth, who went missing in November 1973 and is presumed dead. Then there's Douglas Allen, who was assumed to be dead after he disappeared while hiking near the Carbon River in July 1983. He was found alive during a traffic stop in Mesa, Arizona, in June 2004; the park service calls this a "deliberate disappearance by [the] subject."

And sometimes, even when the circumstances have been laid out in the park's fatality files or in newspaper accounts, all they do is bolster the notion that there's no way to know how or when an unnatural cause will send a person to meet his maker.

Take the case of O. B. Dorsey, who died a "sudden death" near Shaw Creek in November 1928. A written account of a conversation with his wife, Mrs. Mable Dorsey, found in the fatality files, offers a cryptic description of what befell the man. The two were driving a truck with a shovel and stopped so that Mr. Dorsey could put oil in the vehicle. "As Mr. Dorsey was cranking the truck the shovel [came] back up," recorded district ranger H. W. Hall. "She [Mrs. Dorsey] saw what was about to happen and screamed to stop the shovel but not in time." There was "hair, blood, and some flesh" on the front of the truck upon inspection. "From what information I could get from Mrs. Dorsey the shovel backed up against the truck and crushed his head," Dorsey wrote. "She is the only person that claims to have seen the accident."

Then there's the story of logger Oscar Borg, who succumbed to anaphylactic shock in September 1933 after being stung by yellow jackets at the White River Campground. Borg was a single man, forty-seven years old, and a Civilian Conservation Corps (CCC) worker, according to his fatality file. He and a partner were taking down snags—standing dead trees—when the incident occurred. Borg was starting to "limb a snag" when the swarm of wasps attacked, stinging him in his nose and neck, according to notes in the file. "He immediately starting cursing, stating, 'Every time that I get stung by a bee I get sick.' Fifteen minutes later he became unconscious and started frothing at the mouth," his companion told authorities. By the time a doctor arrived thirty minutes later, Borg was dead.

Another CCC worker, John Moskin (or Moskim, from the superintendent's report) died in September 1937 in what the park called a "premature dynamite blast" in the Ohanapecosh Campground. The twenty-one-year-old from Newark, New Jersey, was setting a charge to remove a stump when the explosive was detonated; the committee that investigated the incident determined that the young man blew the charge by "using a metal crowbar" to tamp it down.

Falling Trees

Those who aspire to the summit of Mount Rainier generally don't worry about falling trees; after all, they are above timberline, and they have other falling objects to worry about, like rocks and snow. But lower down, "widowmakers"—limbs swept from trees by wind, stumps undermined by construction, or falling trees themselves—have exacted a toll.

Ida Ella Floe, Stephen Floe, and their granddaughter, Claudette Bline, were crushed when a tree fell on their car near the park's northern boundary in June 1957. The profound family tragedy was brought on when the giant fir, undermined by the flow of the White River, smashed the moving vehicle, according to a story by the Associated Press. The Floes, husband and wife, both fifty-eight and residents of Seattle, were "killed outright." Mrs. Bline, twenty years old and a resident of Yakima, died in the hospital. The sole survivor of the accident was Bline's infant daughter, Kerri.

Water wasn't the culprit in the undermining of a "root-studded tree stump" that tumbled onto a tour bus stopped on a park road. It was construction work on a nearby bridge, the Associated Press reported, explaining work done the previous autumn at the site had loosened the massive stump. The incident, which occurred in August 1959, resulted in the death of twenty-three-year-old Marilyn Friedman of Brooklyn, New York. She and her husband were chaperones with a party of "41 vacationers, who call themselves the Rolling Stones." The group reportedly toured the park each year, and was returning to Seattle when the accident occurred. Three teenagers were also hurt, and other "passengers in the bus were showered with glass."

In what a family friend called a "freak accident," gusty winds snapped off the top of a hemlock tree, sending a thirty-foot-long section of the trunk, which measured twenty inches in diameter, onto Jason and Kellie Cosner's car in November 2001. The Seattle couple, both twenty-six years old and celebrating their first wedding anniversary in the park, probably never saw it coming. The accident killed the husband and badly injured his wife, who was transported to the hospital from the scene of the accident, about a mile and a half east of the Nisqually entrance. "If they had been five seconds faster or five seconds slower, it wouldn't have happened. It would have missed," the friend told the *Seattle Times*.

Falling Rock

Rock dropping out of ice forever ended the marriage of another couple in June 1924. Earl Kummer, along with his wife and mother, had headed out to take a look at the snout of the Nisqually Glacier, which at the time was an impressive wall of rock-studded frozen snow not far from the Glacier Bridge below Paradise. Though the park had identified a safe zone for sightseers, according to superintendent O. A. Tomlinson, the Kummer family "ventured past the warning signs and into the danger zone near the end of the glacier."

Both wife and husband were struck down by rocks melting out from the towering toe of the ice river. Mr. Kummer's mom, who wasn't injured, ran for help. A couple of visitors moved the bleeding man out of the line of fire, observing that "stones were dropping on all sides, and it was extremely dangerous." The rescuers also noted that the injured man's head was "crushed and was bleeding profusely."

"Mr. Kummer was unconscious . . . and his wife, who had been holding the injured man's head out of the water where he had fallen, fainted as soon as her husband was carried away by rescuers," the superintendent reported.

Both Kummers were taken back to Longmire, and a doctor was summoned. The physician determined that Mr. Kummer had fractured his skull and was hemorrhaging; he "was beyond medical help." The husband perished of his injury. The wife suffered broken ribs, bruises, and shock, and the dying man's mother also suffered "nervous breakdown due to shock."

The superintendent's letter makes note of the fact that on that warm day, "stones, debris, etc. were falling from the melting glacier at frequent intervals and plainly visible to anyone approaching." Hence the warning signs that the Kummers had ignored. In the wake of the accident, however, the park strung barbed wire to keep people out of the rockfall zone, and more danger signs were set up "to try to impress on the thoughtless and [ad]venturous the real danger of the situation."

The fate of Douglas Nash is reminiscent of those who've been killed on park roads by fallen trees. In his case the widowmaker was a boulder, which "crushed the cab" of his pickup truck as he was traveling on WA 410 at Cayuse Pass in June 1963. The operator of a service station in Enumclaw, Washington, Nash had three passengers in the vehicle who "escaped injury," according to a newspaper report.

Random rockfall was also at play in July 1964, when two teenaged girls on a guided tour in the Nisqually Canyon were killed as the group came under fire. Fourteen-year-old Elyse Starr died instantly, according to the park record; eighteen-year-old Janet Leettola perished shortly after the event.

Remembering Those Who Died of Unnatural Causes

In August 1933 Duff Broseau was killed by a falling tree about five miles from Longmire.

Clifford Gabby was working on the Glacier Bridge in September 1960 when he fell from the span and was killed.

In October 1965 hunter Chester Carver (spelled Carber in the park record) was asphyxiated when toxic fumes filled his "house trailer." According to a newspaper account, he'd pulled off WA 410 to spend the night and lit a kerosene heater in his "home-made" trailer to fend off the "night chill." His body was discovered by other hunters the following morning.

In July 2012 Tacoma businessman Stephen Albers was riding in the annual RAMROD (Ride Around Mount Rainier in One Day) event when he crashed on Stevens Canyon Road and sustained head injuries that would later claim his life. A local newspaper noted that, in addition to being an "athlete and outdoorsman," the sixty-year-old grandfather was "deeply involved in civic life," serving on the boards of a number of charitable organizations. The ride (not a race) follows narrow park roads, passes through a number of small towns, and involves about ten thousand feet of elevation change on its 150-mile-plus circuit of the park. Albers's accident took place on a steep descent between Inspiration Point and Box Canyon.

Homicides and Suicides
Without doubt, deaths by homicide or suicide are unnatural, and among the hardest to reconcile. Regrets abound in their wakes, compounded by

uncertainty and, in the case of murder, questions that may remain unanswered and motivations that may be unfathomable.

In many cases, details surrounding suicide are held close by grieving families. When a loved one takes his or her own life, it leaves a wound unlike any other, laced with guilt and "if onlys." When a loved one is murdered, the circumstances, again, may be held close, to protect the victim, the family, or an ongoing investigation or prosecution.

While every death chronicled in this book deserves special care, these have been approached with an intentionally light touch. A stigma often attaches itself to the victims of suicide and violent deaths, as well as to their families. Probing too deeply, getting it wrong, or, however inadvertently, passing judgment carries the untenable risk of exacerbating the wounds carried by survivors. The list below is culled mostly from the park record.

In Memory

Brian Behm committed suicide in October 1984 by driving his car into a rock wall at Oh My Point.

Mary Carlton died in July 1986 in a homicide, but no location is specified and the park notes an "unfounded reporting party."

Otto Papke, 39, committed suicide by driving over a cliff in Stevens Canyon in June 1987.

In September 1987 an unknown male—no name or age is provided in the park record—was found dead south of the tunnel on WA 123, the victim of a gunshot wound.

John Kiler committed suicide in March 1988 on the Nisqually River Plain; the thirty-one-year-old took what was called an "acute overdose of drugs."

Leland Eugene Ney died in a vehicle accident about a quarter-mile below Windy Point in June 1989. The park considers this a possible suicide, and notes there was a felony warrant out for his arrest.

In an apparent suicide, James Tindall died of asphyxiation due to carbon monoxide poisoning in his camp at Sunrise in April 1993.

In November 1994 Stacy Stoddard committed suicide by taking an overdose of prescription drugs; she died in the parking lot at Longmire.

In December 1994 Michael Thomas died of a self-inflicted gunshot wound on the Trail of Shadows in Longmire.

Sheila Kearns's remains were discovered in the Old Longmire Campground in May 1997. The park service record notes that an investigation into her death is ongoing.

David Rivera died of a self-inflicted gunshot wound to the head on the Wonderland Trail in June 1997.

Ronald Sarff, a National Park Service employee, committed suicide at the Tahoma Woods housing complex in July 1997.

In July 1999 thirty-six-year-old Billy Boyd and his seven-year-old son, Nicholas, died in an apparent homicide-suicide, according to park records and newspaper reports. The two had been on a camping trip in the park, and were reported missing by the boy's mother when they didn't return home as expected. The deaths took place at Christine Falls; both bodies were found below the bridge in Van Trump Creek. The elder Boyd, a carpenter from Tacoma, left suicide notes, which indicated "he thought his son was going to have a difficult life, as he had," park officials told the *Seattle Times*. By another account, relatives who read the father's notes believed he "felt deserted and wanted to kill himself. But he didn't want to leave his son behind, so [he] planned to kill the boy, too."

Erin Beth Gordon committed suicide via a self-inflicted gunshot wound at the National Park Inn in November 2001.

Valerie Martin died in an apparent suicide after jumping off the Glacier Bridge in August 2002. Her body was found on the riverside rocks.

In July 2005 Timothy Cole's remains were discovered in the park; he'd gone missing in December 2004. He died of exposure, and his death is considered a suicide.

Zachery Weston is a presumed suicide. His clothing and camping equipment were found in the vicinity of Wapowety Cleaver in August 2005, but his remains have never been found.

James Longworth died of a self-inflicted gunshot wound in October 2008 at the Kautz Creek picnic area.

In April 2010 Robert Casper committed suicide at the Carbon River Entrance Station. The method is not disclosed by the National Park Service.

In September 2012 Linda Fong committed suicide in a fall from Ricksecker Point.

Robert Congeli disappeared on the Wonderland Trail in September 2013 and is a suspected suicide.

Epilogue: Surviving Mount Rainier

I STOOD ON THE LOW RIDGELINE ABOVE THE SNOWPLAY AREA AT PARAdise. Only three cars were in the parking lot, and one of them was mine. It was midweek in mid-March, and the weather was sketchy. Dark clouds were advancing on the Tatoosh Range, and the summit of Mount Rainier was obscured. A pair of skiers set off into the woods to the southeast, staying low. I had no idea where the occupants of the other car were.

I was alone on the stormy shoulder of the mountain.

I looked up toward the peak, where snowfields melted into steely, low-slung clouds. A rope marked the edge of the groomed area, and I traced it toward where the route to Camp Muir began. Someone could be up there, I supposed. But there was no sign. No trail. No track to follow.

I wanted to walk onward and upward, but I'd done enough research for this book to know I had already broken several cardinal rules of travel on the mountain, especially in winter. No matter that I carried the basics for safe wilderness travel on my back; I was solo, and no one knew where I was. To go beyond the play area boundary, beyond the thin rope strung on wands that delineated known terrain from unknown, would place me firmly in the foolhardy category.

This was a short hike; the only way to go now was down. This decision was reinforced when I turned around and saw how black the clouds gathering behind the Tatoosh Range were. It wasn't cold, it wasn't windy, and there wasn't a whiteout . . . yet.

But it was time to retreat.

I fell in love with Mount Rainier more than twenty-five years ago, after editing a book about trails and climbing routes in the park. The *Adventure Guide to Mount Rainier* is long out of print, but the setting enchanted me. I appropriated the name Laughingwater for my company from Laughingwater Creek. No babbling, no roaring, no tinkling or thundering waterway for me. Laughing water. I could hear it in my heart long before I actually heard it with my ears.

On my first visit to the park with my new husband, we followed the Ohanapecosh River to its confluence with Laughingwater Creek straight away; somewhere there's a picture of me before the sign. Then we explored the lowlands on the east side. The idea of dying in the park didn't occur to us. And it shouldn't have. For most visitors Mount Rainier National Park is a joyous, tremendous place, beautiful like nowhere else on the planet. Though this book records all of the things that can be terrifying and deadly, the upshot is that the park is a place where living well is amplified. The water laughs. The trees and shrubs swell with moisture. The wildflowers are gaudy, flaunting their colors like bridesmaids. We were passing through, and we left properly awed and amazed.

That said, those who attempt to climb the peak, and those who walk the Wonderland Trail or head off into the backcountry, would be foolish not to temper their excitement with caution. On any mountain, or deep in any wilderness, experience, preparedness, and common sense are necessary. If you lack the prerequisites, you should travel with someone who does possess them, whether a friend or a professional guide or outfitter. That way, if the random bad thing happens, you'll stand a good chance of surviving. You'll come out of the woods, or down off the glacier, with a good story to tell.

My story, on that stormy day in March, ended with an eventless meander back down to the car—now one of only two in the lot. Someone else, like me, had decided to retreat. On my way back to the Whittaker Bunkhouse in Ashford, I checked out Narada Falls, looked up toward the snowy toe of the Nisqually Glacier from Glacier Bridge, saw Christine Falls, and wandered through the historic village at Longmire. My final stop was at a pullout near the entrance station, where I stood on the edge of the Nisqually River and watched the water flow through braided channels and around deadfall. No danger, no fear, only a faint regret that it was time to go.

I have struggled with the idea that writing about Rainier's dead does a disservice to the park, and with the idea that the dead should be left to rest in peace. I expressed this to a friend who had just lost his wife, also my friend, to cancer. But don't you think, he said, that perhaps the families are glad the departed are not forgotten?

I hope that's true. I hope these loved ones are OK with the stories I've told. I hope they rest not only in peace, but that their spirits sometimes gather along the banks of Laughingwater Creek, just hanging out, forever enchanted by the music of the mountain.

Safe Travels

The exploration of any national park, including Mount Rainier, is safer and more enjoyable if you educate yourself before setting out. Visit the park's website at www.nps.gov for the latest information and to get information on any alerts—road closures, weather advisories, status updates on facilities—that might be in effect during your visit.

Here are some basics to keep you safe on any excursion.

For the Driver
- Obey speed limits.
- If you are in a vehicle traveling slower than the posted speed limit, pull over to let cars stacked up behind you pass.
- Used designated pullouts for sightseeing. Be sure to pull completely off the road so you do not impede traffic.
- Be aware of wildlife, especially when traveling at dawn or dusk. Slow down along stretches of roadway posted for wildlife crossings.
- In winter, Mount Rainier requires all visitors to carry snow chains in their vehicle. Four-wheel-drive vehicles are not exempt. Tire chains are available for rent at various locations around the park if you do not own them. Visit www.nps.gov/mora/planyourvisit/tire-chain-faq.htm for more information.
- Carry an emergency kit in your car that contains water, food, spare clothing, blankets, a first-aid kit, flashlight, radio, and batteries.

For the Hiker
No matter how short or long your hike, you should carry a backpack or day pack containing these items, at a minimum:
- Water
- Food
- A Swiss Army knife or other knife/multitool

- First-aid supplies, including aspirin or over-the-counter pain reliever, antibacterial ointment, antiseptic swabs, butterfly bandages, adhesive tape, adhesive strips, two triangular bandages, two inflatable splints, Second Skin for blisters, three-inch gauze, a CPR shield, rubber gloves, a sewing needle and thread, and first-aid instructions
- Layers of clothing
- An emergency blanket
- An emergency whistle, which can be used to alert searchers of your location if you become lost or you can't make it back to the trailhead for another reason, like an injury
- A compass and good topographic map (and know how to use them)

For longer excursions, you should consider carrying a kit that contains:
- A GPS unit (be sure to carry extra batteries)
- A signal mirror
- A flashlight
- Aluminum foil
- Water purification tablets
- A space blanket

Also carry the following, but only use them in conditions when fire danger is minimal:
- Matches in a waterproof container
- A cigarette lighter
- A candle
- Fire starter
- A flare

The next best piece of safety advice is to hike with a partner or a party. If you choose to hike alone, tell somebody where you're going and when you plan to return.

Before you set out on any hike, consider physical conditioning. Being fit makes any walk more fun and much safer.

Here are a few more tips:

- Check the weather forecast. Be careful not to get caught at high altitude in a bad storm or along a stream in a flash flood. Watch cloud formations so you don't get stranded on a ridgeline during a lightning storm. Avoid traveling during prolonged periods of cold weather.

- Keep your party together; move only as fast as your slowest companion.

- Before you leave for the trailhead, find out as much as you can about the route, especially the potential hazards. Rangers at visitor centers, ranger stations, or on the trail are your best resource for up-to-date reports on conditions.

- Don't wait until you're confused to look at your maps. Follow them as you go, maintaining a continual fix on your location.

- If you get lost, don't panic. Sit down, relax, check your map, and get your bearings.

- Confidently plan your next move. If necessary, retrace your steps until you find familiar ground, even if you think that might lengthen your trip. If you calmly and rationally determine a plan of action, you'll be fine.

- If you are genuinely lost, stay put.

For the Climber

Much of what applies to the hiker also applies to the mountain climber, whether the goal is Columbia Crest or Camp Muir. Most aspiring summiters will (and should) seek out an experienced guide service to acquaint them with the necessaries of a summit attempt. Otherwise, be sure to consult the climbing resources on the park's website, at www.nps.gov/mora/planyourvisit/things-to-know-before-you-climb.htm. These guidelines are the backbone for any ascent.

Climbers are required to pay a climbing cost recovery fee and register with the park prior to making a summit attempt. The fees help cover staffing high camps with climbing rangers, maintaining services and facilities at high camps (including flying human waste off the mountain), environmental protection, and the provision of rapid response to emergencies, including rescues.

All climbers should respect the Blue Bag Rule. It's actually a Golden Rule. You don't want to deal with the other climbers' poop, so don't make them deal with yours. Use the blue bag, and pack it out.

Here is some basic advice:

- Don't underestimate the mountain or overestimate yourself. Be realistic about your abilities and experience when selecting a route. Approach any climb humbly, but with confidence.
- Train. Build your physical fitness. Rainier is steep and high, and any summit attempt requires strength and endurance. Climbing less technical glaciated peaks (other Cascade volcanoes, or even high peaks in the Sierra Nevada or the Rockies) is good practice and recommended by the park.
- Learn and hone techniques for glacier travel, including the use of crampons, snow anchors, and ice axes, and methods of self-rescue and self-arrest.
- Complete a course in avalanche awareness.
- Complete a course in wilderness first aid.
- Familiarize yourself with the symptoms of altitude sickness. In its most severe forms high-altitude pulmonary edema (HAPE; the accumulation of fluid in the lungs) and high-altitude cerebral edema (HACE; the accumulation of fluid on the brain) altitude sickness is a killer. Symptoms generally manifest themselves at about ten thousand feet and include nausea and vomiting, and headache. These alone may not be severe enough to necessitate descent, but should symptoms escalate, including shortness of breath when resting (a sign of HAPE) or alterations in mental function (laziness, confusion, and emotionality are all signs of HACE), the victim should be moved to a lower elevation immediately.
- Get the beta on your selected route. Check out the Mount Rainier Climbing blog, maintained by the park's climbing rangers, at mountrainierclimbing.blogspot.com.

- Don't conflate not reaching the summit with defeat. You learned something, whether it's that you need more time to acclimate, or that the mountain is, indeed, fully capable of conjuring whiteout conditions from a bluebird sky . . . or that getting to Camp Muir was all you really wanted to do after all. It's all good.

Three guide and instruction services were certified as concessioners on the mountain at the time of this writing:
- Alpine Ascents International; (206) 378-1927; www.alpineascents .com/index.html
- International Mountain Guides; (360) 569-2609; www .mountainguides.com/rainier.shtml
- Rainier Mountaineering Inc; (360) 569-2227; www.rmiguides .com/mt-rainier

For Your Health

Hikers, climbers, and wanderers in Mount Rainier National Park will encounter all kinds of weather, some of which can not only be uncomfortable, but also potentially life-threatening. Perhaps the biggest worry is hypothermia (exposure), a condition in which the body's internal temperature drops below normal. This is a demonstrated killer high on the mountain. Here are some tips for avoiding this ailment:
- Stay dry. If hiking in wet weather, wear rain clothes that cover the head, neck, body, and legs, and that provide good protection against wind-driven rain. Rain gear that allows sweat to escape is best (think Gore-Tex); venting is also an option.
- Don't be fooled by the temperature. Most hypothermia cases develop in air temperatures between thirty and fifty degrees Fahrenheit, but hypothermia can develop when it is warmer, and is certainly a danger when temperatures drop significantly below freezing.
- Be aware of the symptoms of hypothermia. These include uncontrollable fits of shivering; vague, slow, slurred speech; memory lapses; incoherence; fumbling hands; frequent stumbling or a lurching gait; drowsiness; exhaustion; and inability to get up after a rest. When a member of your party has hypothermia, he or

she may also deny the problem.

If you suspect a member of your party is hypothermic, take these steps immediately:

- Get the victim out of the wind and rain.
- Strip off all wet clothes and get the victim into warm clothing. To boost warming a more severely hypothermic companion, crawl into a sleeping bag with the victim.
- If the victim is mildly impaired, provide warm drinks.
- Seek medical attention as quickly as possible.

Another potential hazard for summertime visitors are heat-related illnesses like heat exhaustion and heatstroke. There are no recorded incidents of heat having killed anyone in the park, but it's something to watch for regardless. Warning signs of heat-related illness include nausea and/or vomiting; headache, light-headedness, and/or fainting; weakness, fatigue, and/or a lack of coordination; loss of concentration; and flushed skin. If you or a member of your party exhibits these symptoms, seek shade, lie down and elevate the feet and legs, apply wet cloths to the head and neck (and other parts of the body, if you can), and drink cool liquids.

Heatstroke is life-threatening. Hikers who lose consciousness; vomit; have red, hot skin (moist or dry); a weak pulse; and shallow breathing are in danger of convulsions, coma, and death. Cool the victim by any means possible, as quickly as possible, and call for emergency medical aid.

Wildlife

Remarkably, no deaths have occurred in Mount Rainier National Park due to encounters with wild animals. I say "remarkably" because some visitors maintain an unhealthy disregard for best practices around the animals, big and small, and because the park is home to critters fully capable of causing injury and death, including bears, mountain lions, and deer.

Some cautionary tales: In July 1939 a well-meaning priest from Providence Hospital in Oakland was injured in the park in a bear encounter. According to park records, the priest had been feeding the bear from his automobile window. When the food was gone, the bear refused to move on. It wanted more. To shoo the bruin away, the priest smacked it on the nose. In response, the bear "swung a paw across the man's face." A couple of days later, a woman from Berkeley, California, was "severely scratched on her arm by a bear." Still later in the month, a bear broke into a car to get at the food left inside, despite the family having been warned against doing that.

Sound familiar? Stories like these have been told over and over again in parks where bears abide with humans. Other stories involve deer getting ornery when the handouts end, and encounters with coyotes, squirrels, and jays.

The practices listed below—some of which have been elevated to regulations and laws—have been developed to protect both the wildlife and the human:

- Stay clear of all wild animals. A good rule of thumb is to maintain a distance of one hundred yards from "safe" wildlife like deer, coyotes, and bobcats, and three hundred yards from larger, more dangerous wildlife like bears and mountain lions.

- Make sure you know how best to deal with encounters with a black bear or a mountain lion. The park's recommendations can be found online at www.nps.gov/mora/planyourvisit/wildlife.htm.

- Do not feed any wild animal, no matter how cute or how much it begs. Acclimating birds, chipmunks, deer, and larger mammals like bears to human food is not only dangerous for humans, but also reduces the animals' ability to survive when the people offering handouts have gone home.

Tips and Courtesy

There's no way to avoid it. The beauty of Mount Rainier National Park is a siren call to all kinds—hikers, walkers, birders, skiers, snowshoers, photographers, history buffs, sightseers, anglers, tourists, and more. To make sure everyone has a chance to find what they seek, consider this advice for sharing the "resource," as park management might say.

To avoid traffic snarls and increase your odds of finding parking in designated lots, shoot for the proverbial "alpine start." The earlier you get to the trailhead, the better chance you have of getting a good parking place and a reasonably uncrowded hike.

If you must park outside designated lots, be sure to choose a space that's safely off access roads and doesn't block access to driveways, fire hydrants, gates, and public walkways or trailheads.

If you are hiking in a group, make way for hikers coming in the opposite direction. On a narrow trail that means hiking single file. This is about safety as well as courtesy: If the trail has a drop-off, forcing hikers walking the opposite direction to hug the edge can be dangerous. In general, uphill hikers have right of way.

Use your earbuds if you choose to listen to music on the trail. No matter how fabulous your music selection, others shouldn't be forced to listen to it.

Better yet, don't listen to your device at all. You'll be able to hear not only the sounds of nature, but also of approaching wildlife, rockfall, or avalanche.

Put your cell phone on vibrate, and then tuck it deep into your pack so you aren't tempted to use it. It's nice to have a phone for an emergency, but using it on the trail, particularly on speaker, to discuss business or personal affairs can wait.

Leave No Trace

If I had my way, the principles of Leave No Trace would be taught in schools alongside reading, writing, and arithmetic. They are that important. Here are the basics:

- Be sure you leave nothing, regardless how small, along the trail, along the road, in a parking lot, or at a campsite. If there are no trash receptacles available, pack everything out, including orange peels, cigarette butts, and gum wrappers. Pick up any trash that others leave behind.
- Follow main trails. Avoid cutting switchbacks and walking on vegetation beside the trail.
- Don't pick up "souvenirs," such as rocks, antlers, or wildflowers. The next person wants to see them too, and collecting souvenirs violates park regulations.

- Avoid making loud noises on the trail (unless you are in bear country) or in camp. Be courteous—remember, sound travels easily on the trail, especially across water.
- Use restrooms if they are available. If not, carry a lightweight trowel to bury human waste six to eight inches deep and at least two hundred feet from any water source. Pack out used toilet paper in a ziplock bag.
- Go without a campfire if you can't find an established fire pit. Carry a stove for cooking and a flashlight, candle lantern, or headlamp for light. For emergencies, learn how to build a no-trace fire.
- Camp in obviously used sites when they are available. Otherwise, camp and cook on durable surfaces such as bedrock, sand, gravel bars, or bare ground.

For more information, visit the Leave No Trace Center for Outdoor Ethics website at https://lnt.org.

ACKNOWLEDGMENTS AND AUTHOR'S NOTE

Discussions with park officials, who were reticent to participate in the production of this book given that living in the park is far more important to them than dying in the park, nonetheless pointed me toward the important stories and stressed that what is presented here should also include lessons on how visitors can stay safe. I thank them for their service and their reluctance, and hope I've done justice to the stories that are most important to them.

This work would not have been possible without the help of the curators and archivists in Mount Rainier National Park and at the National Archives and Research Administration in Seattle, who assisted me with researching park records. The volunteers working in these offices were helpful and generous with their time.

Thanks to the colleagues who have supported me as I worked on this project, whether overtly or just by listening. These include Randi Minetor, Jim Shere, Ann Peters, Arthur Dawson, Becca Lawton, and Patrice Fusillo. You bucked me up when I bogged down.

Thanks to Lou Whittaker, for taking the time to review the manuscript for accuracy, and to Mike Gauthier, for being receptive even though circumstances precluded a review.

The staff and editors at Lyons Press and Rowman & Littlefield demonstrated incredible patience and care in the production of this book. Thank you, Holly Rubino, for your faith in me. Thank you, Stephanie Scott, for your careful review of the first draft. And thank you Emily Chiarelli for shepherding the book through the production process.

Thanks to my family, especially my sons Jesse, Cruz, and Penn, who've always been behind me in my work as a writer.

Thanks also to my Nana. It's complicated, but I know you had my back on this one.

A special shout-out to my mom. She totally got it when I told her that, upon returning home after spending a week in the park researching these tales of the dead, I sat down on my front porch and had a good, long cry. She gets me, and I love her for that.

Finally, I want to acknowledge how researching and writing this book has deepened my understanding of my calling as a storyteller. Without question, this is the hardest book I've ever written. I've never been so conscious of trying to do right by people, whether dead or surviving. Many of these names had drifted out of consciousness until I typed them into a search engine or found them in a file box. Sussing out the details felt shallow at first, but gradually I grew to understand that, through these stories, the people who died on Rainier could reach out and touch another human being again, if only for a moment, if only in a few words. I feel good about that. And I'll say it again: If I got anything wrong, or I missed anything important, I invite family, friends, or others who care to set me straight.

Appendix A:

LIST OF DEATHS 1893–2016

The chart was derived from the Mount Rainier Fatality List (http://mountrainierclimbing.us/sar/fatalities.php). Any errors of omission or in transcription are mine. If I could find ages or confirm the spelling of names via other sources, they have been added here. It should also be noted that the date of death may reflect the date a person went missing.

If the death occurred on a Mount Rainier summit attempt, it is noted. Other summits have been listed in the Location column. Blanks in the Age column indicate that those items were blank on the formal list and I was unable to ascertain the information from other sources.

DATE OF DEATH	NAME	AGE	CAUSE/ACTIVITY	LOCATION
Jan. 1, 1893	E. H. Hudson		Gunshot wound	Longmire
July 27, 1897	Edgar McClure		Fall	Muir Snowfield
Jan. 1, 1907	Nils Brown Crescent (first name unknown) A boy surnamed Prestline		Traumatic injuries suffered in an avalanche while hiking; working for Starbo Mining Corp.	Buried in Glacier Basin
Aug. 14, 1909	Joseph W. Stevens T. V. Callaghan		Missing and presumed dead (summit)	Summit crater
Aug. 1, 1911	Legh Osborn Garrett		Disappeared (summit)	Location unknown; attempt via the Success Cleaver
May 12, 1912	Ruth Dory		Vehicle accident	Unknown
Aug. 12, 1912	Charlotte Hunt		Fall	Pinnacle Peak
Aug. 18, 1915	Gilbert Ordway		Hit on the head by a rock	Cowlitz Cleaver
Sept. 2, 1915	C. W. Ferguson		Collapse in ice cave	Paradise Ice Caves
Sept. 18, 1916	J. A. Fritsch		Crevasse fall (summit)	Above Gibraltar Rock
Sept. 14, 1917	Dorothy Haskell	14	Crevasse fall	Paradise Glacier
Aug. 16, 1921	Jack Meredith	24	Fall	Little Tahoma
Aug. 21, 1923	Elle Kolbinson		Drowned	Reflection Lake
June 9, 1924	Earl Kummer		Rockfall	Snout of the Nisqually Glacier
July 25, 1924	Sadie Jordan		Fall while hiking	Van Trump Creek
July 26, 1924	Sidney Cole		Rockfall	Gibraltar Ledge
Aug. 22, 1924	Paul Moser		Fall	Unicorn Peak

DATE OF DEATH	NAME	AGE	CAUSE/ACTIVITY	LOCATION
Aug. 14, 1925	Mrs. Charles Johnson		Heart attack	No details
Aug. 28, 1925	Mrs. L. G. Vitous		Vehicle accident	Dry Creek bridge
Jan. 8, 1927	John Parker		Heart attack	No details
Sept. 14, 1927	Gust Johnson		Heart attack	Longmire Campground
Feb. 15, 1928	Unknown		Unknown	Panther Creek
Sept. 9, 1928	Hiski Tanttu (aka H. Stanley)		Vehicle accident	Unknown
Nov. 12, 1928	O. B. Dorsey		Unknown; "sudden death"	Unknown
July 2, 1929	Forrest Greathouse		Fall (summit)	Ingraham Glacier
	Edwin Wetzel			
Nov. 19, 1929	W. Bacon		Vehicle accident	Unknown
	Peter Espland			
Aug. 17, 1930	Joseph Murphy		Unknown	No details
May 14, 1931	Harry Hagadorn		Heart attack	No details
July 5, 1931	Robert Zinn		Fall (summit)	Above the Nisqually Ice Cliff
Sept. 13, 1931	Clifford Byland		Vehicle accident	No details; "may not have died; records unclear"
Feb. 20, 1932	Richard Pearce	28	Avalanche	Unknown
May 28, 1933	Peter Dyrendahl		Heart attack	No details
Aug. 21, 1933	Duff Broseau		Falling tree	Five miles from Longmire
Sept. 13, 1933	Oscar Borg	47	Bee stings	White River Camp
Sept. 13, 1933	Joseph Tobits	24	Drowned	Reflection Lake
Jan. 11, 1934	Edward Bulgar		Heart attack after skiing	National Park Inn
June 12, 1934	Louis Foss		Vehicle accident	Two miles inside the Nisqually Park entrance
June 15, 1934	H. E. O'Neill (park superintendent)		Heart attack	Camp Tahoma
July 14, 1934	John Berquist	76	Heart attack after hiking	Paradise Valley Camp
Jan. 1, 1936	Delmar Fadden		Fall (summit)	Emmons Glacier at 13,000 feet
Mar. 26, 1936	John Northrop		Avalanche	Unknown
Aug. 23, 1936	Peter Sater		Rockfall on a hike	Stevens Canyon
Jan. 7, 1937	Mrs. Frank Greer		Unknown	Longmire
Feb. 20, 1937	Frank Messo	38	Heart attack after hiking	Narada Falls
June 22, 1937	Louis Santucci	18	Drowned	Ohanapecosh River
July 9, 1937	Peter Olaf Holland	75	Heart attack	Ohanapecosh Hot Springs
July 18, 1937	John Farris	18	Fall/drowned	Mount Wow
Aug. 16, 1937	Elizabeth Wecker	57	Heart attack	Longmire Campground
Sept. 20, 1938	Edward English		Vehicle accident	No details
Sept. 20, 1938	Katherine Donahoe	77	Drowned	Ohanapecosh Hot Springs
June 30, 1939	Unknown		Vehicle accident	No details
June 30, 1939	Unknown		Drowned	Ohanapecosh Hot Springs
July 29, 1939	John Janskowski	19	Vehicle accident	Carbon River
Sept. 6, 1939	John Moskin		Explosion	Ohanapecosh Campground
Sept. 13, 1940	Sigurd Hall	25	Skiing accident	Muir Snowfield
July 21, 1940	Jean Baunsgard	54	Heart attack	Van Trump Trail
August 1940	T. B. Brockway	54	Heart attack	Tipsoo Lake picnic area
Aug. 10, 1941	Leon Brigham Jr.	21	Fall (summit)	Russell or Carbon Glacier
Aug. 31, 1941	C. B. Brockway		Heart attack	Unknown
Apr. 1, 1944	Noland O'Neil		Plane crash	Unknown

DATE OF DEATH	NAME	AGE	CAUSE/ACTIVITY	LOCATION
Dec. 10, 1946	Duane Abbott		Marine air transport plane	South Tahoma Glacier
	Robert Anderson		crash	
	Joe Bainter			
	Charles Criswell			
	Robert Reilly			
	Alben Robertson			
	Leslie Simmons Jr.			
	Harry Skinner			
	Wallace Slonin			
	Lawrence Smith			
	Buddy Snelling			
	Bobby Stafford			
	William St. Clair			
	Walter Stewart			
	John Stone			
	Albert Stubblefield			
	William Sullivan			
	Chester Taube			
	Harry Thompson Jr.			
	Duane Thornton			
	Keith Tisch			
	Eldon Todd			
	Richard Trego			
	Charles Truby			
	Harry Turner			
	Ernesto Valdovin			
	Gene Vremsak			
	William Wadden			
	Donald Walker			
	Gilbert Watkins			
	Duane White			
	Louis Whitten			
May 2, 1948	Myrtle Neyhart		Avalanche	Unknown
July 10, 1949	John Thompson		Drowned	Carbon River
June 29, 1951	C. E. Ringenback		Vehicle accident	No details
July 27, 1951	Harold Carpenter		Vehicle accident	Unknown
	Mrs. Harold Carpenter			
	Dennis Carpenter (son)			
Aug. 6, 1951	Joann Ramey	17	Fall	Naches Peak
Aug. 23, 1951	Ralph Fisher		Vehicle accident	No details
Aug. 31, 1951	Lester Bloom		Vehicle accident	No details
July 5, 1954	Lewis Aycock		Unknown	Unknown
Aug. 11, 1954	Clare Combat		Fall into a crevasse	Meany Crest
Apr. 30, 1956	Richard Olson		Vehicle accident	Unknown
Aug. 18, 1956	William Purcell	42	Vehicle accident	No details
Aug. 18, 1956	Russell Miller		Asthma attack	Unknown

DATE OF DEATH	NAME	AGE	CAUSE/ACTIVITY	LOCATION
June 4, 1957	Claudette Bline	20	Tree fell on the car	Near the north park boundary
	Ida Ella Floe	58		on WA 410
	Stephen Floe	58		
July 29, 1957	Catherine Crowther		Heart attack	Unknown
Sept. 1, 1957	William Haupert	20	Fall (summit)	Disappointment Cleaver
Oct. 24, 1957	No name		Vehicle accident	No details
Nov. 30, 1957	Lowell Linn	23	Disappeared while hiking	No details
July 1, 1958	Mary Sovereign		Heart attack	No details
July 23, 1958	Kenneth Stetson	20	Drowned	Fan Lake
Aug. 1, 1959	Irvan Scalf		Vehicle accident (not clear	Unknown
	Coreen Goble		if one accident or two)	
Aug. 6, 1959	Marilyn Friedman	23	Fallen tree	Nisqually Bridge
Sept. 2, 1959	Harold Horn	40	Plane crash	Columbia Crest
	Charles Carman	29		
Sept. 3, 1959	C. T. Bressler	45	Pulmonary edema	Columbia Crest
Mar. 26, 1960	Elmer Branch		Heart attack	Unknown
June 18, 1960	Brian Crecelius	14	Fall	Edith Creek Basin
Aug. 20, 1960	Wayne Henry		Vehicle accident	Unknown
Sept. 9, 1960	Clifford Gabby		Construction accident	Glacier Bridge
Oct. 6, 1962	Mrs. Harold Carlberg	55	Vehicle accident	Unknown
Oct. 12, 1962	Gayle Stevens		Vehicle accident	Unknown
June 2, 1963	Douglas Nash		Rockfall	WA 410 at Cayuse Pass
Aug. 24, 1963	Percy Thorn		Vehicle accident	Maternity Curve
July 23, 1964	Thomas Pieper		Cerebral hemorrhage	Unknown
July 26, 1964	Elyse Starr	14	Rockfall	Nisqually Canyon
	Janet Leettola	18		
Apr. 23, 1965	Carl Baker		Plane crash	South Mowich Glacier
	Walter Bryant			
	James Middleton			
	Alvin Petry			
	William Newland			
Oct. 17, 1965	Chester Carber		Asphyxiation	Unknown
Apr. 8, 1966	Caroline Jenkins		Asthma	Unknown
Aug. 14, 1966	Helmut Kupfer		Plane crash	Near Grand Park
	Julianne Jonnes			
Aug. 31, 1966	Clay Thompson		Heart attack	Unknown
Nov. 21, 1966	Richard Feldman		Vehicle accident	Unknown
June 29, 1967	Melvin Barklow		Heart attack	Unknown
July 15, 1967	Phyllis Louden	26	Fall	Paradise Ice Caves
	Kelly Louden	5		
	Karen Louden	4		
Aug. 5, 1967	John Hull		Heart attack after hiking	Van Trump Park
Sept. 10, 1967	Elmer Post		Hypothermia	Paradise Glacier
	David Post		Traumatic injuries	
Feb. 18, 1968	Edith Anderson	22	Hiking	Near Paradise Ice Caves
Apr. 15, 1968	Ivan O'Dell	45	Plane crash	Wapowety Cleaver
	Wilfred Crutchfield	50		
June 15, 1968	James Reddick	51	Exposure	Anvil Rock

DATE OF DEATH	NAME	AGE	CAUSE/ACTIVITY	LOCATION
June 24, 1968	Patrick Chamay	31	Pulmonary edema	Liberty Cap
July 12, 1968	Bruce MacDonald	39	Drowned	Ohanapecosh River
Aug. 8, 1968	Martin Quinn	23	Hiking	Near Ipsut Creek Campground
Sept. 12, 1968	Milton Armstrong		Climbing (summit)	Cowlitz Cleaver
Mar. 9, 1969	John Aigers		Avalanche	Panorama Point
June 15, 1969	George Dockery	37	Rockfall	Curtis Ridge
July 13, 1969	Mark Kupperberg	25	Fall while climbing	Winthrop Glacier
	David Stevens			
Aug. 13, 1969	Walter Truesdale		Heart attack	Paradise Inn
Sept. 27, 1969	David Woodward		Heart attack	Near Berkeley Park
July 30, 1970	Eric Weigel	18	Fall while climbing	Pinnacle Peak
Aug. 20, 1970	Susan Bullinger	9	Drowned	Ohanapecosh River
Aug. 27, 1970	Eric Bruce	10	Drowned	Christine Falls
Sept. 6, 1970	Bruce Wahler	13	Hypothermia	Spray/Seattle Park area
Aug. 1, 1971	Michael Ferry	24	Fall (summit)	Disappointment Cleaver
Oct. 6, 1971	Charles Moore	41	Vehicle accident	Near State Camp
Jan. 13, 1972	Bill Steitz		Plane crash	Cowlitz Glacier
	Kenneth Fry			
	Kenneth Bride			
Aug. 2, 1972	Phillip Englund		Hiking	Owyhigh Lake Area
May 27, 1973	Robert Linderman		Sledding accident	Edith Creek Basin
June 26, 1973	Mark Wolstoncroft	22	Fall	Mount Wow
Sept. 7, 1973	Rendle Moore	35	Plane crash	Backbone Ridge
	Chris McKay	24		
Sept. 8, 1973	Eugene Sullivan	21	Fall	Panorama Point
Sept. 14, 1973	Gordon Barry	58	Plane crash	Pyramid Peak
	Louise Barry	55		
	Robert Henry			
	Violet Henry	49		
Nov. 13, 1973	Hepworth		Missing; presumed dead	No details
Nov. 18, 1973	David Taylor	23	Avalanche	Success Cleaver
July 31, 1975	Florence Veall	75	Heart attack	Paradise Inn
Aug. 14, 1975	Mark Jackson	17	Rockfall	Mowich Face
Nov. 11, 1975	Arnold Manthey	50	Skiing	Paradise Valley Road
Feb. 7, 1976	Robert Anderson	14	Sledding accident	Paradise Valley Road entrance
Feb. 16, 1977	Jack Wilkins	55	Fall while glissading (summit)	Pyramid Glacier
June 16, 1977	Margaret Muerer	18	Fall over waterfall	Dead Horse Creek
June 19, 1977	Moises Alvarez	39	Vehicle accident	Windy Point on WA 410
June 30, 1977	Julie Fillo	20	Hiking	Cowlitz Chimneys
July 6, 1977	Dean Klapper	33	Fall (summit)	Winthrop Glacier
Aug. 12, 1977	Craig Perky	21	Vehicle accident	Mile 7 in North Stevens Canyon
Aug. 30, 1977	William Hershey	19	Fall	Faraway Rock
Sept. 7, 1977	Mary Gnehm	47	Fall (summit)	Ingraham Glacier
Sept. 10, 1977	Jacques Jackson	16	Fall	Silver Falls
Dec. 31, 1977	Michael McNerthney	17	Fall (summit)	SW Face of Panorama Point
Mar. 26, 1978	Marvin Skillman	34	Hiking	Paul Peak Trail

DATE OF DEATH	NAME	AGE	CAUSE/ACTIVITY	LOCATION
May 21, 1978	Peter Lepard	2 mos.	Crib death	Longmire Campground
May 31, 1978	Todd Davis	24	Avalanche (summit)	Fuhrer's Finger
June 24, 1978	Rexford Norton		Heart attack	Cougar Rock Campground
Aug. 8, 1978	John Stenson	59	Heart attack	Pinnacle Peak saddle
Sept. 8, 1978	Shirli Voight	30	Exposure	Disappointment Cleaver
	Guillermi Mendoza	28	Exposure	
Oct. 14, 1978	Joan Webber	49	Rockfall	Sluiskin Mountain
Mar. 4, 1979	Willi Unsoeld	52	Avalanche	Cadaver Gap
	Janie Diepenbrock	21		
Sept. 1, 1979	Dale Click	27	Fall into crevasse	Inter Glacier
Aug. 30, 1980	Marie Olinares	5	Vehicle accident	Stevens Canyon Road
May 24, 1981	Doug Fowler	21	Fall (summit)	Liberty Ridge
	Bruce Mooney	20		
June 21, 1981	Jonathan Laitone	27	Avalanche (summit)	Ingraham Glacier
	Mark Ernlund	29		
	Ronald Farrell	41		
	Craig Tippie	28		
	Ira Liedman	30		
	Michael Watts	36		
	David Boulton	29		
	David Kidd	29		
	Gordon Heneage	42		
	Henry Matthews	38		
	Tom O'Brien	19		
July 16, 1981	Peter Brookes	26	Unknown	Liberty Ridge
July 22, 1981	Nicholas Kuhnhausen	6	Hiking	White River
Aug. 1, 1981	Murray Falkin		Heart attack while hiking	Muir Snowfield
July 4, 1982	Deborah Wetherald	31	Hiking	Edith Creek Basin
July 24, 1982	Warren Mullinnex	56	Heart attack	Ohanapecosh Campground
Mar. 21, 1983	Donald Olson	32	Plane crash	Success Glacier
	William Hayes	41		
	Ivan Choi	43		
	William Mortison	32		
	Richard Rocker	21		
May 7, 1983	Douglas Vercoe	34	Fall (summit)	Muir Snowfield
May 29, 1983	Christopher Blight	25	Fall (summit)	Emmons Glacier
June 11, 1983	Harold Spiess	26	Fall	Ricksecker Point
July 7, 1983	Robert Jacob	67	Camping	Cougar Rock Campground
July 16, 1983	Martin Richey	25	Fall while hiking	Cowlitz River
July 23, 1983	Douglas Allen		Disappearance	Carbon River
July 31, 1983	Nancy Keaton		Heart attack	Unknown
Sept. 5, 1983	Patrick Hill	26	Fall (summit)	Disappointment Cleaver
	Douglas Velder	19		
July 26, 1984	Alfred Westburg	54	Heart attack	Summerland area
Oct. 1, 1984	Fuat Dikmen	28	Summit climb	Liberty Ridge
Oct. 19, 1984	Brian Behm	24	Suicide	Oh My Point
Aug. 17, 1985	Jackie Brown	20	Vehicle accident	Stevens Canyon

DATE OF DEATH	NAME	AGE	CAUSE/ACTIVITY	LOCATION
Apr. 5, 1986	James Rodgers	45	Skiing	Paradise
July 3, 1986	Mary Carlton		Homicide	Unknown
Aug. 1, 1986	Christopher Pennington	24	Waterfall	Comet Falls
May 31, 1987	Don Wiltberger	31	Asphyxiation	Liberty Ridge
	John Weis	31		
June 4, 1987	William Hutson	43	Unknown	Paradise
June 12, 1987	Otto Papke	39	Suicide	Stevens Canyon
June 27, 1987	Kurt Fengler	34	Asphyxiation	Emmons Glacier
Sept. 11, 1987	Robert Goodwin	49	Vehicle accident	Deadwood Creek
Sept. 26, 1987	Unidentified male		Homicide	South of the tunnel on WA 123
Oct. 17, 1987	Jeremy Anderson	52	Fall	Naches Peak
Mar. 7, 1988	Pamela Lee	28	Avalanche	Plummer Peak
Mar. 19, 1988	William Saul		Plane crash	Willis Wall
Mar. 20, 1988	John Kiler	31	Suicide	Nisqually River plain
May 13, 1988	Craig Adkison	32	Fall (summit attempt)	Liberty Ridge
	Greg Remmick	32		
	David Kellokoski	30		
July 5, 1988	Andre Genereux	26	Fall	Unicorn Peak/Snow Lake
July 19, 1988	Merle Huibregtse	64	Vehicle accident	WA 410 near Ghost Lake
Oct. 2, 1988	Phyliss Newton	71	Heart attack	Maternity Curve
May 11, 1989	Richard Mooney	33	Hypothermia	Liberty Ridge
May 11, 1989	Peter Derdowski	26	Fall	Liberty Ridge
June 19, 1989	Leland Ney		Vehicle accident/possible suicide	Windy Point on WA 410
July 2, 1989	Fred Ogden		Vehicle accident	Windy Point on WA 410
Jan. 2, 1990	Ronald McDonald	53	Plane crash	Summit crater
	Randall Bates	45		
June 22, 1990	Lyle Longaker	70	Natural causes	Ohanapecosh Campground
June 28, 1990	Vicen I. Pfost	23	Drowned	Paradise River
July 2, 1990	Harry Card	50	Plane crash	Kautz Glacier
	Mike Curran	25		
	Randy Dierlam	29		
	David Bowen	28		
	David Smith	31		
Aug. 5, 1990	Pamela Johnson	24	Vehicle accident	Kautz Creek
Oct. 28, 1990	James Kampe		Skiing	Muir Snowfield
Jan. 4, 1991	Mark Fogerty	26	Skiing	Muir Snowfield
May 17, 1991	James Tuttle	44	Crevasse fall (summit)	Ingraham Glacier
Aug. 7, 1991	Laura Siebert		Vehicle accident	Ohana View on Stevens Creek
Aug. 19, 1991	Margit Haugerudgraathen		Vehicle accident	Ohana View on Stevens Creek
Aug. 19, 1991	Kristine Sitton		Fell over waterfall	Silver Falls
Sept. 1, 1991	Karl Feichtmeir	38	Fall (summit)	Disappointment Cleaver
Sept. 2, 1991	Ken Seifert	41	Fall (summit)	Disappointment Cleaver
Sept. 26, 1991	Kenneth Cardy	64	Heart attack while hiking	First Burroughs Mountain, Sunrise
Oct. 21, 1991	Arceo, Adrian		Drowned	Ohanapecosh River
Feb. 29, 1992	Gregory Terry	27	Fall (summit)	Fuhrer Finger/Wilson Glacier
	Jeffry Vallee	26		

DATE OF DEATH	NAME	AGE	CAUSE/ACTIVITY	LOCATION
June 21, 1992	Michael Price		Fall (summit)	Emmons Glacier
Mar. 26, 1993	James Ruby		Heart attack (skiing)	Paradise at Barn Flats
Apr. 15, 1993	James Tindall		Suicide	Sunshine Point Campground
June 18, 1993	Robert Bartlett		Hiking	Myrtle Falls Trail
Sept. 26, 1993	Robert Hyde	46	Vehicle accident	WA 410 at Deadwood Creek
	Mary Hyde	41		
Oct. 24, 1993	Anne Bavette		Fall	Pinnacle Peak
July 26, 1994	William Olson		Drowned	Carbon River
Aug. 24, 1994	Jerald Wentlandt		Vehicle accident	WA 123 at Cayuse Pass
Nov. 2, 1994	Stacy Stoddard		Suicide	Longmire
Dec. 11, 1994	Michael Thomas		Suicide	Trail of Shadows at Longmire
Aug. 12, 1995	Sean Ryan		Fall (summit)	Emmons Glacier
	Philip Otis			
Aug. 20, 1995	Scott Porter		Fall (summit)	Emmons Glacier
	Karl Ahrens			
Aug. 30, 1995	Miwako Suzuki	21	Vehicle accident	Ghost Lake curve on WA 410
	Keisuke Masumori	24		
July 12, 1996	Jeremy Zaccardi		Asthma attack	Emmons Glacier
May 10, 1997	Sheila Kearns		Homicide	Old Longmire Campground
June 4, 1997	David Rivera		Suicide	South Mowich River, Wonderland Trail
July 7, 1997	Ronald Sarff		Suicide	Tahoma Woods Housing
July 29, 1997	Donald McIntyre	51	Fall (summit)	Emmons Glacier
Oct. 17, 1997	Nicholas Giromini	25	Fall (summit)	Upper Cowlitz Glacier
Nov. 13, 1997	Chet Hanson		Hiking (disappeared)	Owyhigh Lakes
Nov. 16, 1997	Donald Pettigrew	84	Vehicle accident	Windy Point on WA 410
June 11, 1998	Patrick Nestler	29	Avalanche (summit)	Disappointment Cleaver
May 16, 1999	John Repka	51	Hiking	Muir Snowfield
May 24, 1999	David Persson	31	Fall (summit)	Black Pyramid/Liberty Ridge
June 20, 1999	William Tietjen	27	Unknown	Muir Snowfield
July 8, 1999	Joseph Lee Wood Jr.	34	Unknown	Van Trump Trail
July 30, 1999	Nicholas Boyd	7	Homicide	Christine Falls
	Billy Boyd	36	Suicide	
Oct. 7, 1999	Donald Campbell	73	Hiking	Carbon River Trail
Nov. 11, 1999	Chris Hartonas	40	Hiking	Probably near Camp Muir
	Raymond Vakili	48		
Mar. 24, 2000	Kent Swanson	57	Hiking	Carbon River suspension bridge
Sept. 18, 2000	James Beslow		Vehicle accident	Ghost Lake curve on WA 410
	Scott McEachin			
Nov. 5, 2000	Yuri Glavan		Vehicle accident	A mile inside the Nisqually entrance
Mar. 21, 2001	Randall Lane		Plane crash	Lost Creek drainage
	Phillip Cruise			
Aug. 2, 2001	Lawrence Minard		Heart attack (summit attempt)	Disappointment Cleaver
Sept. 7, 2001	Dale Collins		Heart attack	Frozen Lake
Nov. 11, 2001	Erin Beth Gordon		Suicide	National Park Inn

DATE OF DEATH	NAME	AGE	CAUSE/ACTIVITY	LOCATION
Nov. 24, 2001	Jason Cosner	26	Vehicle accident	1.5 miles from the Nisqually entrance
May 29, 2002	Keeta Owens	21	Fall (summit)	Liberty Cap
	Grit Kleinschmidt	26	Hypothermia (summit)	
	Cornelius Beilharz	26	Fall (summit)	
June 6, 2002	Benjamin Hernstedt	25	Fall (summit)	Ingraham Glacier
	Jeff Dupuis	21		
Aug. 18, 2002	Valerie Martin		Suicide	Nisqually River Glacier Bridge
Sept. 13, 2002	Marie McClafun		Heart attack	Sourdough Ridge Trail
Sept. 13, 2002	Ed Hommer		Rockfall (summit)	Disappointment Cleaver
July 10, 2003	Erica Smith		Asthma	Jackson Visitor Center
Sept. 7, 2003	Alvin Craver		Heart attack	Dewey Lake Trail
May 15, 2004	Peter Cooley	39	Fall (summit)	Black Pyramid, Liberty Ridge
June 3, 2004	Jonathan (Peter) Cahill	40	Fall (summit)	Liberty Ridge
June 12, 2004	Luke Casady	29	Avalanche (skiing/summit)	Liberty Ridge
	Ansel Vizcaya	29		
July 26, 2004	William Bowey		Drowned	Sylvia Falls
Oct. 24, 2004	Aaron Koester	21	Avalanche (summit)	Ingraham Glacier
Oct. 29, 2004	Samuel Neimoyer		Vehicle accident	Windy Point on WA 410
Nov. 13, 2004	Vasily Kozorezov	16	Fall while hiking	Eagle Peak
May 23, 2005	Timothy Stark	57	Hiking	Paradise Glacier
	Greg Stark	27		
June 9, 2005	Dorothy Kennedy		Vehicle accident	Milepost 59 on WA 410
June 10, 2005	Mike Beery		Fall (summit)	Gibraltar Chute
July 20, 2005	Timothy Cole		Suicide	Nickel Creek
Aug. 2005	Zachery Weston		Suicide	Wapowety Cleaver
June 2006	Darcy Quick		Fall	Comet Falls
Feb. 24, 2007	Stanley Quande	54	Avalanche	Crystal Mountain
Mar. 19, 2007	Frances Blakely	47	Hiking	Ipsut Creek
	Robert Blakely	44		
June 16, 2007	Brian (Jeff) Graves	47	Hiking	Eagle Peak
Dec. 18, 2007	Kirk Reiser		Hiking (snowshoeing)	Edith Creek Basin
Mar. 17, 2008	Devin Ossman	45	Hiking	Kautz Creek Trail
June 11, 2008	Eduard Burceag	31	Hiking	Muir Snowfield
Oct. 13, 2008	James Longworth		Suicide	Kautz Creek picnic area
Nov. 10, 2008	Timothy Swift		Hiking	Spray Falls
July 7, 2009	Dennis Newton		Heart attack	Crystal Creek Trailhead
Aug. 10, 2009	Richard Dawson		Heart attack	Milepost 62 on WA 410
Apr. 2, 2010	Robert Casper		Suicide	Carbon River Entrance Station
June 6, 2010	Mark Wedeven	29	Avalanche (summit)	Ingraham Glacier
July 1, 2010	Eric Lewis	57	Unknown (summit)	Ingraham or Nisqually Glacier
July 27, 2010	Lee Adams	52	Fall (summit)	Emmons Glacier
Aug. 12, 2010	Jason Russell	11	Drowned	Northern park boundary
May 10, 2011	Tucker Taffe	33	Fall (summit)	Nisqually Glacier
June 12, 2011	Robert Plankers	60	Fall (summit)	Liberty Ridge
June 26, 2011	Michael Hendrickson		Unknown	GSI Glacier Dorm at Paradise
Sept. 13, 2011	Roger Wagner		Fall	Christine Falls

DATE OF DEATH	NAME	AGE	CAUSE/ACTIVITY	LOCATION
Sept. 13, 2011	Richard Hudson	82	Unknown	Paradise parking lot
Dec. 12, 2011	Brian Grobois		Hypothermia	Stevens Creek
Jan. 1, 2012	Benjamin Barnes		Unknown	On Paradise Road above Narada Falls
Jan. 1, 2012	Margaret Anderson		Homicide	On Paradise Road above Narada Falls
Jan. 15, 2012	Seol Hee Jin	52	Climb (summit)	Unknown
Jan. 15, 2012	Eunsork Yang	52	Climb (summit)	Paradise Glacier
Jan. 15, 2012	Michelle Trojanowski	30	Climb (Camp Muir)	Paradise Glacier
Jan. 15, 2012	Mark Vucich	37	Climb (Camp Muir)	Muir Snowfield
June 21, 2012	Nicholas Hall		Fall (rescue operation)	Winthrop Glacier
July 4, 2012	David Watson		Glissading	Edith Creek
July 26, 2012	Stephen Albers		Bicycling	Stevens Canyon Road
Sept. 23, 2012	Linda Fong		Suicide	Ricksecker Point
June 22, 2013	Ahamed Asiri		Drowning	White River Campground
July 1, 2013	David Toarmina		Heart attack	Skyline Trail near Paradise
July 14, 2013	Stan Sattelberg		Heart attack	Paradise
Sept. 26, 2013	George Merriam		Fall	Pinnacle Peak Trail
Sept. 18, 2013	Alan Burgestahler		Heart attack	Cougar Rock Campground
Sept. 20, 2013	Robert Congeli		Suicide	Wonderland Trail
May 30, 2014	Matt Hegeman	38	Climbing (summit)	Liberty Ridge
	Eitan Green	29		
	Erik Kolb	34		
	Mark Mahaney	26		
	Uday Marty	40		
	John Mullally	40		
June 19, 2014	Karen Sykes	70	Hiking	Owyhigh Lakes Trail
July 12, 2014	Eric Hansen		Vehicle accident	Stevens Canyon Road
July 13, 2014	Edwin Birch	64	Hiking	Wonderland Trail
Sept. 11, 2014	Thomas Casias	64	Vehicle accident	Stevens Canyon Road
Dec. 28, 2014	Louis Landry	37	Snowshoeing	Paradise Area
June 12, 2015	Kyle Bufis	25	Climbing (summit)	Mount Rainier Summit
Aug. 1, 2015	Jack Kipp	63	Heart attack	Paradise Area
Sept. 14, 2015	Timothy Hagan	62	Fall (hiking)	Crescent Lake (Sluiskin Range)
Mar. 26, 2016	Arvid Lahti	58	Climbing (summit)	Beehive
Aug. 13, 2016	Craig Falk	54	Hiking	Nachez Loop Trail
July 3, 2017	Dmitri Pajitnov	30	Skiing	Pebble Creek
July 13, 2017	Burt Meyer	75	Hiking	Eagle Peak Trail
July 16, 2017	Mark Naiman	42	Skiing	Emmons Glacier

Appendix B

REFERENCES AND RESOURCES

Mount Rainier National Park has kept meticulous records of fatalities on the mountain. A searchable resource of 420 deaths on the mountain is available online at www.mountrainierclimbing.us/sar/fatalities.php. This resource is the backbone of the events described in this book.

Wonderland: An Administrative History of Mount Rainier National Park, by Theodore Catton, provides an in-depth overview of park history, as well as addresses the steps that the park has taken over the years to mitigate the dangers of climbing, hiking, skiing, and exploring in the park. It is available online at www.nps.gov/mora/learn/historyculture/upload/Catton_1996_-Wonderland_An_Administrative_History_of_Mount_Rainier_National_Park-2.pdf.

The park maintains a decade-by-decade historic time line that records significant events including major climbing accidents and rescues, as well as tragedies like the loss of the thirty-two marines in a plane crash in 1946. The time line is available online at www.nps.gov/features/mora_cenn/timeline.htm.

Other important resources that informed compilation of these stories included information culled from aides such as:

Records of Mount Rainier National Park; https://archive.org/stream/recordsofmount ra00shad/recordsofmountra00shad_djvu.txt
Inventory of the Records of the National Park Service, Record Group 79; www.nps.gov/aboutus/foia/upload/NPSrg79_inventory-5.pdf
Mount Rainier Search and Rescue Reports, 1997 to 2004; www.nps.gov/mora/planyour visit/search-and-rescue-reports.htm#PennHancockSAR
Mount Rainier Annual Climbing Statistics; www.nps.gov/mora/learn/management/upload/climbing-stats-thru-2010.pdf
Mount Rainier National Park *Nature Notes*; www.nps.gov/parkhistory/online_books/mora/nn-vol.htm
Mount Rainier Climbing Photos by Mike Gauthier; www.nps.gov/media/photo/gallery.htm?id=5AF80928-155D-4519-3E3FAAAE2F7A3EBF
The Tahoma News; the most current editions of the park newspaper are posted at www.nps.gov/mora on the Publications page.
The Mountaineers Annuals Archives; www.mountaineers.org/about/history/the-mountaineer-annuals/the-mountaineer-annuals

The *American Alpine Journal*, a publication of the American Alpine Club, posts reports on mountaineering accidents around the globe, not only to document the events, but also to highlight lessons to be learned. I've included individual links to stories I researched as part of the documentation for chapters compiled below. To do your own research on Mount Rainier, or on other peaks and climbs that American alpinists have attempted, successfully or not, the website, http://publications .americanalpineclub.org is searchable and fascinating.

Newspaper archives, when not available online through the publications themselves, were accessed via Newspapers.com. Other newspaper sources included the Washington State Library links to newspapers in Washington (www.sos.wa.gov/library/wa_newspapers.aspx) and Washington Online Historical Newspapers (https://sites.google.com/site/ onlinenewspapersite/Home/usa/wa).

I did not reach out to the families or friends of the deceased in the compilation of this book. First, it seemed like an intrusion; second, it would have taken too much time, with more than four hundred families to track down and contact. If family or friends would like to contact me, either to clarify facts or to add remembrances of the dead for subsequent editions, I encourage them to reach out through my publisher.

Books

Davidson, Jim, and Kevin Vaugh. *The Ledge: An Inspirational Story of Friendship and Survival.* Ballantine Books, 2011.

Farabee, Charles "Butch," Jr. *Death, Daring, and Disaster: Search and Rescue in the National Parks.* Taylor Trade Publishing, 2005.

Filley, Bette. *The Big Fact Book About Mount Rainier.* Dunamis House, 1996.

Forgey, William. *Wilderness Medicine: Beyond First Aid.* 7th ed. FalconGuides, 2017.

Haines, Aubrey. *Mountain Fever: Historic Conquests of Rainier.* University of Washington Press, 1999. First published 1962 by Oregon Historical Society.

Molenaar, Dee. *The Challenge of Rainier: A Record of the Exploration and Ascents, Triumphs and Tragedies on the Northwest's Greatest Mountain.* 4th (40th anniversary) ed. Mountaineers Books, 2011. First published in 1971.

Muir, John. *Steep Trails.* Includes the essay "An Ascent of Mount Rainier." Edited by William Frederic Badé. Houghton-Mifflin, 1918.

Whittaker, Lou, and Andrea Gabbard. *Memoirs of a Mountain Guide.* Mountaineers Books, 1994.

Online and Periodical References by Chapter

I have listed most of the articles or documents I referred to in compiling these stories. Information from one source may have been used in the compilation of multiple stories. All stories were compiled from multiple sources if available.

Introduction

Mount Rainier Annual Visitor Statistics, 1967–2010. www.nps.gov/mora/learn/manage
 ment/upload/vis-stats-1967-2010-2.pdf.
Mount Rainier National Park Visitation Statistics. https://irma.nps.gov/Stats/
 SSRSReports/Park%20Specific%20Reports/Annual%20Park%20Recreation%20
 Visitation%20(1904%20-%20Last%20Calendar%20Year)?Park=MORA.
Olympian. "Mount Rainier, Olympic See Slight Rises in Visitation." February 10, 2016.
 www.theolympian.com/outdoors/article59665396.html.
University of Washington, University Libraries, Special Collections. "Mount Rainier
 National Park: 100 Years in Paradise." www.lib.washington.edu/specialcollections/
 collections/exhibits/rainier.

A Brief History of Peak and Park

Bishop, Julie A. "Geologic Hazards of Mount Rainier." May 1975.
Brockman, C. Frank. *The Geological Story of Mount Rainier*, Book One. ca. 1930s.
Coombs, Howard A. *The Geology of Mount Rainier National Park*. Seattle: University of
 Washington, 1936.
Crandell, Dwight R. *The Geologic Story of Mount Rainier*. US Geological Survey, 1969.
Driedger, Carolyn L. "Geology in Action—Jokulhlaups on Mount Rainier." US Geo-
 logical Survey, 1988. https://pubs.er.usgs.gov/publication/ofr88459.
"The Glaciers of Mount Rainier." IUGG Glacier Study Tour, September 25, 1963.
 Edited by Mark F. Meier of the US Geological Survey.
Mount Rainier Annual Visitor Statistics. www.nps.gov/mora/learn/management/
 upload/vis-stats-1967-2016.pdf.
National Park Service. "Glaciers." Includes references to subpages on specific glaciers,
 debris flows, and glacial monitoring. www.nps.gov/mora/learn/nature/glaciers.htm.
National Park Service. "November 2006 Flood." https://www.nps.gov/mora/learn/news/
 november-2006-flooding.htm.
Reese, Gary Fuller. Mount Rainier National Park Place Names (online pdf). 2009.
Sisson, Thomas W. "History and Hazards of Mount Rainier, Washington." US Geological Survey. https://pubs.usgs.gov/of/1995/0642/of95-642.pdf.
University of Washington Publications in Geology. "The Mount Rainier Volcanics."
 https://www.nps.gov/parkhistory/online_books/geology/publications/state/wa/
 uw-1936-3-2/sec1d.htm.

USGS Cascades Volcano Observatory. "First Ascent of Mount Rainier, Washington, August 17, 1870." https://volcanoes.usgs.gov/observatories/cvo/Historical/first_ ascent_rainier_1870.shtml.

Part One: To the Summit

Chapters 1 through 7

American Alpine Journal. "Asphyxiation, Weather, Fatigue, Washington, Mount Rainier." 1988. http://publications.americanalpineclub.org/articles/13198805002/ Asphyxiation-Weather-Fatigue-Washington-Mount-Rainier.

American Alpine Journal. "Avalanche, Bad Weather, Washington, Mt. Rainier." 1980. http://publications.americanalpineclub.org/articles/13198004002/ Avalanche-Bad-Weather-Washington-Mt-Rainier.

American Alpine Journal. "Avalanche, Washington, Mount Rainier." 1999. http://publications.americanalpineclub.org/articles/13199907002/ Avalanche-Washington-Mount-Rainier.

American Alpine Journal. "Avalanche, Washington, Mount Rainier, Ingraham Glacier." 2005. http://publications.americanalpineclub.org/articles/13200510302/ Avalanche-Washington-Mount-Rainier-Ingraham-Glacier.

American Alpine Journal. "Avalanche, Washington, Mount Rainier, Liberty Ridge." 2005. http://publications.americanalpineclub.org/articles/13200509700/ Avalanche-Washington-Mount-Rainier-Liberty-Ridge.

American Alpine Journal. "Donald D. McIntyre, 1946–1997." 1998. http://publications .americanalpineclub.org/articles/12199841301/Donald-D-McIntyre-1946-1997.

American Alpine Journal. "Exhaustion—Possible AMS or HACE, Fall on Ice/Snow, Weather, Washington, Mount Rainier, Liberty Ridge." 2012. http://publications .americanalpineclub.org/articles/13201208500/Exhaustion-Possible-AMS-or -HACE-Fall-on-IceSnow-Weather-Washington-Mount-Rainier-Liberty-Ridge.

American Alpine Journal. "Falling Ice, Washington, Mount Rainier." 1982. http://publications.americanalpineclub.org/articles/13198205500/ Falling-Ice-Washington-Mount-Rainier.

American Alpine Journal. "Fall into Crevasse and Fall into Crevasse, Unroped, Inadequate Equipment, Inexperience, Washington, Mount Rainier." 1984. http://publications .americanalpineclub.org/articles/13198405100/Fall-Into-Crevasse-and-Fall-Into -Crevasse-Unroped-Inadequate-Equipment-Inexperience-Washington-Mount -Rainier.

American Alpine Journal. "Fall into Crevasse, Inadequate Belay, Inadequate Equipment, Washington, Mount Rainier." 1992. http://publications.americanalpineclub.org/ articles/13199204400/Fall-into-Crevasse-Inadequate-Belay-Inadequate -Equipment-Washington-Mount-Rainier.

American Alpine Journal. "Fall into Crevasse—Inadequate Protection, Weather and Stranded—Weather, Exposure—Hypothermia, Washington, Mount Rainier, Ingraham Glacier." 2003. http://publications.americanalpineclub.org/

articles/13200308800/Fall-into-Crevasse-Inadequate-Protection-Weather
-and-Stranded-Weather-Exposure-Hypothermia-Washington-Mount-Rainier
-Ingraham-Glacier.

American Alpine Journal. "Fall into Crevasse, Snow Bridge Collapse, Washington, Mount Rainier." 1988. http://publications.americanalpineclub.org/articles/13198805500/ Fall-Into-Crevasse-Snow-Bridge-Collapse-Washington-Mount-Rainier.

American Alpine Journal. "Fall Off Cornice, Fall into Crevasse, Bad Weather, Washington, Mount Rainier." 1984. http://publications.americanalpineclub.org/articles /13198404701/Fall-Off-Cornice-Fall-Into-Crevasse-Bad-Weather-Washington -Mount-Rainier.

American Alpine Journal. "Fall on Snow/Ice, Climbing Alone and Unroped, Faulty Use of Crampons, Washington, Mount Rainier." 1992. http://publications.americanalpine club.org/articles/13199205600/Fall-on-SnowIce-Climbing-Alone-and-Unroped -Faulty-Use-of-Crampons-Washington-Mount-Rainier.

American Alpine Journal. "Fall on Snow, Inexperience, Weather, Washington, Mount Rainier." 1989. http://publications.americanalpineclub.org/articles/13198906600/ Fall-on-Snow-Inexperience-Weather-Washington-Mount-Rainier.

American Alpine Journal. "Fall on Snow—Unable to Self-Arrest, Fall into Crevasse, Washington, Mount Rainier, Emmons Glacier." 2011. http://publications.american alpineclub.org/articles/13201109402/Fall-on-Snow-Unable-to-Self-Arrest-Fall -into-Crevasse-Washington-Mount-Rainier-Emmons-Glacier.

American Alpine Journal. "Fatal Mountaineer: The High-Altitude Life and Death of Willi Unsoeld, American Himalayan Legend." 2003. http://publications.american alpineclub.org/articles/12200343600/Fatal-Mountaineer-The-High-Altitude -Life-and-Death-of-Willi-Unsoeld-American-Himalayan-Legend.

American Alpine Journal. "Fatigue, Exposure, Exceeding Abilities, Hypothermia, Slip or Fall on Snow, Washington, Mount Rainier." 1990. http://publications.ameri-canalpineclub.org/articles/13199006000/Fatigue-Exposure-Exceeding-Abilities-Hypothermia-Slip-or-Fall-on-Snow-Washington-Mount-Rainier.

American Alpine Journal. "Patrick David Chamay, 1937–1968, In Memoriam." 1969. http://publications.americanalpineclub.org/articles/12196949700/ Patrick-David-Chamay-1937-1968.

American Alpine Journal. "Slip on Snow, Inadequate Equipment, Inexperience, Washington, Mount Rainier." 1984. http://publications.americanalpineclub.org/articles /13198405700/Slip-on-Snow-Inadequate-Equipment-Inexperience-Washington -Mount-Rainier.

American Alpine Journal. "Washington, Mt. Rainier" (Dockery accident report). 1970. http://publications.americanalpineclub.org/articles/13197001300/ Washington-Mt-Rainier.

American Alpine Journal. "Washington, Mt. Rainier" (Kupperberg/Stevens accident report). 1970. http://publications.americanalpineclub.org/articles/13197001400/ Washington-Mt-Rainier.

Arai, Michiko. "Danger Zones: Mt. Rainier; Where & Why Accidents Happen." *American Alpine Journal*, 2014. http://publications.americanalpineclub.org/articles/13201212568/Danger-Zones-Mt-Rainier.

"Arvid, My Loyal Friend." Video posted to YouTube by Monique Richard in April 2016. www.youtube.com/watch?v=HwN0bh3TQWM&feature=youtube.

Associated Press. "1 Dies, Friend Survives Rainier Fall." *Seattle Times*, May 20, 1991. http://community.seattletimes.nwsource.com/archive/?date=19910520&slug=1284183.

Associated Press. "2 Killed in Fall on Mt. Rainier; 3 Others Rescued From Crevasse." *Los Angeles Times*, June 8, 2002. http://articles.latimes.com/2002/jun/08/nation/na-dead8.

Associated Press. "6 Mount Rainier Climbing Victims Won't be Immediately Recovered because of Ice, Rock Fall Danger." *Oregonian*, June 1, 2014. www.oregonlive.com/pacific-northwest-news/index.ssf/2014/06/6_mount_rainier_climbing_victi.html.

Associated Press. "Bodies of Climbers Retrieved." *Lansing State Journal*, May 29, 1981. www.newspapers.com/image/210173033/?terms=Doug%2BFowler%2BBruce%2BMooney.

Associated Press. "Climber Likely Dead from Hypothermia on Mount Rainier." *Seattle Times*, March 28, 2016. www.seattletimes.com/seattle-news/rescue-under-way-for-climbers-snowshoer-on-mount-rainier.

Associated Press. "Climber's Body Recovered on Mount Rainier." Fox News, June 18, 2004. www.foxnews.com/story/2004/06/18/climber-body-recovered-on-mount-rainier.html.

Associated Press. "Climbers Trapped on Mount Rainier." *Greenwood (SC) Index-Journal*, September 4, 1979. www.newspapers.com/image/70395387/?terms=Dale%2BClick.

Associated Press. "Climbers Who Died on Mount Rainier Left Videotape of Their Trek." *Arizona Republic*, June 10, 1987. www.newspapers.com/image/121010528.

Associated Press. "Climbing Accident Betrays Four Friends; Two Die in Mount Rainier Fall, Severing Friendship of Adventure." *Spokesman-Review* (Spokane, WA), August 28, 1995. www.spokesman.com/stories/1995/aug/28/climbing-accident-betrays-four-friends-two-die-in.

Associated Press. "Climbing Deaths Underscore Danger of Mount Rainier." May 21, 1988. www.apnewsarchive.com/1988/Climbing-Deaths-Underscore-Danger-of-Mount-Rainier/id-af186c53e4c560591f6720dd55cfa984.

Associated Press. "Deaths Are on Rise in Rainier National Park." *Daily News* (Port Angeles, WA), September 19, 1977. www.newspapers.com/image/25633246.

Associated Press. "Father: Climber Found Dead on Mount Rainier Had Gone Back to Get Cook Stove." *Seattle Times*, June 15, 2015. www.seattletimes.com/seattle-news/father-climber-found-dead-on-mount-rainier-had-gone-to-get-cook-stove.

Associated Press. "Friends Say Dead Climbers Were Experts." *Berkeley Daily Planet*, June 1, 2002. www.berkeleydailyplanet.com/issue/2002-06-01/article/12367.

Associated Press. "Guide Says His Slip Triggered Avalanche That Killed Climber." *Hazleton (PA) Standard-Speaker*, June 14, 1998. www.newspapers.com/image/59731792/?terms=James%2BRuby%2Bmount%2BRainier.

Associated Press. "Mount Rainier Rangers Renew Recovery Effort for Climber Swept Away in Avalanche." *Oregonian,* June 8, 2010. www.oregonlive.com/news/index .ssf/2010/06/lost_mount_rainier_climber_an.html.

Associated Press. "Sitka Climber Dies in Rainier Avalanche." *Sitka Daily Sentinel,* June 1, 1978. www.newspapers.com/image/12193290.

Barcott, Bruce. "The Secret Life of Guides." *Outside,* December 1, 1999. www.outside online.com/1928636/secret-life-guides.

Batcheldor, Matt. "Climber Sought Adventure, Social Justice before Death." *Spokesman-Review* (Spokane, WA), June 27, 2010. www.spokesman.com/stories/2010/jun/27/ climber-sought-adventure-social-justice-before.

Brewer, Christopher. "Skier Dies at Mount Rainier." *Chronicle* (Lewis County, WA), May 11, 2011. www.chronline.com/news/skier-dies-at-mount-rainier/article_ ffbac3dc-7bf6-11e0-a59b-001cc4c03286.html.

Butler, Katherine. "Mark Wedeven Struck Down by Avalanche on Mount Rainier." Mother Nature Network, August 5, 2010. www.mnn.com/health/fitness-well-being/stories/ mark-wedeven-struck-down-by-avalanche-on-mount-rainier.

CBS News. "Surviving Rainier Climber Rescued." May 17, 2004. www.cbsnews.com/ news/surviving-rainier-climber-rescued.

Chicago Tribune. Gregory B. Terry obituary. March 15, 1992. http://articles.chicagotribune.com/1992-03-15/ news/9201240304_1_mr-terry-rainier-national-park-recreational-equipment.

Climbing. "Ueli Steck Found Dead on Nuptse." April 30, 2017. www.climbing.com/ news/ueli-steck-found-dead-on-nuptse.

Daily News (Port Angeles, WA). "Rainier Rescuers Isolated." November 22, 1974. www .newspapers.com/image/25634462.

Daily Reporter (Dover, OH). "Search for Wooster Ranger Is Resumed on Mt. Rainier." November 21, 1974. www.newspapers.com/image/19815112.

Devlin, Sherry. "Family Recalls Climber's Passion." *Missoulian,* July 17, 2004. http:// missoulian.com/news/local/family-recalls-climber-s-passion/article_0c80e296 -c0ae-5713-9213-d1c6394cf296.html.

Dininny, Shannon. "Mount Rainier Makes Changes after Ranger's Death." *Seattle Times,* June 4, 2013 (updated June 5, 2013). www.seattletimes.com/seattle-news/ mount-rainier-makes-changes-after-rangerrsquos-death.

"Everest 1953: On Willi Unsoeld." Video posted to Vimeo by *Outside* magazine, March 29, 2013. https://vimeo.com/62971964.

Firehouse. "Washington Firefighter Loses Life Climbing On Mount Rainier." October 26, 2004. www.firehouse.com/news/10516575/ washington-firefighter-loses-life-climbing-on-mount-rainier.

Florida Today. "Avalanche Kills Climber." January 1, 1978. www.newspapers.com/ image/125414763.

Fort Lauderdale News. "Searchers Give Up Efforts to Recover Bodies on the Mountain." June 24, 1981. www.newspapers.com/image/233416915/?terms=Mount%2BRain ier.

Gintzler, Ariella. "Kilian Jornet Summits Everest Twice, but Did He Set a Record?" *Trail Runner,* May 28, 2017. http://trailrunnermag.com/people/news/kilian-jornet -summits-everest.html.

Glenn, Stacia, and Craig Hill. "Norwegian Climber Missing on Mount Rainier Identified." *News Tribune* (Tacoma, WA), March 30, 2016 (updated March 31, 2016). www.thenewstribune.com/news/local/article69004122.html.

Green, Sarah Jean. "Mount Rainier Claims Third Life This Year." *Seattle Times,* June 11, 2005. http://community.seattletimes.nwsource.com/archive/?date=20050611&slug =rainier11m.

Hill, Craig. "Rescuers Fear Climber Took 'Unsurvivable' Fall on Mount Rainier's Liberty Ridge." *News Tribune* (Tacoma, WA), June 14, 2011. http://blog.thenewstribune.com/adventure/2011/06/14/ rescuers-working-to-save-olympia-man-on-mount-rainiers-liberty-ridge.

Hill, Craig. "Valor Award: Richards Tells One of Rainier's Saddest Stories." *News Tribune* (Tacoma, WA), November 8, 2010. http://blog.thenewstribune.com/ adventure/2010/11/08/valor-award-richards-tells-one-of-rainiers-saddest-stories.

Huck, Janet. "Chimacum Firefighter Dies in Mount Rainier Accident." PTleader.com, June 15, 2005. www.ptleader.com/news/chimacum-firefighter-dies-in-mount -rainier-accident/article_ce734ea0-ce3d-5446-8b71-d01c69c2c158.html.

Jenks, Jayson. "Screams in the Silence: A Story of Love, Loss and Eternal Friendship on Mount Rainier." *Seattle Times Pacific NW Magazine,* July 21, 2016 (updated March 2, 2017). www.seattletimes.com/pacific-nw-magazine/screams-in-the-silence-a -story-of-love-loss-and-eternal-friendship-on-mount-rainier.

Kamb, Lewis, and Sam Skolnik. "Orting Climber Dies on Mount Rainier." *Seattle Post-Intelligencer,* June 3, 2004. www.seattlepi.com/local/article/Orting-climber-dies-on -Mount-Rainier-1146438.php.

King, Wayne. "11 Climbers Missing on Mt. Rainier in Fall of Ice Wall." *New York Times,* June 22, 1981. www.nytimes.com/1981/06/22/us/11-climbers-missing-on-mt -rainier-in-fall-of-ice-wall.html.

Ko, Michael. "Experienced Mountaineer Dies on Mt. Rainier's Liberty Ridge." *Seattle Times,* June 4, 2004. http://community.seattletimes.nwsource.com/archive/?date=20 040604&slug=climber04m.

Lewis, Mike. "Mount Rainier Accident Kills Monroe Man." *Seattle Post-Intelligencer,* October 25, 2004. www.seattlepi.com/local/article/Mount-Rainier-accident-kills -Monroe-man-1157628.php.

Los Angeles Times. "Descent into Horror: Mt. Rainier Avalanche Victims Recount Dramatic Rescue." June 19, 1998. http://articles.latimes.com/1998/jun/19/sports/ sp-61616/2.

LouWhittaker.com. Climber and author pages. http://louwhittaker.com.

Mayor, Jeff. "Seattle Man Dies while after Falling into Mount Rainier Crevasse." *News Tribune* (Tacoma, WA), July 28, 2010. http://blog.thenewstribune.com/adventure/2010/07/28/ seattle-man-dies-while-after-falling-into-mount-rainier-crevasse.

McClary, Daryl C. "Avalanche Kills 11 Climbers as They Ascend Mount Rainier on June 21, 1981." HistoryLink.org, August 23, 2014. www.historylink.org/File/10796.

Mountain Zone. "Body on Mount Rainier Positively Identified." October 28, 1997. www.mountainzone.com/news/rainier3.html.

Mount Rainier National Park. *Nature Notes* 15, no. 2 (June 1937). www.nps.gov/park history/online_books/mora/notes/vol15-2h.htm.

National Geographic. "Exclusive: Climber Completes the Most Dangerous Rope-Free Ascent Ever." June 3, 2017. www.nationalgeographic.com/adventure/features/athletes/alex-honnoldmost-dangerous-free-solo-climb-yosemite-national-park-el-capitan.

National Park Service. "Two Climbers Recovered from Paradise Glacier; Another Remains Missing." September 8, 2012; www.nps.gov/mora/learn/news/two-climbers-recovered.htm.

New York Times. "Jack Wilkins, 55, Dies in Fall from Mountain; A Reporter in Seattle." February 18, 1977. www.nytimes.com/1977/02/18/archives/jack-wilkins-55-dies-in-fall-from-mountain-a-reporter-in-seattle.html.

New York Times. "Mountain Climbers Rescue 2 Men Hurt in Plane Crash atop Glacier." December 21, 1981. www.nytimes.com/1981/12/21/us/mountain-climbers-rescue-2-men-hurt-in-plane-crash-atop-glacier.html.

O&P Edge. "Mountaineer Hommer Dies." September 26, 2002. https://opedge.com/Articles/ViewArticle/news_2002-09-26_01.

Perry, Nick, and Susan Gilmore. "Mount Rainier Climber Killed after Fall into Crevasse." *Seattle Times,* July 28, 2010. www.seattletimes.com/seattle-news/mount-rainier-climber-killed-after-fall-into-crevasse.

Philadelphia Inquirer. "Penna. Student Is Killed by Fall on Mt. Rainier." September 2, 1957. www.newspapers.com/image/178016515.

Reno Gazette-Journal. "2nd Tahoe climber's body found on Rainier." May 14, 1989. www.newspapers.com/image/149814309.

RMI Expeditions. "RMI's History." www.rmiguides.com/about-us/history.

Schaffer, Grayson. "Fifty Years Later: An Interview with Tom Hornbein." *Outside,* April 13, 2012. www.outsideonline.com/1899251/fifty-years-later.

Seattle Times. "Lafayette Grad among Rainier Dead." June 5, 2014. Via the *Morning Call* (Allenstown, PA), www.newspapers.com/image/273155567/?terms=Uday%2BMarty.

Seattle Times. "Lucky Survivors Tell 6-Hour Ordeal of Killer Avalanche on Mt. Rainier." June 14, 1998. Via the *Chicago Tribune,* http://articles.chicagotribune.com/1998-06-14/news/9806140073_1_rainier-mountaineering-climbers-lou-whittaker.

Seattle Times. "Missing Climbers Died on Rainier." March 11, 1992. http://community.seattletimes.nwsource.com/archive/?date=19920311&slug=1480477.

Seattle Times. "Mount Rainier Victim Was Seasoned Climber." September 4, 1991. http://community.seattletimes.nwsource.com/archive/?date=19910904&slug=1303514.

Seattle Times. "Mt. Rainier Victim Was Avid Climber—Reno Man Had More Than 20 Years' Experience as Mountaineer." July 31, 1997. http://community.seattletimes .nwsource.com/archive/?date=19970731&slug=2552334.

Seattle Times. "Retrieving Bodies of Mount Rainier Climbers, Including Colby Graduate, Could Take Months." June 2, 2014. Via the *Bangor Daily News,* http://bangor dailynews.com/2014/06/02/news/nation/search-scaled-back-for-climbers -including-colby-graduate-missing-on-mount-rainier.

SFGate. "Petaluma Hiker Fell to Death Just Before He Reached Safety." October 29, 1997. www.sfgate.com/news/article/Petaluma-Hiker-Fell-To-Death-Just -Before-He-2798663.php.

Sharma, K. K. "'I Am Going to Die,' Whispered Nanda Devi on the Mountain She Regarded as Her Own." *People,* October 4, 1976. http://people.com/archive/i-am -going-to-die-whispered-nanda-devi-on-the-mountain-she-regarded-as-her-own -vol-6-no-14.

Solomon, Chris, Eric Sorensen, and David Bowermaster. "Treacherous Night on Rainier; Climbers Killed on Mount Rainier." *Seattle Times,* May 29, 2002. www.i-world .net/oma/news/accidents/2002-05-29-rainier.html.

Summitpost.org. "Mount Rainier." Created March 28, 2001; edited May 6, 2015. www .summitpost.org/mount-rainier/150291.

United Press International. "A Mountain Climber Was Killed and His Teenager Daughter . . ." June 27, 1987. www.upi.com/Archives/1987/06/27/A-mountain-climber -was-killed-and-his-teenager-daughter/1524551764800.

United Press International. "Authorities Thursday Found the Bodies of Three Climbers amid . . ." May 19, 1988. www.upi.com/Archives/1988/05/19/ Authorities-Thursday-found-the-bodies-of-three-climbers-amid/3894580017600.

United Press International. "Park Rangers Issue Warning." June 1, 1985. www.upi.com/ Archives/1985/06/01/Park-rangers-issue-warning/8678486446400.

Unsoeld, Jolene. "The Unsoeld Story." *Smokejumper Quarterly Magazine,* February 14, 2003. http://smokejumpers.com/index.php/smokejumpermagazine/getitem/ articles_id=8.

Watson, Emmett. "Dynamic Coach Leon Brigham Was Years Ahead of His Time." *Seattle Times,* November 26, 1992. http://community.seattletimes.nwsource.com/arc hive/?date=19921126&slug=1526823.

Williams, Allison. "Jim and Lou Whittaker." *Seattle Met,* August 2012. www.seattlemet .com/articles/2012/7/18/jim-and-lou-whittaker-august-2012.

Part Two: Elsewhere in the Park

Chapters 8 through 16

American Alpine Journal. "Falling Rock, Off Route, Exceeding Abilities, Washington, Unicorn Peak." 1989. http://publications.americanalpineclub.org/articles /13198907102/Falling-Rock-Off-Route-Exceeding-Abilities-Washington -Unicorn-Peak.

American Alpine Journal. "Falls on Snow and Ice, Inadequate Equipment—Crampons Wrong Size and Broken, Moderate Experience, Washington, Mount Rainier." 1996. http://publications.americanalpineclub.org/articles/13199606902/Falls-on-Snow-and-Ice-Inadequate-EquipmentCrampons-Wrong-Size-and-Broken-Moderate-Experience-Washington-Mount-Rainier.

American Alpine Journal. "Slip or Fall on Snow, Party Separated, Washington, Mt. Rainier." 1992. http://publications.americanalpineclub.org/articles/13199204201/Slip-or-Fall-on-Snow-Party-Separated-Washington-Mt-Rainier.

American Alpine Journal. "Weather, Exhaustion, Hypothermia, Inadequate Clothing, Washington, Mount Rainier, Muir Snowfield." 2006. http://publications.americanalpineclub.org/articles/13200606600/Weather-Exhaustion-Hypothermia-Inadequate-Clothing-Washington-Mount-Rainier-Muir-Snowfield.

American Alpine Journal. "Washington, Mt. Rainier" (Linn accident report). 1958. http://publications.americanalpineclub.org/articles/13195802700/Washington-Mt-Rainier.

American Alpine Journal. "Washington, Mt. Rainier (Post accident report). 1968. http://publications.americanalpineclub.org/articles/13196801900/Washington-Mt-Rainier.

Archbold, Mike. "Boy Who Drowned in White River Is Identified. *News-Tribune* (Tacoma, WA), August 12, 2010. http://blog.thenewstribune.com/crime/2010/08/12/boy-falls-in-white-river-rescue-efforts-underway.

Associated Press. "Accidents Kill Eight." *Daily Chronicle* (Centralia, WA), June 3, 1963. www.newspapers.com/image/5715154/?terms=Douglas%2BNash.

Associated Press. "Body Found in Search for Mount Rainier Snowshoer." *Seattle Times,* December 29, 2014 (updated December 30, 2014). http://blogs.seattletimes.com/today/2014/12/search-at-mount-rainier-for-missing-snowshoer.

Associated Press. "Climber Killed in Mount Rainier Fall Was Bellevue Man, 62." *Seattle Times,* September 16, 2015 (updated September 17, 2015). www.seattletimes.com/seattle-news/climber-killed-in-mount-rainier-fall-was-bellevue-man.

Associated Press. "Fall Kills Hiker." *Kansas City Times,* August 31, 1968. www.newspapers.com/image/51183063.

Associated Press. "Falling Stump Kills Woman." *Times* (San Mateo, CA), August 7, 1959. www.newspapers.com/image/38999789.

Associated Press. "Family of Jew Who Died on Mount Rainier Sets Off Debate on Whether Religious Rites Trump Autopsy Concerns." *Oregonian,* December 26, 2011. www.oregonlive.com/pacific-northwest-news/index.ssf/2011/12/family_of_jew_who_died_on_moun.html.

Associated Press. "Father Apparently Killed 7-Year-Old Son in Murder-Suicide at National Park." San Diego Source, August 3, 1999. www.sddt.com/News/article.cfm?SourceCode=n9908031n#.WVroQjOZNUM.

Associated Press. "Five Hunters Killed on First Weekend." *Port Angeles News,* October 18, 1965. www.newspapers.com/image/16653636/?terms=Chester%2BCarver.

Associated Press. "Inexperience, Equipment Cited in Rainier Tragedy." *Spokesman-Review* (Spokane, WA), October 18, 1995. www.spokesman.com/stories/1995/oct/18/inexperience-equipment-cited-in-rainier-tragedy.

Associated Press. "Kentucky Man Presumed Dead after Navy Airplane Crashes." *Courier-Journal* (Louisville, KY), March 24. 1983. www.newspapers.com/image/10 9543383/?terms=William%2BMortison.

Associated Press. "Man Dies When Tree Falls on Car at Rainier." *Everett Herald,* November 27, 2001. www.heraldnet.com/news/ man-dies-when-tree-falls-on-car-at-rainier.

Associated Press. "Missing Minnesota Hiker Found Dead on Mount Rainier." Minnesota Public Radio News, June 20, 2007. www.mprnews.org/story/2007/06/20/ hikerfound.

Associated Press. "Motorcycle Accident Suit Settled. Bus Crash Victims, Relatives Offered More Than $2 Million." *Spokesman-Review* (Spokane, WA). October 7, 1997. www.spokesman.com/stories/1997/oct/07/ motorcycle-accident-suit-settled-bus-crash.

Associated Press. "Mount Rainier: Search Continues for Missing Climber." *Kitsap Sun* (Bremerton, WA), May 20, 1999. http://web.kitsapsun.com/ archive/1999/05-20/0012_mount_rainier__search_continues_f.html.

Associated Press. "Mount Rainier: Search Suspended for Missing Hiker." *Kitsap Sun* (Bremerton, WA), November 17, 1997. http://web.kitsapsun.com/ archive/1997/11-17/0013_mount_rainier__search_suspended_f.html.

Associated Press. "Second Hiker's Body Retrieved." *Spokesman-Review* (Spokane, WA), March 21, 2007. www.spokesman.com/stories/2007/mar/21/ second-hikers-body-retrieved.

Associated Press. "Skier Killed in Race Fall." *Petaluma Argus-Courier,* April 14, 1940. www.newspapers.com/image/219153310/?terms=Sigurd%2BHall.

Associated Press. "Skier Killed when He Strikes Boulder." *Santa Rosa Press Democrat,* April 14, 1940. www.newspapers.com/image/276269752/?terms=Sigurd%2BHall.

Associated Press. "State Naval Officer Killed in Hiking Fall." *Bridgeport Telegram,* August 31, 1968. www.newspapers.com/image/32354539.

Associated Press. "Storms Continue." *Port Angeles Daily News,* December 2, 1975. www .newspapers.com/image/25650450/?terms=Arnold%2BManthey.

Associated Press. "Three Climbers Edge toward Plane Wreck." *Arizona Republic,* September 8, 1959. www.newspapers.com/image/117153396/?terms=C.%2BT.%2BBr essler.

Associated Press. "Tree Crashes, Kills 3 Persons." *Poughkeepsie Journal,* June 3, 1957. www.newspapers.com/image/114716504/?terms=Stephen%2BFloe.

Associated Press. "Two Dead Fliers Left on Rainier." *Statesman-Journal* (Salem, OR), September 10, 1959. www.newspapers.com/image/81232169/?terms=C.%2BT.%2 BBressler.

Associated Press. "Woman Dies after Night in Snow Cave." *Port Angeles Evening News,* February 19, 1968. www.newspapers.com/image/17917160/?terms=Edith%2BAnd erson.

Barcott, Bruce. "The Devil on Paradise Road." *Outside,* September 12, 2012. www.out sideonline.com/1903756/devil-paradise-road.

Burkitt, Janet. "Nicholas 'Was Precious'—Boy Killed in Mount Rainier Creek by Suicidal Father." *Seattle Times,* August 3, 1999. http://community.seattletimes .nwsource.com/archive/?date=19990803&slug=2975321.

Bush, Evan. "Hiker Found Dead at Mount Rainier National Park." *Seattle Times*, July 14, 2017. www.seattletimes.com/seattle-news/hiker-killed-in-rockfall-at-mount-rainier-national-park.

Bush, Evan. "The Wild Survival Story about an Air Force Pilot Who Got His Plane Stuck atop Mount Rainier." *Seattle Times*, April 12, 2017. www.seattletimes.com/seattle-news/the-wild-survival-story-about-air-force-pilot-who-got-his-plane-stuck-atop-mount-rainier-in-stunt.

Chicago Tribune. "Hunt Missing Marine Plane; 32 Men on Board." December 11, 1946. http://archives.chicagotribune.com/1946/12/12/page/1/article/hunt-missing-marine-plane-32-men-aboard.

Clarridge, Christine. "Hiking Pair Who Died near Mount Rainier Inseparable to the End." *Seattle Times*, March 21, 2007. www.seattletimes.com/seattle-news/hiking-pair-who-died-near-mount-rainier-inseparable-to-the-end.

Clarridge, Christine. "If They Had Used Flagged Log, Would Drowned Hiking Couple Still Be Alive?" *Seattle Times*, March 20, 2007. http://community.seattletimes.nwsource.com/archive/?date=20070320&slug=webhikers20m.

CNN. "Body Identified as Man Sought in Mount Rainier Park Ranger Shooting." January 2, 2012. www.cnn.com/2012/01/02/justice/washington-ranger-killed/index.html.

Daily Chronicle (Centralia, WA). "Accidents Claim Five." October 8, 1962. www.newspapers.com/image/25387467/?terms=Carlberg.

Daily Chronicle (Centralia, WA). "Accidents Kill Eight." August 22, 1960. www.newspapers.com/image/25389928/?terms=Wayne%2BHenry.

Daily Chronicle (Centralia, WA). "East Lewis Crash Kills Randle Pair." August 3, 1959. www.newspapers.com/image/25400540/?terms=Coreen%2BGoble.

Daily Chronicle (Centralia, WA). "Hiker Drowns." August 21, 1970. www.newspapers.com/image/25416641/?terms=susan%2Bbullinger.

Daily Chronicle (Centralia, WA). "Injuries Are Fatal." August 29, 1970. www.newspapers.com/image/25418156/?terms=Eric%2BBruce.

Daily Chronicle (Centralia, WA). "Man Killed at Rainier." October 8, 1971. www.newspapers.com/image/25453488/?terms=Charles%2BMoore.

Daily Chronicle (Centralia, WA). "Missing AF Jet Trainer Located on Mt. Rainier." April 16, 1968. www.newspapers.com/image/31162953/?terms=Wilfred%2BCrutchfield.

Daily Chronicle (Centralia, WA). "Search Noted." July 18, 1968. www.newspapers.com/image/31186073/?terms=Bruce%2BMcDonald.

Daily Chronicle (Centralia, WA). "Skier Killed: Avalanche on Slopes of Mt. Rainier." December 1, 1975. www.newspapers.com/image/25477979/?terms=Arnold%2BManthey.

Dmitri Pajitnov memorial website. http://dmitripajitnov.com.

Doughton, Sandi. "Under the Ice, Above the Clouds." National Parks Conservancy, Winter 2015. www.npca.org/articles/1111-under-the-ice-above-the-clouds#sm.0001o4gs0v1eod5w118bm9qgfy7wr.

Elwood (IN) Call-Leader. "Body May Be Anderson Man's." March 29, 1978. www.newspapers.com/image/88320647/?terms=Marvin%2BSkillman.

Evening Statesman (Walla Walla, WA). "Dead Miners Are Found." April 8, 1907. www.newspapers.com/image/194813191/?terms=Mount%2Brainier.

Fairbanks Daily News-Miner. "Youth Dies on Climb." June 22, 1961. www.newspapers
 .com/image/10426855.

Fort Meyers News-Press. "Crash Victim's Body Recovered." March 25, 1983. www.news
 papers.com/image/212152245/?terms=William%2BMortison.

From a Glaciers Perspective (blog). "Paradise Glacier Ice Caves Lost." April 29, 2010.
 https://glacierchange.wordpress.com/2010/04/29/paradise-glacier-ice-caves-lost.

Gaddis, Ashley Ryan. "Rainier's Terrible Lessons." *Seattle Times,* August 12, 2005.
 http://community.seattletimes.nwsource.com/archive/?date=20050812&slug=pacif
 icprainier14.

Gilmore, Molly. "It Takes a Lot of Celebrating to Say Goodbye to Musician Burt
 Meyer." *Olympian,* July 28, 2017 (updated August 1, 2017). www.theolympian.com/
 news/local/article164304742.html.

Ginsberg, Rachel. "Tracks of Fate." *Mishpacha Jewish Family Weekly,* January 4, 2012.
 http://chabadpiercecounty.com/media/pdf/605/jiZN6056645.pdf.

Glenn, Stacia. "Body Found on Mount Rainier Is Missing Tacoma Hiker." *News
 Tribune* (Tacoma, WA), August 3, 2015. www.thenewstribune.com/news/local/
 article29887330.html.

Glenn, Stacia. "He Left His Friends on a Mount Rainier Trail. They Heard the Rockfall
 That Killed Him." *News Tribune* (Tacoma, WA), July 14, 2017 (updated July 17,
 2017). www.thenewstribune.com/news/local/article161447723.html.

Glenn, Stacia. "Man Killed near Mount Rainier in Jeep Crash Identified. Rescued Passenger in Critical Condition." *News Tribune* (Tacoma, WA), June 19, 2017. www
 .thenewstribune.com/news/local/article156962184.html.

Great Falls (MT) Tribune. Donald F. Pettigrew obituary. November 22, 1997. www
 .newspapers.com/image/242224948/?terms=Donald%2BPettigrew.

Green, Aimee. "Memorial Moved for 32 Dead Marines Still on Rainier." *News Tribune* (Tacoma, WA), August 27, 1999. www.network54.com/Forum/3897/
 thread/939180222/last-1017932129/View+Thread.

Guillen, Tomas, Devin Smith, and Jack Broom. "Controllers Warned Pilot—But Plane
 Crashed Into Mount Rainier Glacier; 5 Dead." *Seattle Times,* July 3, 1990. http://
 community.seattletimes.nwsource.com/archive/?date=19900703&slug=1080341.

Harrell, Debera Carlton. "Missing Hiker's Body Is Found at Rainier." *Seattle Post-
 Intelligencer,* June 19, 2007. www.seattlepi.com/local/article/Missing-hiker-s-body
 -is-found-at-Rainier-1241129.php.

Hill, Craig. "Body of Florida Man Who Fell near Mount Rainier's Christine Falls Recovered." *News Tribune* (Tacoma, WA), September
 13, 2011. http://blog.thenewstribune.com/adventure/2011/09/13/
 body-of-man-who-fell-near-mount-rainiers-christine-falls-recovered.

Hill, Craig. "Son Remembers Parents Who Died at Mt. Rainier." *News Tribune*
 (Tacoma, WA), March 21, 2007. Via the *Olympian,* www.theolympian.com/news/
 article25227568.html.

Indianapolis Star. "Triple Services Planned for Mt. Rainier Victims." July 19, 1967. www
 .newspapers.com/image/105681228/?terms=Louden.

Karen's Trails (blog). http://karenstrails.blogspot.com.

Kitsap Sun (Bremerton, WA). Samuel Neimoyer obituary. November 5, 2004. http://web
.kitsapsun.com/archive/2004/11-05/16007_samuel_neimoyer.html.

Krell, Alexis. "Man Found Dead on Mount Rainier Identified." *News Tribune* (Tacoma,
WA), December 30, 2014. www.thenewstribune.com/news/local/crime/article
25911151.html.

Lewis, Mike. "Two Bodies Recovered from Mount Rainier." *Seattle Post-Intelligencer,*
May 23, 2005. www.seattlepi.com/local/article/Two-bodies-recovered-from
-Mount-Rainier-1174217.php.

Los Angeles Times. Doug Campbell obituary. October 13, 1999. http://articles.latimes
.com/1999/oct/13/news/mn-21798.

Los Angeles Times. News In Brief, September 9, 1973. www.newspapers.com/image/1641
80995/?terms=Rendle%2BMoore.

Los Angeles Times. "Woman's Death Starts Inquiry." August 9, 1924. www.newspapers
.com/image/158045656/?terms=Sadie%2BJordan.

Lundin, John W. "Sigurd Hall—Ski Racer & Mountaineer." 2016. www.alpenglow.org/
climbing/sigurd-hall-2006/JLundin-paper-on-Sigurd-Hall-20161027.pdf.

Lynn, Adam. "Boy Who Drowned in White River Identified as
Saudi Arabia Resident." *News-Tribune* (Tacoma, WA), June
24, 2013. http://blog.thenewstribune.com/crime/2013/06/24/
boy-who-drowned-in-white-river-identified-as-saudi-arabia-resident.

Manus, Elizabeth. "Writer Lost on Mt. Rainier Driven by Sense of Mission." Observer, August 2, 1999. http://observer.com/1999/08/
writer-lost-on-mt-rainier-driven-by-sense-of-mission.

Mayor, Jeff. "Body Found on Mount Rainier Identified as Michelle Trojanowski." *News
Tribune* (Tacoma, WA), September 10, 2012. http://blog.thenewstribune.com/
adventure/2012/09/10/awaiting-ids-on-bodies-found-on-mount-rainier.

McClary, Daryl C. "A Curtis Commando R5C Transport Plane Crashes into Mount
Rainier, Killing 32 U.S. Marines, on December 10, 1946." HistoryLink.org, January
29, 2006. www.historylink.org/File/7820.

Minneapolis Star. "Mountain Hiker from City Killed. August 4, 1972. www.newspapers
.com/image/191425532/?terms=Phillip%2BEnglund.

National Park Service. Annual Snowfall Totals at Paradise, 1920 to 2017. www.nps.gov/
mora/planyourvisit/annual-snowfall-totals.htm

National Park Service. Mount Rainier National Park Weather. www.nps.gov/mora/
planyourvisit/weather.htm.

National Park Service. "Mount Rainier Roads and Bridges" (brochure). http://npshistory
.com/publications/highways/mount_rainier/mount-rainier.pdf.

National Park Service. NPS 2016 Traffic Count Query Builder Report. https://irma
.nps.gov/Stats/SSRSReports/National%20Reports/Query%20Builder%20for%20
Traffic%20Counts%20(1985%20-%20Last%20Calendar%20Year).

National Park Service. "Pebble Creek Recovery." Press release, August 19, 2017. www
.nps.gov/mora/learn/news/sar-pebble-creek-update-8-19-17.htm.

National Park Service. "Rainier Ranger Shot on New Years Day in 2012." www.nps.gov/
mora/learn/news/anderson-memorial.htm.

National Park Service, US Department of the Interior. "Supplementary Case Incident Record for Reiser Avalanche Fatality at Paradise." January, 5, 2008. http://media .nwac.us.s3.amazonaws.com/media/filer_public/44/d8/44d8776c-7370-4643 -8dc2-500fcec18cf5/mora_nps_edit_ck_avalanche_narrative_final.pdf.

National Park Service. "Visitor Fatality at Paradise on Mount Rainier." News release, July 5, 2012. www.nps.gov/mora/learn/news/visitor-fatality.htm.

News Tribune (Tacoma, WA). "Arizona Man Identified as Victim in Mount Rainier Motorcycle Crash." September 16, 2014. www.thenewstribune.com/outdoors/ article25881931.html.

News Tribune (Tacoma, WA). "Body of Mount Rainier Skier Missing since July Has Been Found." Aug. 20, 2017. www.thenewstribune.com/news/local/article 168263417.html.

News Tribune (Tacoma, WA). "He Reached the Top of Mount Rainier. On the Way Down, Skier Fell 150 Feet into Crevasse." July 17, 2017. www.thenewstribune.com/ news/local/article161873348.html#storylink=cpy.

News Tribune (Tacoma, WA). "Ranger Shot, Killed at Mount Rainier National Park." January 1, 2012. www.thenewstribune.com/news/special-reports/article25859659. html.

News Tribune (Tacoma, WA). "Rescuers' Efforts Save Woman Clinging to Cliff after Fatal Jeep Crash near Mount Rainier." June 18, 2017. www.thenewstribune.com/ news/local/article156890229.html.

News Tribune (Tacoma, WA). "Tacoma Businessman and Civic Leader Steve Albers Hurt Badly in Mount Rainier Bike Event." July 27, 2012. http://blog.thenews tribune.com/business/2012/07/27/tacoma-businessman-and-civic-leader-steve -albers-hurt-badly-in-mount-rainier-bike-event.

Pearce, Matt. "Seattle Hiking Writer Karen Sykes, 70, Died Pursuing Her Passion." *Los Angeles Times,* June 24, 2014. www.latimes.com/nation/nationnow/la-na-nn -washington-hiker-20140624-story.html.

Pittman, Mitch. "Loved Ones, Memorial Honors Marines Killed in 1946 Crash." KMOS News, August 31, 2014. http://komonews.com/news/videos/ loved-ones-memorial-honors-marines-killed-in-1946-crash.

Port Angeles Evening News. "Three Hurt as Auto Plunges over 200-Foot Chinook Pass Cliff." August 15, 1956. www.newspapers.com/image/16320243/?terms=William% 2BPurcell.

Porterfield, Elaine. "Snowboarder's Remains Found Two Years after He Vanished on Rainier." *Seattle Post-Intelligencer,* July 19, 2001. www.seattlepi.com/local/article/ Snowboarder-s-remains-found-two-years-after-he-1060360.php.

Pulkkinen, Levi. "Rainier Hiker 'Sacrificed His Life for his Wife.'" *Seattle Post-Intelligencer,* June 11,2008. www.seattlepi.com/local/article/Rainier-hiker -sacrificed-his-life-for-his-wife-1276217.php.

Rackley, Jason. "Farewell to the King . . . Bill Bowey." Oregon Kayaking, July 26, 2004. www.oregonkayaking.net/passages/bb/bb.html.

Repanshek, Kurt. "Missing Snowshoer's Body Found on Mount Rainier." National Parks Traveler, December 22, 2007. http://ftp.nationalparkstraveler.com/2007/12/missing-snowshoers-body-found-mount-rainier.

Richard, Terry. "Paradise at Mount Rainier National Park Lives Up to Its Name during Summer." *Oregonian,* April 20, 2014. www.oregonlive.com/travel/index.ssf/2014/04/paradise_at_mount_rainier_nati.html.

Sanders, Eli. "On Rainier, Choices Are Life and Death." *Seattle Times*, November 11, 1999. http://community.seattletimes.nwsource.com/archive/?date=19991111&slug=2994646.

Schiller, Dane. "Texas Climbers Recount Death-Defying Fall on Mount Rainier." *Houston Chronicle,* June 23, 2013. www.houstonchronicle.com/news/houston-texas/houston/article/Texas-climbers-recount-death-defying-fall-on-4616804.php.

Seattle Star. "Jack Meredith, of Portland, Meets Death in Plunge." August 16, 1919. www.newspapers.com/image/174771389/?terms=Jack%2BMeredith.

Seattle Times. "Florida Man Dies after Fall at Mount Rainier." September 13, 2011. www.seattletimes.com/seattle-news/florida-man-dies-after-fall-at-mount-rainier.

Seattle Times. "Mount Rainier Plane Crash Kills Two Men." January 22, 1990. http://community.seattletimes.nwsource.com/archive/?date=19900122&slug=1052130.

Seattle Times. "Outdoors Writer Karen Sykes' Death Traced to Hypothermia." June 23, 2014. www.seattletimes.com/seattle-news/outdoors-writer-karen-sykesrsquo-death-traced-to-hypothermia.

Seattle Times. "Victims of Fatal Crash Identified." September 1, 1995. http://community.seattletimes.nwsource.com/archive/?date=19950901&slug=2139317.

Seattle Times. "Wenatchee Woman Missing in River." August 20, 1991. http://community.seattletimes.nwsource.com/archive/?date=19910820&slug=1301005.

Seattle Times. "Youth, 16, Falls to His Death in Mount Rainier Park." November 14, 2004. http://community.seattletimes.nwsource.com/archive/?date=20041114&slug=dige14m.

Seven, Richard. "10 Marines Died on Mount Rainier." *Seattle Times,* July 26, 1996. http://community.seattletimes.nwsource.com/archive/?date=19960726&slug=2341079.

Seven, Richard, and Jack Broom. "Crash Victims Chasing Prizes—Rigorous Rodeo Slate Put Cowboys in Plane." *Seattle Times,* July 4, 1990. http://community.seattletimes.nwsource.com/archive/?date=19900704&slug=1080457.

Skoog, Lewis. "The Legend of Sigurd Hall." http://alpenglow.org/climbing/sigurd-hall-2006/index.html.

Skoog, Lewis. "The Silver Skis: America's Wildest Ski Race." www.alpenglow.org/skiing/silver-skis-2005.

Smith, Carol. "Bill Bowey, Dead at 48: Kayaker Was Pioneer of the Creek Less Traveled." *Seattle Post-Intelligencer,* July 29, 2004. www.seattlepi.com/local/article/Bill-Bowey-dead-at-48-Kayaker-was-pioneer-of-1150518.php.

St. Louis Post-Dispatch. "Julie Fillo; Vanished on Hike in Rainier Park 7 Years Ago." September 21, 1984. www.newspapers.com/image/140841353/?terms=Julie%2BFillo.

Statesman-Journal (Salem, OR). "Lake Yields Youth's Body." August 25, 1958. www
.newspapers.com/image/81235065/?terms=Kenneth%2BStetson.

Statesman-Journal (Salem, OR). "New Zealand Man Dies on Mount Rainier Hike."
September 28, 1991. www.newspapers.com/image/198462912/?terms=Kenneth%2
BCardy.

Statesman-Journal (Salem, OR). "Suit Blames FAA for Cowboys' Death in Crash." July
22, 1992. www.newspapers.com/image/201772303/?terms=Cowboys%2Bplane%2B
crash%2BMount%2BRainier.

Stiffler, Lisa. "Remains of 3 Men to be Returned to Families after 30 Years on Mount
Rainier." *Seattle Post-Intelligencer,* September 17, 2001. www.seattlepi.com/local/
article/Remains-of-3-men-to-be-returned-to-families-after-1066052.php.

Strickland, Daryl. "2 Motorcyclists Killed by Bus in Mt. Rainier Park—Four Others
Injured in Traffic Accident." *Seattle Times,* September 27, 1993. http://community
.seattletimes.nwsource.com/archive/?date=19930927&slug=1723231.

Summitpost.org. "Mount Wow." Created May 30, 2005; edited June 22, 2009. www
.summitpost.org/mount-wow/154146.

Tahoe Daily Tribune. "Friends, Family Remembering Heavenly Mountain Resort Ski
Patroller Missing in Mount Rainier National Park." July 18, 2017. www.tahoedaily
tribune.com/trending/memorial-tonight-for-heavenly-mountain-resort-ski
-patroller-missing-in-mount-rainier-national-park.

United Press International. "Bodies of Two Fliers Found." *Bend Bulletin,* September 9,
1959. www.newspapers.com/image/92244864.

United Press International. "Teenager's Body Found in Wash. Park." November 14,
2004. www.upi.com/Teenagers-body-found-in-Wash-park/57001100480610.

University of Washington, University Libraries, Moving Image Collection. "Paradise
Ice Caves Tour, Mt. Rainier," ca. 1957. http://digitalcollections.lib.washington.edu/
cdm/ref/collection/filmarch/id/713.

Washington Trails Association. "Mount Wow." www.wta.org/go-hiking/hikes/mt-wow.

Webber, Joan Malory. "Jumping the Gap: The Epic Poetry of Milton—and After." *Milton Quarterly,* October 1979. http://onlinelibrary.wiley.com/doi/10.1111/j.1094
-348X.1979.tb01157.x/abstract?systemMessage=Wiley+Online+Library+%27Journ
al+Subscribe+%2F+Renew%27+page+will+be+down+on+Wednesday+05th+July+st
arting+at+08.00+EDT+%2F+13.00+BST+%2F+17.30+IST+for+up+to+75+minutes
+due+to+essential+maintenance.

Welch, Craig, Steve Miletich, and Mike Carter. "Suspect's Downward Spiral Ended
with Killing at Rainier." *Seattle Times,* January 3, 2012. www.seattletimes.com/
seattle-news/suspects-downward-spiral-ended-with-killing-at-rainier.

Westside Seattle. "Backcountry Avalanche Kills Skier from Burien." March 6, 2007. www
.westsideseattle.com/robinson-papers/2007/03/06/backcountry-avalanche.

Wreckchasing Message Board. "Mountain with the Most Wrecks." Created March 30, 2015. https://pacaeropress.websitetoolbox.com/post/
mountain-with-the-most-wrecks-7343243.

Index

A

Abbott, Duane 93
Adams, Lee 51
Adkison, Craig 47
Adkison, Lori 47
Ahrens, Karl 48
Aigers, John 142
airplane crashes 55, 89, 94, 95, 96, 97, 98, 99, 100
airplane rescue 96
Albers, Stephen 159
Albright, Horace 10
Allen, Douglas 155
alpenstocks 54, 135
Alpine Ascents International 4, 14, 170
Alvarez, Moises 129
anaphylactic shock 156
Anderson, Edith 136
Anderson, Eric 105
Anderson, Jeremy 87
Anderson, Margaret 105
Anderson, Robert 93, 133
Arceo, Adrian 118
Armstrong, Milton 55
Asiri, Ahamed 115
asphyxiation 29, 159, 161
asthma attacks 149, 150, 152
automated external defibrillator (AED) 125, 147, 148
automobile restrictions 120
automobiles in the park 120
autopsy 77
avalanche accidents 15, 18, 34, 47, 50, 56, 57, 58, 102, 140, 141, 142, 143

avalanches 139
Aycock, Lewis 155

B

Backbone Ridge 99
Bacon, W. 126
Bainter, Joe 93
Baker, Carl 94
Barcott, Bruce 90
Barklow, Melvin 150
Barnes, Benjamin 105
Barn Flats 152
Barrier Peak 80
Barry, Gordon 100
Barry, Louise 100
Bartlett, Robert 152
Bates, Randall 98
Baunsgard, Jean 149
Bavette, Anne 88
Beckter, David 57
Beehive 9, 20
Beery, Mike 39
Behm, Brain 160
Beilharz, Cornelius 49
Bennett, Jeff 112
Berkeley Park 150
Bernstein, Jeremy 19
Berquist, John 149
Beslow, James 130
bicycling accident 159
Birch, Edwin 81
Black Pyramid 22, 143
Blakely, Chris 116
Blakely, Frances Annette 116
Blakely, Robert 116
Blight, Christopher 46

ABOUT THE AUTHOR

Tracy Salcedo is the author of *Historic Yosemite National Park* and *Historic Denali National Park and Preserve*. She has also written guidebooks to a number of destinations in California and Colorado, including *Hiking Through History San Francisco, Hiking Waterfalls in Northern California, Hiking Lassen Volcanic National Park, Best Hikes Near Reno–Lake Tahoe,* and *Best Hikes Sacramento*. In addition, she has written *Best Easy Day Hikes* guides to Lake Tahoe, Reno, Sacramento, San Jose, Fresno, Boulder, Denver, Aspen, and San Francisco's Peninsula, North Bay, and East Bay. She lives with her family in California's Wine Country. You can learn more by visiting www.laughingwaterink.com.